Natural Table

of the Relationships which exist between God, Man and the Universe

"To explain things through man, and not man through things." (Of Errors & Truth)

Louis-Claude de Saint-Martin

Translated by
Piers A. Vaughan

June 2018

This book is dedicated to all my Brothers and Sisters of the Martinist Order of Unknown Philosophers in particular, and all English-speaking Martinist Brothers and Sisters, in the hope that, in making some of the fundamental French documents available in English, this will help them in their personal journeys along the Path to Reintegration.

© Piers A. Vaughan 2018
All rights reserved. No part of this publication may be reproduced, distributed, or transmitted in any form or by any means, including photocopying, recording, or other electronic or mechanical methods, without the prior written permission of the publisher, except in the case of brief quotations embodied in critical reviews and certain other non-commercial uses permitted by copyright law. For permission requests, write to the publisher at the address below.

ISBN 978-1-947907-03-4

Rose Circle Publications
P.O. Box 854
Bayonne, NJ 07002, U.S.A.
www.rosecirclebooks.com

Table of Contents

Table of Contents 3
Foreword 5
Papus' Introduction 9
Original Editors' Note 15
Aleph (א) – Truth Is In Man 17
Beth (ב) – Disorder In Creation 26
Gimel (ג) – Man, Visible Sign of God 36
Daleth (ד) – Man Emanated from God 47
Heh (ה) - The Fall, Loss of the Light 57
Vav (ו) - Temporal Life 67
Zayin (ז) – The Works of Man 78
Heth (ח) – The Universal Law of Reaction 89
Teth (ט) – Rehabilitation: Thought, Will, Action 104
Yod (י) – Religions and Myths: Natural Human Needs 122
Kaph (כ) – Original Intent of Traditions and Myths 137
Lamed (ל) – Religions, Signs of the One Tradition 149
Mem (מ) - From Genesis to the Flood 168
Nun (נ) – From the Flood to Moses 184
Samekh (ס) – From the Tabernacle to the Temple 198
Ayin (ע) – From the Prophets to the Wanderings 212
Peh (פ) – Knowledge and Teaching 226

Tzaddi (צ) – 1, 4 and 10, The Book of Man 242

Qoph (ק) – The Work of the Repairer 256

Resh (ר) – The Acts of the Repairer...266

Shin (ש) – The End of Time 284

Tau (ת) – Search Your Being 297

Appendix I – The Martinist Pantacle..307

Foreword

Seven years after he wrote *Of Errors & Truth*, Louis-Claude de Saint-Martin wrote this book in 1782. Now he was writing as a far more confident man, having enjoyed the success of his first book, and established as a prominent Masonic and Thosophical author who was also a Philosopher devoted to countering the attacks of the Deists and Atheists.

His Master, Martinez de Pasqually had been dead for eight years, and as a man of independent means at the age of 39, Saint-Martin's style had developed, he had traveled widely and was far more confident in his theosophical approach. While his ideas still adhered closely to Pasqually's *Treatise*, he had moved it towards a more understandable system, and his encounter with the works of Jakob Böhme, the 17th Century German Christian mystic, was still some years off. 1782 was also the year of the Convent of Wilhelmsbad, when Jean-Baptiste Willermoz' attempt to encapsulate the teachings of Pasqually, no doubt influenced by his long talks and correspondence with Saint-Martin, came to fruition, and he succeeded in obtaining the authority to rewite the rituals of the Order of Strict Observance to that end.

While *Of Errors & Truth* was – and is, even in French – a difficult book, notwithstanding it became the *de facto* mainland European book on Masonic philosophy of the late 18th Century, by the time of his second book Saint-Martin's style had matured, and he attempted not only to reiterate his Master's teachings and to develop them, but continued his excursions into Pasqually's theosophy by better explaining his theories, now more explicitly referring to God, and to the character called 'Héli' or Elias as 'the Repairer', whom he explicitly identified with Christ, as both the person described as the one who took Adam's place when he fell to Earth, and as the one who voluntarily took on material form to redeem mankind. However, this Repairer was an Avatar rather than a Redeemer, and his role was to show man the Path to Reintegration and to have him follow his example, rather than to suffer simply to wipe out sin for mankind. This was again a departure from orthodox Catholicism and shows how Saint-Martin was moving away from the traditional dogma of the Church. This sweeping tale not only continues the discussion of the relationship between God, Man and Nature; it also looks at history and early Religions and superstitions, taking a line through the Old Testament in reflection of Pasqually's *Treatise*, and ends with a look at the acts of the *Repairer* and the End of Times, Saint-Martin's personal take on the Apocalyse.

Again, since this is a philosophical book, we need to remind ourselves how to interpet terms used by the author, particularly the words Principle, Agent, Virtue and Law. In general, I have capitalized these words as is usually done in the text of the book, with the addition that the word *virtue* is almost always italicized by Saint-Martin.

For our purposes, a Principle can be understood as a directing or governing entity, a power which can make things happen, normally by means of Agent. These Agents are also powers, but intermediary, and particularly on the material world at the will of a Principle. If an active Being is implied in the word 'Principle' it will be capitalized, and where the word suggests a rule or law, the word 'principle' will not. However, understand that this is subjective in a philosophical text, and is only done to make the text flow more easily. A Law is simply a Law of Nature, and as we will see, most actions require only only one Law to be put into effect. Finally, a virtue is usually synonymous with a power, and in the majority of cases the word 'power' can be substituted. However, in many places this word carries an extra quality, as we know from the much-quoted Cardinal Virtues (Prudence, Justice, Temperance and Fortitude) and Theological Virtues (Faith, Hope and Charity or Love), which are specific powers which are often depicted in anthropomorphic form as women bearing an appropriate symbol, such as an anchor for Faith, a pair of scales for Justice, and a sword for Fortitude. In these cases, the word '*virtue*' will be left intact, and italicized as in the original text. It is also interesting to note that the word 'Cause', used extensively in his first book, is almost entirely missing from this second book. One last comment: the word 'Éternel' is normally rendered in English as 'Lord': however, the term has been translated so often as 'O Eternal' in Élus Cohen rituals it seemed produent to retain that word.

While Papus himself, in his introduction, takes time to link the fact that the book has twenty-two chapters with the Major Arcana of the Tarot, there is no evidence that this was Saint-Martin's intention. Indeed, he is quite explicit about his linking of the letters to the Hebrew alphabet, and Footnote 6 also points out that Papus was probably so dazzled by Éliphas Lévi's Tarot discussions as to miss the point of the chapter numbering system.

Saint-Martin himself draws attention to the two languages spoken in heaven, the language of Creation, composed of 4 letters (clearly יהוה or *Yod-Heh-Vav-Heh*), and the language of communication or Angelic language of 22 letters, which clearly refers to the Hebrew alphabet. In line with this, and following the tradition of Psalm 119, whose verses are divided up into twenty-two stanzas, each preceded by a Hebrew letter, and given Pasqually and Saint-Martin's fascination with numbers in the story of the Creation, I have numbered the chapters for the Hebrew alphabet. If I may be permitted to extend the analogy, I found it interesting that the chapters referring to Aleph, Mem and Shin, which by correspondence represent Air (or Spirit), Water and Fire, concern themselves respectively with *Truth is in Man*, *Genesis to the Flood*, and *The Work of the Repairer*. In other words, the Air/Spirit chapter discusses God as the First Principle; the Water chapter discusses the flood; and the Fire chapter discusses the Repairer or Christ, whose name, יהשוה, or *Yehesuah*, represents the letter Shin or fire decending from above into the Divine Name, *Yod-Heh-Shin-Vav-Heh*. This seems more than coincidental. In this vein I have also included descriptive titles of the chapters which have been in common use in modern French editions, which makes navigation easier: the original book simply had roman numerals to distinguish each chapter.

As in the translation of *Of Errors & Truth*, I have included copious footnotes. I prefer footnotes to endnotes, since that means the Reader can simply look at the bottom of the page, instead of having to interrupt the flow while turning to the back of the book. These footnotes are varied in content, ranging from expanded explanations of the theosophical points, to contextual explanations of the history or biblical passages being cited. They have been written to help a person unfamiliar with Saint-Martin or his themes to better understand the book: those with an existing background will perhaps not need to read them.

Finally, while I state the usual apology that any typos, misinterpretation or errors are mine alone, I must take responsibility for one further sin: that of the common title in English. Some sixteen years ago, when I first made some of the chapters available in English for the first time I called the book 'Natural Table'. In truth, the title would be more accurately called 'Natural Portrait' or 'Natural Picture', since the book attempt to paint an image, not unlike that of Pasqually's representation of the Universe, but which in a way is more in line with the operas of the time, where the curtain would go up and the audience was meant to gasp at the *Tableau*, or scene which presented itself – normally of gods on wires in the rafters, mortals who were often kings and queens in wonderful attire in the center, and demons in the lower parts of the stage in a frozen image, before the *recitatives* and *arias* began. I have no doubt that, by using this title, Saint-Martin was similarly hoping to conjure up an image of a great image of God, Agents or Angels, and Man. However, my titling of the book has grown 'legs' in modern parlance, and I am advised that changing the name at this stage would simply have people saying: "It's great that you've translated 'Natural Portrait'. Now, when are you going to translate 'Natural Table'?" And so, the name remains the same…

Piers A. Vaughan
Bayonne, New Jersey
Feast of St. John the Baptist, 2018

Papus' Introduction

Very Dear Brothers,

All the Members of this Great Knighthood of the Ideal which constitutes the Martinist Order, all the Soldiers of Christ who compose our Groups and our Lodges, work to the best of their ability towards the spiritual evolution of their Brothers and Sisters, as well as that of the Profane.

The Desire to perfect oneself through proof and sacrifice, the zeal brought to studies which are often dry, and the constant study of oneself to avoid judging others too severely, since one is tolerant enough of one's own faults, gives rise, little by little, to mysterious abilities[1] in the Man of Desire which are going to make of him a New Man.[2]

It is generally through individual action, through giving moral assistance to a despairing Brother or Sister, that contemporary Martinism exercises a savage and pitiless battle against material pleasures.

And in this life, we have no better guide than the Unknown Philosopher, and his incarnation in our Master Louis-Claude de Saint-Martin.[3]

But the Master's works are rare, and not readily available given the financial means of the members of an Order in which physical poverty is a virtue.

---

[1] In French the term normally used is 'facultés', which could translate to 'faculties' or 'abilities'. However, since the term is used in terms of being able to accomplish an action, the terms 'ability' and 'abilities' will be used throughout.

[2] Saint-Martin termed those who weren't awake to the spiritual journey 'Men of the Stream'. On awakening to the works required to resstablish one's original rights, the person became a 'Man of Desire', working on himself to become a 'New Man', or enlightened individual. Finally, on reaching the end of the Path the seeker became 'Spirit-Man', when the material part of his composite form was finally shed.

[3] Unfortunately, Papus was not strictly correct in this, as Arthur Edward Waite gleefully pointed out in his biography of Saint-Martin some thirty years later. Eight years after the publication of his second book (this one), Saint-Martin was invited back to Lyon by Jean-Baptiste Willermoz, his friend, who was holding séances to communicate with an entity called the 'Agent Inconnu', or *Unknown Agent*, from whom he belived he was receiving important instructions (although he changed his mind later and burned most of the automatic writing transmitted through the medium). It appears that Papus conflated this later involvement of the *Agent Inconnu* with Saint-Martin's *nom-de-plume* of the *Philosophe Inconnu* and believed that the Agent was taking over Saint-Martin and writing through him.

And we should thank our Masters, who have chosen you to be the instrument of diffusing their ideas, by inspiring in you the idea of making "Natural Table" available to all our Brothers and Sisters.

We are sufficiently aware of the honor associated with this function of dispensing truths, and being chosen by the Invisible Ones, to need to reward you with the praise which your modesty and desire to remain unknown would not tolerate.

But let me at least thank those guides who support the Order against all attacks, and who know the appropriate time to give it necessary growth.

As Soldiers of the Christian Ideal in an age of skepticism and materialism given out by all the current centers of faithless instruction, we are raising ourselves up above the emptiness of positivity towards illuminism, assigning Reason and Free Inquiry the important place to which they have a legitimate right.

And if we set aside the superstitions and errors spread amongst the various members of the clergy, we understand that we must challenge the clericalism of Loyola as much as that of Voltaire, and that we should not fly from the domain of blind Faith only to fall into the slavery of an equally blind Negation and Atheism.

Simple Soldiers of a Great Cause, poor children on the farm of the Great Farmer, we aspire to establish the realm of Our Lord here, where the Prince of this World presently reigns, that God of Money and Egotism who guides the majority of terrestrial beings.

And by this action, we know that we can do nothing by ourselves, crushed under the weight of our fault and ignorance, without assistance from On High.

Indeed, it is when man understands that the keys of present-day science are the "Keys of Silver" of which Louis-Claude de Saint-Martin speaks, and that the "Keys of Gold" are within us and not in books, and it is when man has complete consciousness of his inferiority that the Veil of Isis is raised and illuminism comes to reward courage in the face of trials, and true humility and unshakeable confidence in the help offered by the Repairer.[4]

---

[4] The 'Repairer' was Saint-Martin's name for the Christ, who came to earth joined into material form to repair the harm done by man as a result of his original prevarication and the sins of his posterity.

Then earthly knowledge abruptly vanishes in the intense vitality of the Universal Knowledge which is immediately perceived; then this world of wrongs, battles and calumnies moves far away when we reach that plane where Pardon and Pity demonstrate the Peace of the Soul.

It is there that one should seek an explanation for that tranquility of the soul with which Saint-Martin, imprisoned twice during the most dangerous moments of the Revolution, alone concerned himself with when he discussed the importance of the involvement of the Celestial Virgin in the generation of the Living Word within us.

The "Unknown Philosopher" was no more concerned about his physical life than does a chicken; for he lived completely in another life.

He was a "Paricipant in Two Planes", a twice-born, a *Dvija*.[5]

One may imagine how such discussions at such a moment astonished the critics, how such abilities baffled and disconcerted them.

And our old Master wrote *"The Crocodile"* for their sake, since he knew how to enclose his thoughts within the triple initiatic veil whenever he desired to do so.

And in none of his works did this ability manifest itself more perfectly than in this *"Natural Table of the Relationships which exist between God, Man and the Universe"*, based on the secret keys of the twenty-two Arcana of the primordial Alphabet of the Tarot.[6]

One of the greatest contemporary intellectual masters, Saint-Yves d'Alveydre, with the unceasing assistance of an angel from the invisible realm, has reconstituted all the keys of that Archeometer which was THEBA and in which, reading from right to left A-Be-Th (Aleph-Beth-Tau), all the living knowledge of antiquity was contained.

---

[5] *Dvija* means 'twice-born' in Sanskrit. It is a Hindu belief which holds that a person is first born physically, and later reborn spiritually, normally implying an initiatory process (although this idea isn't found in any of the traditional writings or belief systems). However, the enthusiasm with which all Eastern things were being embraced at this time in Europe, and the implication that Saint-Martin had received some form of high initiation prior to his ministry, fit well with Papus' desire to elevate Saint-Martin as a channel for higher communications and a high initiate who was somehow more than human.

[6] This was pure projection on Papus' part: Tarot was barely known in Saint-Martin's time other than as a parlor game, and its elevation into a key esoteric tool didn't truly take place until it was popularized by Éliphas Lévi nearly 80 years later. It is quite clear in this book that the choice of twenty-two chapters was not a coincidence – after all Saint-Martin, like his Master Martinez de Pasqually, had an obsession with numbers – but this referred to the twenty-two letters of the Hebrew language, which have also been referred to as the Angelic language, and which is discussed at length later on in the book.

Without doubt this work will soon appear under the guise of a commentary on the life of Our Lord Jesus Christ and will then be diluted by obfuscation and destroyed by errors.

May every Brother and Sister of the Martinist Order meditate upon these commentaries on the Twenty-Two, written by Saint-Martin, while awaiting the imminent appearance of the other works this famous author of Our Order, which other devoted Brothers are preparing to publish.

Greetings in the Name of Yahweh to all the members of the Order spread throughout the Universe. May they all work to the Glory of the Unknown Philosopher, Our Venerable Master.

PAPUS – Doctor Gérard Encausse

The Archeometer of Alexandre Saint-Yves d'Alveydre

Original Editors' Note

In the margins of the Manuscript of this Work, given to us by an unknown person, there were many additions written in a different handwriting.

Observing that not only did these additions not directly connect to the discourse, but sometimes even interrupted the flow; and since they were also of a style which seemed to differ from that of the overall Work, we thought it necessary to indicate the various pieces of this kind with italics to show they are not by the Author, and that they were added by someone to whom the Mansucript had been given, in order to make each easy to identify.[7]

(Note from the 'Edinburgh' Edition of 1782)

---

[7] But see Footnote 9. Note also that isolated words or short phrases in italics were part of the original text; it is only passages of a sentence or longer in italics which were claimed to be by another hand.

NOTE ON SAINT-MARTIN'S COMMENT ON PAGE 199

While we are used to the occasionally unacceptable comments of our forebears, Saint-Martin makes an observation on page 199 which is simply so egregious I felt it necessary to consult an African Amercian colleague of mine on its inclusion. We decided that, since it was contained in the original publication it was important to include it, but I am including a comment provided by this prominent lecturer and commentator on those times, which he kindly gave permission to be included:

"It is harsh and disappointing to acknowledge that a spiritual visionary like St. Martin could hold such a prejudiced and unsound viewpoint of people of African descent. This is exceptionally difficult as there are scores from that same demographic who are adherents to his esoteric philosophy and teachings over the years. It is therefore in that vein of those on the pathway for spiritual enlightenment, that I strongly encourage the author Piers A. Vaughan to include in his translation project, the offensive sentences where St. Martin negatively comments about those of African descent. Can one separate socially based impurities from the pious nature of the soul? Perhaps or perhaps not. Robespierre was a strong advocate for the abolition of slavery, yet he sent many to the guillotine as well. With that said, accepting the good with the bad places a human value to personalities of our past, present and future."

Dr. E. Oscar Alleyne

Aleph (א) – Truth Is In Man

Fruitful and luminous truths would exist not so much for man's happiness as for his torment, if the attraction he feels for them was a desire he could never satisfy. There would be the same inexplicable contradiction in the *Primum Mobile* Who authored those same Truths if, while wishing to conceal them from our sight, He wrote them into everything which surrounds us, as He has done in the living power of the Elements, in the order and harmony of all of the actions of the Universe, and more clearly still in the distinctive character which is man.

It is far more in line with the Laws of that Primitive[8] Cause, to believe that He hasn't multiplied the rays of His own light to us only to deprive us of the ability to understand and use them, and that, if He has placed so many instructive things both around us and within us, it is to allow us to meditate on them and understand them, and bring us, by this means, to those realizations, at once striking and universal, which can assuage our concerns and our desires.

These Truths would cease to appear inaccessible to us if, through attentive and intelligent care, we learned how to grasp the thread which is constantly offered to us, for then this thread, corresponding to light, would fulfill its main purpose, which is undoubtedly to bring us closer to it and reunite the two extremes.

To contribute to such an important goal, let us begin by dispelling any doubts raised about man's true nature, since it is from this that all knowledge of the Laws and nature of other Beings must result.

Man cannot bring any material work into existence without it being preceded by actions, which are, as it were, Creative Powers, and which, despite operating internally and invisibly, are nevertheless easy to distinguish both by their successive steps and by their different properties: for example, before building an edifice, I plan its design or concept, I adopt this plan, and finally I make the choice as to the best means to accomplish it.

---

[8] Pasqually and Saint-Martin often use the word 'primitive' to designate 'primal' or 'original'. In this translate we will use the word 'primitive' wherever possible, to keep with the style of the original, but where there is any possible confusion we will use the term 'original'.

It is clear that the invisible abilities by means of which I have the power to produce that work are, by their very nature, greatly superior to their outcome, and that they are quite independent of it. For this edifice would not have been able come into existence without those abilities which made me capable of giving life to it being modified. Once it has received them, they continue to be superior; since having the power to destroy it, and then not destroying it is in a way to continue its existence; and finally, if it were destroyed, the abilities which had given it being would still remain what they had been before and during its existence.

Not only are these abilities superior to their productions, but I should also recognize that they are superior to and foreign to my body, since they operate in the silence of all my senses; because my senses may well be their organs and ministers but they are not their source and generating Principle, for my senses act only by impulse, whereas my intelligent Being acts through deliberation because my intellectual abilities have real power over my senses, because they exercise strength and control through the various activities my will may impose on them, whereas my senses have only a passive control over these abilities, that of absorbing them; because ultimately, for example in Geometry, even the most scrupulous and satisfactory precision to the senses still leaves something to be desired to the mind, as in that multitude of figures whose physical connections and relationships we understand, yet whose true numbers and relationships are definitely beyond the world of the senses.

This order in the works of man should educate us on the subject of a Superior Order, for if our material deeds which are most removed from Life take their existence from the stable and permanent Powers which are their necessary Agents, how could we not accept that the most perfect material results – such as the existence of universal and of individual physical Nature – are also the products of Powers superior to those creations? The more a work contains perfection, the more it demonstrates its generative Principle. Why, then, would we challenge this idea which is both simple and vast, which gives us a single Law for the creation of all things, even though they are all distinguished from one another by their action and their basic characteristics?

So, the superiority of Nature's creations still means they are the result of Powers or abilities similar in essence and power to those necessarily manifested in man, when he produces all his works. For, although those works are only created through transpositions or changes, we cannot avoid seeing them as types of creations, since through these various arrangements and combinations of material substances, man creates things which previously existed only in their constitutent parts.

If the universal edifice of Nature must be the visible work of abilities which existed prior to its creation, we have the same certainty concerning the existence of those abilities that we have in the reality of the abilities which manifest in us, and we can be sure that, since Nature's productions are material like ours, though of a Superior Order, the physical components of Universal Nature can be no more aware of the abilities which created and now govern them, than our creations or our bodies know those which we clearly know exist in us.

Just as Nature could never have existed without the universal work of those invisible abilities, it can lose the existence it has received unless those abilities which produced it never lose any of their power or their indestructibility, since they exist independently of their material creations, just as my invisible abilities exist independently of the works I create.

Let us pause for a moment, and read in the Universe itself clear proof of the existence of those physical Powers which are superior to Nature.[9]

Regardless of the center of the orbits of the wandering *stars, their Law gives them all a tendency towards that common center to which they are all equally attracted.*

However, we see them maintain their distance from that center, sometimes coming closer, sometimes going farther away in accordance with regular Laws, yet never touching or joining with it.[10]

In vain can the mutual attraction of these planetary stars be opposed, since each is counterbalanced by the others, so they are mutually supportive and because of this they all resist the central attraction. It still

---

[9] This is one of the sections identified in the Original Editors' Note as being in a different hand, and therefore of unknown origin. While nobody would go so far as to accuse the Publishers of lying, and since all manuscripts would of necessity have been handwritten, making it easy to see differences in style and script, not only does the style in this case seem identical to the rest of the book; it also fits in with the general attempt to communicate an ambience of received knowledge and higher truth. Most scholars are agreed that it is all by Saint-Martin, and in the unlikely possibility that these sections were indeed written in different handwriting, this probably only meant that Saint-Martin dictated it to another person. The Translator is unaware of any manuscript copies still existing, in which case it would be easy to at least verify if the marginalia were in a different hand.

[10] Wandering stars are comets, and it has long been observed thay man have elliptical orbits which take the body far out into space, while swinging around a planet or other central point at quite a close range.

remains to ask why the mutual and individual attraction of these stars doesn't firstly make them all come together, then precipitate them all towards the common center of their general attraction; since, if their balance and support depends on their several aspects and their specific respective position, it is evident that in their daily movements this position varies, and that for a long time, therefore, their Law of Attraction would have to vary, as would the character of permanence attributed to them.

We could appeal to the fixed stars, which, despite the enormous distance they are from the other stars, can influence them, and attract them as those attract their common center, so maintaining them in their movements. This argument would seem to be powerful and wise, and it would also appear to follow the simple Laws of sound Physics: but in reality it only adds to our difficulties.

Although the fixed stars appear to maintain the same position, we are so far removed from them that on this point we only have conjecture to rely on.

In the second instance, while it may be true that they are fixed, as they seem to be, we can't deny that new stars have appeared in several places in the sky, which have then ceased to show themselves; and I will quote but one example which was noted by several astronomers in 1572 in the constellation of Cassiopeia. Firstly, that star equalled the size of Vega in the Lyre in magnitude, then Sirius, and next became almost as large as Venus at perigee, so that it could be seen with the naked eye in daytime. But after losing its light little by little, it was never seen again. According to other commentaries, it was presumed that it had made previous appearances, that its period could be around three hundred and something years, and that it could therefore reappear at the end of the 19th Century.[11]

If we can observe such revolutions, such changes among the fixed stars, there can be no doubt that some of them have movement. It is also certain that a variation in only one of these stars must influence the region

---

[11] This observation was made by a large number of astronomers, including Tycho Brahé (in whose honor this supernova is called *Tycho's Supernova*), John Dee, Thomas Allen and others. Indeed, Queen Elizabeth I summoned Allen, the Court Astronomer, to explain its meaning; and it had a profound affect in local news and events in a number of other countries. Ultimately the contemporary theories proved incorrect: being a supernova it was the last, massive explosion of an aging star before it faded into a remnant forever.

to which it belongs and carry enough preponderance there to disrupt the local harmony.

If the local harmony can be disrupted in one of the regions of the fixed stars, this disruption may extend to all regions. They could therefore cease constantly maintaining their respective positions and succumb to the power of general attraction which, reuniting them together with all the other stars into a common center, would successively destroy the system of the Universe.

We have never seen such a disaster take place, and if Nature changes, it is slowly, which still shows us that an apparent order is in charge. There is therefore an invisible physical power reigning over the fixed stars, like those over the planets, which maintains them in their space, just as they maintain all living Beings within their respective bounds. Now, joining this evidence to the similar points we have already established, we repeat that the Universe exists only because of creative abilities invisible to Nature, just as the physical things made by man can only be produced by means of his invisible abilities; and further, that the creative abilities of the Universe have a necessary existence which is independent of the Universe, just as my invisible abilities necessarily exist and are independent of my material works.

Everything comes together here to demonstrate the superiority of man, since it is in his own abilities that he discovers what raises him up to demonstrate the active and invisible Principle from Whom the Universe receives its existence and its Laws; since in the works, even material, that he has the power to produce, he finds evidence that his being is of an imperishable nature.

Let nobody argue against these reflections by citing those physical and material actions common to both man and beast. In speaking of such works, we are not talking at all about those natural actions he has in common with animals, but those acts of genius and intelligence which always distinguish him through their notable characters and unique signs.

Since this difference between man's intellectual Being and his physical Being was shown with clear evidence in the writings from which I drew the epigraph for this book[12], here we will limit ourselves to pointing out that we cannot execute the least of our desires without

---

[12] *"To explain things through man, and not man through things."* He is quoting from his own first book, which he uses as the epigraph for his second book.

accepting that we carry everywhere within us the *Principle of Being and Life*. Now, how could the *Principle of Being and Life* perish?

However, despite this distinctive character, man is completely dependent on his physical and sensory thoughts. It cannot be denied that he carries in him all the abilities analogous to the objects that he can know, for what are all our discoveries, if not the intimate perception and secret sense of the connection which exists between our own genius and the objects themselves? Nevertheless, we cannot have a notion of any physical object if that object doesn't communicate its impressions to us, and we have evidence of this when a failure of our senses deprives us, either completely or in part, of a knowledge of the objects which relate to them.

It is true that often, though comparison or analogy alone, original thoughts lead us to secondary thoughts, and that, through a kind of inference, an understanding of things which are near us leads us to form theories about things which are further away; but then, we are still subject to the same Law, since it is always the first thing that is known to us which serves as the vehicle for these thoughts, and without it neither the second nor the original thought would have been produced in us.

It is therefore certain that concerning physical things and those thoughts connected with them man is in true servitude, a concept from which we will draw fresh insights into its true Law later on.

As well as the thoughts which man is always acquiring from physical things through the action of those objects on his senses, he has thoughts of another kind: he has thoughts inspired by a Law, a Power which directs the Universe and those same material things; he has thoughts inspired by the Order which should govern him; finally, he is drawn – as if by natural movement – towards that harmony which appears to give rise to them and govern them.

He cannot create a single thought himself; however, he has that of a Superior Power and Wisdom which is both the goal of all Laws, the place of all harmony, and the pivot and center from whence everything emanates and to which all the *powers* of Beings lead. Because this is the true conclusion of all systems, all dogmas, all opinions – even the most absurd – concerning the nature of things and that of their Principle. There is no doctrine, except Atheism, which doesn't have this amazing *Unity* for its goal, as we will see later.

If these thoughts form an Order which is completely different from the Order which we have for physical things: if no physical objects can produce them, since even the most perfect animals clearly cannot manifest anything similar even though, like man, they all live among these things; if, at the same time, no thought can be awakened in man without means outside of him; it follows that man is dependent for his intellectual thoughts as well as his physical thoughts, and that, in both Orders, although he has the seed of all these thoughts within him, he is compelled to wait for external reactions to come to animate and give birth to them. He is neither their master nor their author, and when he tries to focus on anything, he cannot, despite his efforts, be certain of accomplishing his goal and avoid being distracted by a thousand competing thoughts.

We are all subject to involuntarily receiving those unruly, troublesome and intrusive thoughts which, despite ourselves, pursue us with concerns and doubts of all kinds, and which come to interfere with our most satisfying intellectual enjoyment.

From all of these facts, it follows that if the material works of man have shown that he contains invisible and immaterial abilities, both preceding and necessary for the realization of those works, and that, for the same reason, the work of the material Universe or physical Nature has shown us the creative invisible and immaterial abilities outside of that same Nature and which indeed created it; so man's intellectual abilities are indisputable proof that there exists an Order superior to theirs, and to those which create all the material things in Nature: that is to say that, regardless of the universal creative abilities of physical Nature, there exist, still outside of man, intelligent and sentient abilities analogous to his Being and which produce thoughts in him; for since the motives behind his thoughts aren't his, he can only discover these motives in an intelligent source connected with his Being; for without this connection these motives would have no effect on him, and the seed of his thought would remain inactive, and consequently fruitless.

However, although man is as passive in his intellectual ideas as in his physical ideas, he always retains the privilege of examining the thoughts submitted to him, to judge them, to adopt them or reject them, and then to act according to his choice; ever hoping, by taking a careful and consistent path, to come one day to a permanent enjoyment of pure thought; all of which derives naturally from the proper use of his liberty.

But he must clearly distinguish this directed liberty from the slavish will of the inclinations, powers or influences which normally determine man's actions. Liberty is an attribute which is his by right and which belongs to his Being, even though the reasons behind his decisions are foreign to him.

We will therefore consider it from two angles: as Principle and effect. As a *Principle*, liberty is the true source of our decisions, it is this ability which is in us to follow the Law imposed upon us, or to act against that Law. Ultimately, it is the ability to remain faithful to the light that is constantly offered to us. This *principle of liberty* is found in man even when he is a slave to *influences* which are foreign to his Law. Then again, before taking a decision, we see him comparing the various impulses which rule him, setting his habits and his passions against one another, finally choosing the one which has the greatest attraction for him.

Considered as an *effect*, liberty steers him solely towards the Law given to our intellectual nature; and then it assumes independence, a complete exemption from any *action, power* or *influence* contrary to that Law, an exemption which few men have known. From this point of view, where man admits no other reason than that of his Law, all his decisions, all his actions are the result of that Law which guides him, and it is only then that he is truly free, never distracted by any foreign motive concerning what benefits his Being.

As to the Principle Being, that Universal Sentient Power, superior to man, Whose actions we can neither surmount nor avoid, and Whose existence is proven by the passive state we have towards Him regarding our thoughts, this Ultimate Principle also has a liberty which differs essentially from those of other Beings; because being Himself His own Law, He can never be separated from it, and His liberty isn't exposed to any obstacle or foreign impulse. Thus, He doesn't possess that disastrous ability by means of which man can act against the very purpose of his existence. And this demonstrates the infinite superiority of this Universal Principle and Creator of all Laws.

That Supreme Principle, Source of all Powers, Who both enlivens man's thoughts and engenders the visible works of material Nature, that Being necessary to all other Beings, the Source of all actions, from Whom continually emanate all existences, that Final Term towards Which everything moves as if by an irresistible force since everything seeks *Life*: that Being, I say, is He whom men generally call GOD.

Aleph (א) – Truth Is In Man

Whatever the constrained ideas that coarse ignorance has instituted among different Nations, all those men who wish to go into themselves and probe the indestructible feeling that they have of this Principle, will recognize that He is GOOD in His essence, and that all Good comes from Him; that Evil is only what is opposed to Him; that He therefore cannot wish for Evil and that on the contrary He ceaselessly brings to His creations, through the excellence of His nature, every extent of happiness of which they are capable with respect to their various Orders, though the means He uses are still hidden from our eyes.

I won't try make the nature of this Being any clearer, nor will I enter into the Sanctuary of the *Divine Powers*: to do so requires knowledge of some of the numbers which constitute Him; now, how would it be possible for man to submit Divinity to his calculations and to fix His principle NUMBER? To know a principle number, one needs to have at least one of its harmonics[13]; and if, while attempting to represent the immensity of the Divine Powers, we were to fill a book – even the entire Universe – with numerical signs, we would still not have the the first harmonic, since we could always add new numbers: that is to say, we would always discover new *Virtues* in that Being.

Moreover, we should say about GOD what we have said about man's invisible Being. Before contemplating a study to discover His relationships and His laws, we have to convince ourselves of His existence, because existing or having everything in oneself, depending on one's Order, is one and the same thing; so that to recognize a need for and the existence of the Eternal Principle of the infinite is to attribute to Him every ability, perfection and power which that Universal Being must have within Himself, although one can conceive neither their number nor their immensity. These first steps being assured, let us try to discover new relationships by looking at physical Nature.

---

[13] The word used is '*aliquot*', which is best known as a fractional part, normally in music. Indeed, one manufacturer of grand pianos, Blüthner, employed what they called the 'aliquot system' in which a fourth string was added to the usual number of three for each piano key, but which was neither struck by the hammer nor muted, allowing it to vibrate freely in harmony, reputedly giving a richer tone to the sound.

Beth (ב) – Disorder In Creation

Is it possible to contemplate the spectacle of the Universe without admiration? The regular course of those wandering lights, which are like the visible spirits of Nature; that kind of daily Creation which their presence works on all the regions of the Earth, and which renews itself in the same regions across the cycle of the Ages; the inalterable Laws of gravity and movement, rigorously observed even in the most disturbing shocks and stormiest revolutions. These are undoubtedly wonders which would appear to give the Universe a right to man's homage.

But while offering us this majestic spectacle of order and harmony, even more clearly it shows us signs of confusion, and we are obliged in our thoughts to give it the lowest rank: for it has no influence over the active and creative abilities to which it owes its existence, and it has no more direct and necessary link to God, to Whom these abilities belong, than our material creations have to us. The Universe is, so to speak, a Being apart; it is separate to Divinity, though He is neither unknown nor even indifferent to it. Finally, it doesn't share at all in the Divine essence, though God takes care to maintain and govern it. Thus, it doesn't participate in that perfection which we know belongs to Divinity; it doesn't unite with it at all; and consequently, it isn't part of the simplicity of those fundamental Laws specific to Divine Nature.

Also, by observing the characteristics of disorder and deformity throughout the Universe, we see that it is nothing more than a violent assembly of sympathies and antipathies, similarities and differences which force Beings to live in a continual state of unrest in order to draw closer to what is similar to them, and to flee what is their opposite; since they continually strive towards a more peaceful state. General and individual bodies exist only through the subdivision and mixing of their constituent parts; and the death of those bodies only takes place when the emanations of those parts which had been mutually combined, separate and return to their particular unity. Finally, why does everything in Creation consume itself, if not because everything is moving towards that Unity from whence everything came?

We even see a striking example of the confusion and violence which is all of Nature in the physical Law which, four times a day, stirs up the basin of the seas, and which hasn't given them a moment of calm since the origin of things; a characteristic image by which man can, at first glance, explain the enigma of the Universe.

How, then can we find man to be so inattentive as to identify God with that physical Universe: that Being without thought, without desire, whose very actions it manifests are alien to it; that Being which exists only through division and disorder?

Could the compounds with which physical Nature is formed have any relationship with the constitutive character of universal Unity? And could the existence of that composite and limited Being, which is subject to so many vicissitudes, ever be confused with the Principle of ONE, Eternal and Immutable, the Source of life, Whose independent action extends over all Beings and Who preceded everything?

The imperfection attributed to temporal things proves that they are neither equal to nor coeternal with God, and shows at the same time that they cannot be as permanent as Him; for, since their imperfect nature doesn't partake at all in the essence of God, to Whom alone belongs perfection and *Life*, they must be able to lose the life or movement that they had received; because the true right of God in never ceasing to be, is in never having begun.

And indeed, if *life* or movement were essential to matter, it would not have been necessary, as the most famous Philosophers have said, to require matter *and* movement to form a world, since according to this Principle, by obtaining the one, they would necessarily have had the other.[14]

If men have been wrong on these matters, it is because they have closed their eyes to the great Laws of Beings, and because they haven't recognized the essential characteristics which must, in man's mind, separate the Universe and God.

In the intelligent Order of things, it is the superior which nourishes the inferior; it is the Principle of all existence Who maintains in all Beings the life He has given them; it is from the First Source of Truth that intellectual man daily receives his thoughts and the wisdom which enlightens him.

---

[14] It is interesting that one of the prerequisites for recognizing an object as living by Biologists is motion, together with being composed of cells, being capable of growth, reproduction, obtaining and using energy, and reacting to the environment.

Now, this Superior Principle doesn't rely on any of His creations for His life or His sustenance, as He receives everything from Himself, finds everything in Himself, and is always safe from privation, want and death.

On the other hand, in every class in the Physical Order it is the Inferior Orders which nourish and feed the Superior ones: the Vegetable, Animal and Material bodies of man provide us with the clearest evidence. Doesn't the Earth itself sustain its existence by means of its own creations? Isn't it from their remains that it receives fertilization and food? And are the rain, dew and snow which fertilize it anything other than its own exhalations which fall back onto its surface, having received from the atmosphere the powers[15] necessary to perform its fructification?

This, then, is a most striking image of the Earth's impotence and the clearest evidence of the need for its destruction; since being able to retain its generative powers and existence only through the use of its own creations, we cannot believe it to be imperishable unless we were able to see in it, as in God, a basic and limitless ability to create: and if that were so, we would never see sterility or drought within it or on its surface.

Yet the Earth gives evidence daily that it can become sterile, since whole countries can be found which are devoid of plants and the things they formerly possessed in abundance.

So, since the Earth can become sterile, yet can only be fed with its own fruit, what will nourish it when it stops producing anything? And how will it maintain its strength and its existence, if the existence of any Being cannot be maintained without food?

Now, can we imagine anything more hideous than a Being whose life is based on vicissitudes, destruction and death; a Being which, like *matter*, like time, like the Saturn of fable, can exist only by eating its own children, which cannot preserve one part without sacrificing another: in a word, which can only ensure its own existence by having to devour its own brothers?

This is the place to consider the results of all the research which has been made concerning God and matter. Throughout time men have sought to understand what matter is, yet they still haven't been able to grasp it: there are even very advanced languages which have no words to express it. On the other hand, among those who have taken God as the subject of

---

[15] Here Saint-Martin used the term *Virtues*. In instances where the term 'virtue' is used merely to denote powers or a non-religious or non-classical use of the word, the term 'powers' will be used for ease of reading.

their reflections, nobody has been able to say what He *isn't*, since there are no positive names expressing a true attribute or perfection which don't belong to that Universal Being, since He is the original basis of all that is. And if men sometimes give Him negative designations such as *Immortal, Infinite, Independent*[16], we will see, by examining their true meaning, that they express very positive attributes, since in fact these appellations only serve to state that He is exempt from the subjections and limits of matter.

In the Supreme Principle Who ordered the creation of this Universe and sustains its existence, everything is fundamentally order, peace and harmony; so, we shouldn't attribute the confusion which reigns in all parts of our shadowy realm to Him: for such disturbance can only be the result of an inferior and corrupt Cause which can only act separately and outside of the Good Principle, since it is evident that it is worthless and impotent compared to the First Cause, and that it can do nothing to the very essence of the material Universe.

It is impossible for these two Causes to exist together outside of the Order of temporal things. Once the inferior Cause ceased to conform to the Law of the Superior Cause, it lost any union and any communication with Him, for then the Superior Cause, the Eternal Principle of order and harmony let the Inferior Cause which opposed to His unity, fall into the darkness of its own corruption, just as every day He lets us voluntarily lose the extent of our abilities and confine them, through our own actions, within the confines of the vilest attachments to the point of distancing us completely from the things which accord with our nature.[17]

Thus, far from the birth of Evil and the creation of the place in which it had been enclosed producing, in the true order, a greater harmony of things which added to the Immensity, they made specific what should essentially be universal; split up actions which should be united; confined in one place what had been separated from the universal and which should circulate endlessly throughout the entire system of Beings; and finally *manifested* in physical form what had previously existed in immaterial principle: for if we could dissect the Universe and move its coarse envelopes aside, we would find the *principle* seeds and filaments

---

[16] In the sense of *not* mortal, *not* finite, and *not* dependent, which are, grammatically speaking negative words.

[17] So, in Saint-Martin's theosophy, the Superior Cause, or God, gives free will to all His creations, whether outside of time, as the Inferior Agent (what we might perhaps call the Devil); or inside of time, as man.

organized in the same way we find in their fruit and their products; and this invisible Universe would also be as distinct in our mind as the material Universe is to our physical eyes. And that is where the Observers get it wrong when they confuse the invisible Universe with the visible Universe, and claim that the latter is solid and real, when it only belongs to the invisible and *principle* Universe.[18]

This is how the Inferior Cause is limited by the physical and insurmountable ramparts of the pure and vivifying action of the Great Principle, before Whom all corruption sees its efforts destroyed; and if studying such subjects by those who are reading me now have sometimes come at the price of understanding the true Laws of Beings, here they will see why the Sun's revolution gives an annual period of around 365 days; for they would have the right to deny the Principles I am suggesting, if the evidence weren't physically laid out in front of them.

Since that Inferior Cause exercises its action in the dark space to which it has been confined, everything contained there along with it must, without exception, be exposed to its attacks; and while it can do nothing to the First Cause or to the essence of the Universe, it can combat their Agents, putting up obstacles to the results of their actions, and insinuate its dysfunctional action in the smallest disturbances of individual Beings, so as to further increase disorder.

Finally, if we wish to understand temporal nature, let us consider our atmosphere, which exhibits phenomena which allow us to trace its origin. Often, for an entire morning thick fog, or a single mass of vapor spread uniformly in the air, appears to rise up against the light of the daystar and stands in the way of its brightness; but then the full power of the sun breaks through this barrier, dispels the darkness and separates those vapors into a thousand clouds, of which the purest and most buoyant are attracted by its heat, while the coarsest and most unhealthy are

---

[18] In this paragraph Saint-Martin puts forward a distinctly gnostic outlook on man's current status. For him the First Cause or First Principle, God, becomes a rather indifferent God in this process, allowing the Inferior Cause to be the motivator for subdivision, and particularly in crystallizing immaterial bodies into physical forms. In this sense God, by allowing the prevaricating Agent(s) to do this, insulates Himself from any involvement in this act of trapping man in matter and in time. This was possibly Saint-Martin's way to avoiding God having to command his 'good' Agents to perform what was in a way an 'evil' act. While this does not precisely follow Pasqually's vision in his *Treatise*, these thoughts reflect the result of seven years of development and discussion following Pasqually's death. Note also that 'the Observers' is Saint-Martin's term for Deists, Atheists and any Philosophers who don't see God's Hand in all of Creation, as we saw in his first book, *Of Errors & Truth*, which was the reason for his writing it in the first place.

precipitated onto the terrestrial surface, there to join and combine with various mixed, material substances. This physical picture is clearly meant to educate us.

It is important to examine here how the Inferior Cause can be opposed to the Superior Cause, and understanding how it can be that Evil exists in the presence of material phenomena can help us in this study. Firstly, let us observe the difference between these material Beings and the intelligent productions of the Infinite.

The Creator Being endlessly produces Beings outside of Himself, as the corporeal Principles endlessly produce their actions outside of themselves.

The Creator doesn't product composite Beings, since He is ONE, unique in His essence. As a result, if there are any among the creations of that First Principle which can be led into corruption, at least they can neither dissolve nor be destroyed as can corporeal and composite products. That is already a big difference between the nature of these two kinds of Being. We will find an even greater difference in the kinds of corruption to which they are susceptible.

The corruption or disturbance – that is, the evil – of material creations lies in ceasing to appear in the form which is proper to them. The corruption of immaterial creations lies in ceasing to be subject to the Law which constitutes them.

However, the destruction of material creation when they naturally come to the end of their existence is, of course, not evil; it is only a disorder where it's premature; and even then, the evil is less in the Beings delivered to destruction than in the disordered action which results.

Immaterial Beings on the other hand, not being composite, can never be penetrated by any external action; they can neither decompose nor be destroyed. So, any corruption of these Beings cannot come from the same source as that of material creations, since the opposite Law which works on them cannot affect simple Beings.

So, where could this corruption come from, seeing that such physical and immaterial creations both draw their lives from a pure source, each according to its Order? It would be insulting to the *Principle* to suggest the slightest stain in their essence.

From the extreme difference which exists between immaterial and material creations, it follows that since the latter are passive, since they are composite, they are not the Agents of their corruption; they can therefore only be their subject, since this disorder necessarily comes to them from outside.

On the other hand immaterial creations, since they are simple Beings and in their primitive and pure state, can neither be affected nor disrupted by any outside power, since nothing of them is exposed, and they contain their whole existence and their entire Being within themselves, as each one forms its own unity; from which it follows that if there were any which were corrupted, not only would they have been subject to their own corruption, but they must also have been its organ and Agent since it wouldn't have been possible for that corruption to have come into them from outside, since no other Being could have affected them or disturbed their Law.

There are Observers who, only considering man in his present state of degradation, a slave to prejudice and habit, dominated by his appetites and given over to physical impressions, have concluded that it is a necessary part of both all his animal and his intellectual actions; from which they believe themselves authorized to state that Evil exists inside him, or from the imperfection of his essence, or from God, or from Nature, so that his actions themselves would be unimportant. Then, extending the false opinion they have formed about man's liberty across all Beings, they deny the existence of any free Being, and from their theory they conclude that Evil exists as an independent force.

Without stopping to combat these errors, suffice it to point out that they only come to this conclusion by confusing motive, decision and result in the actions of the free Being. Now, in recognizing that the Evil Principle is only able to exercise its freedom on something, it would be just as true that it is the author of the reason for its determination, for the subject or object over which we exercise our decision may be genuine, yet our motives might not be. Every day we form false and corrupt motives regarding the very best things; so, we mustn't confuse the thing with the motive: one is external, and the other took shape within us.

These observations lead us to discover the true source of Evil. For can a Being who draws near and rejoices in seeing the *virtues* of the Sovereign Principle discover a strong notion contrary to the delights of that sublime spectacle? If he turns away from that great sight, or if, while gazing upon those pure creations of the Infinite, while he contemplates them he seeks a notion which is false and contrary to their Laws, can he find it outside of himself, since this notion is evil, and the evil didn't exist at all prior to that criminal thought being born within him, for no creation can exist prior to its generative Principle.

That is how the primitive, pure and simple state of all intelligent and free Beings proves that corruption cannot arise in him without him voluntarily producing its seed and its source. That is how it is clear that the Divine Principle in no way contributes to the evil and disorder which may arise among His creations, since He is purity itself. This, then, shows that He doesn't participate at all: since being simple, like His creations, and moreover being Himself the Law of His own essence and all His works, like them He is, for the most powerful reason, impervious to any external action.

So, by what means could disorder and corruption come to Him, seeing that in the Physical Order itself the powers of free and corrupt Beings, as well as all the rights of their corruption, only extend to secondary objects, and not to their originating Principles? Even the greatest disturbances they can bring to physical Nature don't alter its fruits and its creations, and never reach its supporting columns, which can only ever be shaken by the Hand which established them.[19]

Man's will can control some of his bodily movements, but he cannot control any of the basic functions of his animalistic life, whose needs are impossible to suppress.[20] If he takes his actions too far, and attacks the very basis of his vital existence, he can, it is true, end its apparent course; but he can neither destroy the particular Principle which brought him into existence, nor the Law innate in that Principle, by means of which he must act for a time, while separated from his origin.

If we raise ourselves up a level and contemplate the Laws which operate across universal Nature, we will see the same process.

The Sun's influences vary continually in our atmosphere: sometimes the clouds in the terrestrial region block them, sometimes fresh winds moderate them or hinder them: even man himself can increase or decrease the action of this star locally, by focusing or by blocking its rays. However, the action of the Sun is always the same: it is constantly *projecting* the same light around it, and its active power is always

---

[19] Note the Masonic references to columns holding up Nature, set up by a higher hand, which will be familiar to those who recall the Masonic lecture on the two pillars.
[20] In other words, he can only control voluntary movements, and has no conscious control over his animal functions, such as breathing, digesting and the beating of his heart.

spreading abroad with the same strength and the same abundance, although in our inferior realm we experience its effects quite diversely.

This is a true picture of what happens in the Immaterial Order. Although free Beings, being separate from the Great Principle, can avoid the intellectual influences which descend continuously upon them, although those intellectual influences themselves may suffer some contraction during their journey which may divert their effects, the One Who sends those beneficial gifts never closes His beneficent hand. He always performs the same action. He is always equally strong, equally powerful, equally pure, equally undisturbed by the erring of His free creations, who can plunge themselves into crime and give birth to evil by the sole right of their free will. It would therefore be absurd to claim any participation by the Divine Being in the disturbances of free Beings, and those which take place in the Universe: in a word, God and Evil can never have the slightest relationship.

It would be with the same lack of proof that we might attribute evil to material Beings, since they can do nothing by themselves, and all their actions come from their individual Principle, which is always governed or put in motion by a power separate from them.

Now, if there are only three Orders of Being: God, intelligent Beings and physical Nature; if we cannot find the origin of Evil in the first, Who is exclusively the source of all good, nor in the last, which is neither free nor sentient, yet however the existence of Evil is undisputed, one is necessarily forced to attribute it to man, or to any other Being which, like him, occupies an intermediate rank.

Indeed, it cannot be denied that physical Nature is neither blind nor ignorant, and that it acts regularly and in a certain order, which is fresh proof that it acts under the control of an Intelligence, else it would follow a path of disorder. It cannot be denied that man sometimes does good, sometimes evil; that sometimes he follows the fundamental Laws of his Being, and sometimes he deviates from them. When he does good, he is walking with the light and help of the intellect, and when he does evil, this can be attributed to him alone, and not to the intellect, which is the sole path and the sole guide to good, through which alone can man and all Beings do good.

As to Evil itself, in vain would we would try to make known its essential nature. For Evil to be understood, it would be necessary for it to be true, and then it would cease to be evil, since truth and goodness are the same thing. However, as we have said, to understand it is to perceive the relationship between an object and the order and harmony whose rule we have within ourselves. But if Evil has no relationship with that Order, and is exactly opposed to it, how can we see any similarity between them; and therefore, how could we comprehend it?

Nevertheless, Evil has its own weight, number and measure, like Good, and even here below we can even understand the relationship which the weight, number and measure of Good has with the weight, number and measure of Evil, and this in terms of quantity, intensity and duration. For the relationship of Evil to Good is from *nine to one* in quantity, from *zero to one* in intensity, and from *seven to one* in duration.

If these expressions appear puzzling to the reader, and he wishes for an explanation, I beg him not to ask physical calculators; for they don't understand the practical relationships between things.[21]

We have dwelt long enough on how man should have been able to convince himself of the immaterial existence of his Being, and that of the Supreme Principle; and what he should observe so as not to confuse this Principle with matter and corruption, nor to assign this imperishable Life to visible things, which is the most beautiful privilege of a Being that there has ever been, and in which His direct creations alone participate by right of their origin.

By the simple continuation of these observations, we will soon set forth satisfying theories as to man's destiny, and that of other Beings.

---

[21] Because Saint-Martin is using Theosophical Addition and not Mathematical Addition, so he is telling the Reader not to ask a Mathematician to explain these figures. A fuller outline of how these figures may be arrived at can be found in *Of Errors & Truth*, Saint-Martin's first book, originally published in 1775, as well as his book *On Numbers*, published posthumously.

Gimel (ג) – Man, Visible Sign of God

When a man produces a piece of work, what he does is to create and make visible the plan, thought or design he has formed. He focuses on giving this copy as much conformity with the original that he possibly can, so that his thought might be better understood.

If the people to whom this man wishes to make himself understood could read his thoughts, he wouldn't need physical signs to be understood: everything he conceived would be understood by them as quickly and to the same extent as by the man himself.

But being bound, like him, by material obstacles which limit their intelligence, he is compelled to transmit his idea to them physically; else it would mean nothing to them as it wouldn't be able to reach them.

So, he uses all those physical means and produces all those material works just to communicate his idea to his fellow men, to Beings who are distinct from him, separated from him; just to strive to bring them closer to him, to compare them to an image of himself, and by striving to enclose them in his unity, from which they are separated.

This is how a Writer or Orator physically manifests his thoughts, to engage those who read or hear him to become one with him by accepting his opinion.

This is how a Sovereign assembles his armies and raises up ramparts and fortresses, to impress upon the people a conviction of his power, and at the same time to instil terror in them; so that, as convinced as him of his power, they are all completely of one mind and joined to his cause, and whether through admiration or through fear, they form one whole with him. In the absence of these visible signs, the Orator's opinion and the Sovereign's power would remain concentrated in themselves, without anyone knowing about them.

So it is for all other men, for they don't have, nor will they ever have any goal other than that of acquiring in their thoughts the privilege of domination, universality, unity.

It is that same Universal Law of reunion which produces that general activity and voracity we previously remarked on in physical Nature: for we see a reciprocal attraction between all bodies, by which, on coming together, they substantialize and feed one another. It is for need of this communication that all individuals strive to link themselves with the Beings which surround them, to mingle with them and absorb them into their own unity, so that, as the subdivisions disappear, that which is separated may reunite, that which is at the circumference may return to the center, that which is concealed may reach the light; and that, by means of this, harmony and order will overcome the confusion which holds all Beings in thrall.

Why, if all Laws are uniform, wouldn't we apply to the creation of the Universe the same judgment which we bring to our works? Why wouldn't we regard them as being like the expression of God's thought, since man's thought is expressed in his rough and material works? Finally, why wouldn't we believe that the purpose of God's universal work is the extension and rule of that unity, which we ourselves intend in every one of our actions?

Nothing can stand against the claim we make concerning this analogy between God and man, since we see it in the works of both: indeed, if all the works of God or man are necessarily preceded by internal actions and invisible abilities whose existence we cannot dispute, we are correct in believing that by following the same Law in their acts of creation, they also have the same purpose and the same object.

Without stopping to examine this point further, we will accept that all visible Beings in the Universe are the expression and sign of God's abilities and designs, just as we regard all our creations as being the physical expression of our thoughts and our internal abilities.

When God had recourse to using visible signs, such as the Universe, to communicate His thought, He had to use them simply for the benefit of Beings who are separated from Him. For if all Beings had remained in His unity, they wouldn't have needed those means to read them. Therefore, we recognize that these corrupt Beings who have voluntarily separated from the First Cause and are subject to the Laws of His justice within the visible confines of the Universe, are still the object of His love, since He acts ceaselessly to remove that separation which is so contrary to their happiness.

So it was, indeed, for love of those Beings who had separated from Him that God manifest His abilities and His *Virtues* in all His visible works, in order to reestablish a salutary correspondence between them and Him, which would help them, heal them, and regenerate them through a new Creation; it was to impart to them that outpouring of *life* which alone could draw them back from the state of death in which they had languished from the moment they had become *isolated from Him*. And finally, it was to fashion their reunion with the Divine Source, and to impress on them that character of unity to which we ourselves are attracted with so much activity in all our works.

If the Universe shows the existence of corruption, since it encloses and encompasses it, we should understand from that what the destiny of physical Nature might be, with regard to those Beings separated from unity; *and it isn't without purpose and reason that the terrestrial mass and all bodies are like so many sponges saturated with water, which is violently expressed beneath the pressure of superior Agents.*

Since the Law of moving towards unity applies to all Orders and all Beings, it follows that the least of individuals has the same aim within its species: that is to say, that the universal Principles, both general and specific, each occur in the creations which belong to them, in order to make their powers visible to Beings which are distinct from them, which, being intended to receive the communication and aid of these powers, could not do so without this means.

And so, all the creations, all the individuals of general and specific Creation are, each according to their kind, simply the visible expression and the representative image of the properties of the general or specific Principle which acts in them. They must all carry within them the clear marks of that Principle which constitutes them. They should clearly manifest its type and its power through the actions and the deeds they perform. In a word, they should be its characteristic sign and, as it were, its physical and living image.

All Agents and all things of Nature contain within them the proof of this truth. The Sun is characteristic of the Fire *Principle*, the Moon the Water *Principle*, and our planet that of the Earth *Principle*: all that the Earth produces and contains within it similarly manifests this General Law. The grape indicates the vine; the date, a palm tree; silk, a worm; honey, a bee. Each mineral proclaims the kind of earth and salt which serves as its basis and connection; each vegetable the seed which generated it; without speaking here of the multitude of other natural, fundamental, relative, fixed, progressive, simple, composite, active and passive signs and characteristics by which the whole of the Universe is composed, and which offer the means to explain all of its parts by one another.

We can say as much of our artistic creations and all of man's inventions. Every one of his works proclaims the ideas, tastes, intelligence, and particular profession of the man who is its Agent or creator. A statue leads to the thought of a sculptor; a picture to that of a painter; a palace to that of an architect, because all these creations are but the physical execution of the abilities specific to the genius or the artist who created them, just as the creations of Nature are but the expression of their Principle and only exist to be its true character.

Here we must fight a false theory, resurrected in recent times, concerning the nature of things, by which it is assumed that they have a progressive perfectibility, which can successively bring the most Inferior Orders and species to the highest ranks of elevation in the chain of Beings, so that, in following this doctrine, we would no longer know if a stone couldn't become a tree, if a tree couldn't become a horse, a horse a man, and imperceptibly a Being of an even more perfect nature. This outlook, dictated by error and ignorance of the true Principles, cannot endure when one thinks about it carefully.

Everything is regulated, everything is determined depending on the species, and even down to the individual. For everything that exists there is a fixed Law, an immutable number and an indelible character, like that of the *Principle Being* in which all Laws, all numbers, all characters reside. Each Order, each Family has its barrier which no power can ever cross.

The various mutations which insects exhibit in their forms during their lives don't negate this truth in any way, since there we can still observe a constant Law in the various species of perfect animals, which, each according to their Order are born, live and perish in the same form; for even insects, despite their mutations, never change their Kingdom: indeed, in their lowest form they are still above the plants and minerals; and even in their most distinguished manner of being, they show neither the character, nor the Laws by which more perfect animals are governed. In this respect all we can infer from them is a kind, a Kingdom, a group apart which is most significant, but which they will never leave, and whose Laws they will necessarily follow, as do all other Beings, each according to their Order.

If the life of all Nature's creations didn't have fixed characteristics, how could one determine their purpose and their properties? How could the plans of the Great Principle be accomplished, Who, by laying out

Nature before the Beings who are separated from Him, desires to provide them with enduring and regular indicators by which they might restore their relationship and their connections with Him? If these material signs were variable, if their Laws, their progress, even their forms were not fixed, the work of that Painter would only be a collection of pictures containing muddled objects, in which the mind could find no point on which to focus, and which could never show the purpose of the Great Being.

Finally, that Great Being Himself would only demonstrate powerlessness and weakness, since He would have set forth a plan which He was unable to complete.

If it is true that all the creations of Nature and art have their own specific characteristics, and if it is by means of that alone that they may clearly express their Principles, and if at a single glance a trained eye should be able to determine through which Agent that creation manifests its abilities, man, too, can only exist in accordance with that general Law.

Since man, like all Beings comes from a Principle which is his own, like all Beings he must be the visible representation of that Principle. Like them, he must manifest it visibly, so that nobody might mistake it, and on seeing the image one would recognize the model from which he was derived. Therefore, when observing his nature, let us seek to understand the Principle of which he must be the visible sign and expression.

However, here I am only talking about his intellectual Being; whereas his corporeal Being, like all other bodies, is simply the expression of a non-sentient and immaterial Principle, and being composed of the same essences as those bodies is subject to all the fragility of compound Beings.

To know man, therefore, we must seek in him the signs of a Principle of a different Order.

Irrespective of thought and the other intellectual abilities which we have identified in him, he exhibits things so foreign to matter that one is compelled to attribute to them a Principle other than the Principle of matter. Foresight, combinations of all kinds, the bold knowledge with which he numbers, meaures and weighs the entire Universe to such a degree; those sublime astronomical observations by which, placed between time which is no more and time which has not yet come he reconciles their most distant extremities, verifies the phenomena of the earliest epochs and confidently predicts those of ages to come; the privilege he alone has in Nature of taming and enslaving animals, of sowing and harvesting, of extracting the fire from substances, of subjecting all Elemental substances to his manipulations and use; finally, that activity in which he endlessly seeks to invent and produce new Beings, such that his action becomes a kind of continuous creation: these are the facts which bear witness to an active Principle within him which is completely different from the passive Principle of matter.

If we look carefully at man's works, we find that they are not only the expression of his thoughts, but also that he seeks, so far as he can, to paint himself in his works. He never ceases to multiply his own image through painting and sculpture, and in thousands of the most frivolous artistic creations. Finally, he gives the buildings he erects proportions which relate to his body. This is a profound truth which can reveal a large area for study to intelligent eyes, since this active desire to duplicate his image so much, and to only find beauty in what is similar to him, must forever separate man from all the other Beings of this Universe.

When we make the mistake of trying to attribute all these facts to the working of our sensory organs, we are ignoring the fact that we must then assume that the human species is uniform in its Laws and its actions, just like all animals, each according to their Order. Now, the individual differences we find between animals of the same species doesn't prevent each of them having a character of its own; but there is also a form of living and behaving which is uniform and common to all the individuals which compose it, regardless of the distances between locations, and variations created by differences in climates on all physical, material Beings.

Instead of this uniformity, man shows almost nothing except difference and opposition: it seems as if he bears no resemblance to any of his fellow men. He differs from each of them in his morals, tastes, habits and knowledge. When left to himself he challenges them all in ambition, in greed, in possessions, in talents, in dogmas. Every man is like a Sovereign in his own empire; and every man even strives towards universal domination.

What am I saying? Not only that man differs from his fellow man, but at any instant he even differs from himself. He wants and he doesn't want, he hates and he loves, he takes and rejects the same thing at almost the same time, at almost the same time he is captivated and repelled. Moreover, he sometimes flees from what delights him, and draws near to what he loathes, and seeks out evil, pain, and even death.

If this was simply due to the operating of his sensory organs, if it was always the same impulse which governed his actions, man would show more uniform behavior both in himself and towards others; he would function according to an enduring and peaceable Law, and when he couldn't do things identically, he would at least do them similarly, and in that we would always recognize a single Principle. So, how can people teach that the senses control everything and teach man everything, since on the contrary it is obvious that regarding corporeal things they cannot even measure anything correctly?

Thus, it may be said that in his darkness as well as in his light, man manifests a Principle which is completely different from that which operates and maintains his sensory organs, for as we have already seen, the former can act through deliberation, whereas the latter can only act through impulse.

The proportions of man's body reflect the relationship between his intellectual Being and a Principle superior to that of corporeal Nature.

If we draw a circle in which man's height is the diameter, the line of his two extended arms, being equal to his height, can also be regarded as a diameter of the same circle; now, let us consider whether it is possible to draw two diameters in the same circle without them both having to go through the center of the circle.

Our body, it is true, doesn't have those two diameters passing through the center of the same circle, since the diameter of his height isn't cut into two equal parts on his body by the horizontal diameter formed by his extended arms; and because of this man is, so to speak, connected with to two centers; but this truth simply proves a transposition in man's constituent powers, and not an alteration in the essence of those constituent powers, and so it doesn't in any way destroy the connection we are making; and although these fundamental dimensions are no longer in their natural place, man can always find traces of his greatness and nobility in the proportions of his body.

The animals which most resemble man in their conformity differ completely on this point, since their extended arms give a line which is much longer than that of the height of their body.

These proportions, which are exclusively attributed to man's body, make him the common and fundamental basis of all the proportions and all the powers of the rest of the corporeal Beings, which we should never consider except in relation to the human form.[22]

But these marvels of the mind and these corporeal relationships, whose image we've just presented, are not the most essential of those that may be observed in man. He has yet other abilities and rights which place him above all the Beings of Nature.

Just as there is no elemental substance which does not contain useful properties, according to its type; there is no man in whom the seeds of justice, and even that beneficence which is the primitive characteristic of that Necessary Being, the Sovereign Father and Preserver of all legitimate existence, couldn't develop.

The opposite conclusions which people have claimed to draw from fruitless education are null and abusive. For them to have any value, the teacher would have to be perfect, or at least have the qualities which matched the needs of his pupils; and he would have to be competent in the art of understanding their characters and their needs, in order to show them, in an engaging manner, the kind of support or *power* they lack, without which their moral insensitivity would only grow, they would sink more and more into vice and corruption, and they would be rejected due to the imperfection of their nature, which is in fact only the result of the incompetence and inadequacy of their Master.

If we therefore exclude certain monstrous men – and even their actions only become inexplicable because in the beginning they sought the seat of their heart in vain – there could not exist a Nation or a man in whom we couldn't find a few vestiges of *virtue*. Even the most corrupt associations were founded on justice, and cover themselves with its appearance, at least; and to obtain success in their misguided undertakings

---

[22] This somewhat muddy argument relies on Saint-Martin's obsession with the number 4 as the number of perfection, and its analogous shape, the square, which he sometimes represents as a traditional square, and sometimes as an equal-armed cross, as seen in his first book *Of Errors & Truth*. In effect he is saying that, since man's height is the same as the full extent of his two arms, his center forms the center of a circle in which his height forms one diameter and his extended arms the other diameter, thereby forming 'the angle of a square' (or four right angles), which is a well-known Masonic term. He contrasts this to that of an ape, in which the arms, when extended, are far longer than the height, and uses this as an argument for using man as the exemplar against which all other corporeal Beings should be judged. However, while acknowledging that this doesn't work since man's arms don't come out of the middle of his body, and that such a depiction of man's form requires two circles drawn slightly apart, he goes on to say that this doesn't matter, since man's transcendant self means that part of him is raised up to a higher plane. This somewhat disingenuous argument really destroys the point he is trying to make!

even the perversest men have borrowed the name and outward trappings of wisdom.[23]

The beneficence natural to man would also be manifested universally if we sought its signs elsewhere than in needs which are foreign to us, because it must be exercised on real objects, in order to determine and develop the true *powers* which belong to our essence.

But, regardless of how the Observers incessantly base their experiments on false needs and equally imaginary benefits, they forget that man, left to himself, contents himself with a single *virtue*, which leads him to neglect and forget all the others. Now they only take note of the one he has adopted, and then, not finding the same *virtues* in all individuals and among all Nations, they hastily determine that, since they are not found everywhere, they cannot be a part of man's essence.

It is an unforgivable error to determine a general Law for the human species from various specific examples. We repeat: man has within himself the seeds of all the *virtues*; they are all in his nature, although he only manifests some of them; and what often happens is that, when he appears to have disregarded his innate *virtues*, he has simply substituted some for others.

The savage who violates the fidelity of marriage by offering his wife to his guests experiences only beneficence and pleasure in exercising hospitality.

Indian widows who throw themselves onto the funeral pyre, sacrifice the voice of Nature to the desire to appear to be tender and sensitive, or to the desire to enter into possession of the properties which their religious dogmas make them hope for in another life.[24]

The very Priests who profaned their Religions with human sacrifices, only gave themselves over to those awful crimes to let their piety shine forth through the nobility of the victim, convincing themselves that, through that terrible act of faith, they understood the idea of the greatness and power of the Supreme Agent, or that they would make Him more

---

[23] This seem to say that there was once a sliver of good in even the most corrupt individuals or organizations, who still cover their misguided actions in the guise of wisdom or justice, suggesting that there remains a vestige of those *virtues* left. This seems to extend even to hardened criminals (the 'monsters'), though the language is so obtuse it is difficult to work out whether the comment about the heart extends to them as well as the Nations and individuals mentioned later.

[24] Here he is talking about reincarnation, that Hindu belief which suggests that one who has passed a poor and miserable existence may hope to return in a considerably wealthier state in the following incarnation.

propitious towards the Earth when they believed Him to be angered against it.

It is therefore quite clear that, despite the errors of men, all their Religions, Institutions and customs are based on a truth or a *virtue*.

As an example, may we consider the social conventions of man and his political establishments? They are all intended to repair a disorder which is moral or physical, real or customary. He has – or claims to have – as the object of all his laws, a means to remedy various abuses, to prevent them, or to procure some advantage for his fellow citizens and himself which may contribute towards making them content.

Now, does this not admit that, being superior to those physical Beings which are focused solely upon themselves, here below man must perform functions which are different to theirs? Is it not made apparent through his own actions that he is charged with a divine task, for as God is Good in His very essence, the continual repair of disorder and the preservation of His works must surely be the work of the Divinity?

Finally, we see Sacred Institutions established across the Earth, in which man alone of all the physical Beings participates. We find religious dogmas across all time and in all regions of the Universe [25] which teach man that he can bring his offerings and his tributes up to the Sanctuary of a Divinity that he knows not, but to Whom he is perfectly known, and by Whom he can hope to be heard.

Everywhere, these dogmas teach that the Divine decrees are not always impenetrable to man, that he may, in this respect, participate in some way in the power and in the supreme *virtues*, and everywhere we have seen true men – or impostors – proclaim themselves to be His ministers and organs.

The very signs of those sublime rights can be perceived, not only in all the public Religions of the different Nations; not only in what have been called the *Occult Sciences* where there are mysterious ceremonies and specific formulas to which are attributed secret powers over Nature, diseases, good and evil genies, and over men's thoughts [26]; but also in the

---

[25] In this instance Saint-Martin is referring to the Earth (...*contrées de l'Univers*...), but he is being hyperbolic in his description, rather than suggesting the existence of aliens (!)

[26] While we know that, at this time, Saint-Martin was still a member of the Élus Cohen, it is clear from this slightly sarcastic comment that he was beginning to question his membership in this Order and what it could accomplish. However, it was not until 1785, three years following the publication of this book, that he would formally resign from all his Lodges, all his formal Masonic and Theurgical activities.

simple civil and legal actions of human authorities, which, taking their conventional laws to be the arbiters, regard and consult them as absolute declarations of Truth, and when acting in accordance with those laws, don't fear saying that they possess an enlightened authority and a sound knowledge which is safe from all error.

If it is true that man doesn't have a single thought within him, and yet the notion of such power and such illumination is, so to speak, universal, everything may well be degraded in science and in man's gloomy progress, but not everything is false. This notion therefore shows that there is some analogy, some connection with the Supreme Action, and some vestiges of man's own rights which remain to him, as we have already discovered in man's mind and its clear connections with the Infinite Intelligence and with His *Virtues*.

With all these signs, is it still possible for us to misunderstand the Principle of man? If all the Beings who have received life exist only to manifest the properties of the Agent which gave it to them, can there be any doubt that the Agent from Whom man received his would be the Divinity Himself, since we find in him so many signs of a superior origin and of a Divine Action?

Let us now bring together the consequences of all of the proofs which we have just established, and in the Being Who produced man let us recognize an inexhaustible source of thoughts, knowledge, powers, illumination, strength, powers; and finally an infinite number of abilities for which no Principle of Nature can offer an image, abilities which bring us all into the essence of the Necessary Being when we wish to contemplate His existence.

Since none of these rights seem to be foreign to us; since on the contrary, we find in them traits multiplied in man's abilities, it is clear that we are destined to possess them all, and manifest them to the eyes of those who are unaware of them or who wish to ignore them. Let us therefore state this more clearly: if each of the Beings of Nature is the expression of one of the temporal powers of Wisdom, man is the visible and outward sign or expression of Divinity Himself. It is for that reason that he must have in him all the traits that characterize Him; otherwise the resemblance isn't perfect, and the model could be misunderstood. And in this we can already form an idea concerning the natural relationships which exist between God, Man and the Universe.

Daleth (ד) – Man Emanated from God

The principles I have explained concerning the sublime destiny of man should earn our confidence all the more, since he himself manifests the truth in almost all his actions. Driven by a hidden instinct to dominate, either by force or by the apparent justice of his doctrine, by this he appears to be concerned solely with proving the existence of a God, and to present Him to his fellow man.

Those who declare themselves to be against the idea of an eternal and infinitely just Being, Source of all felicity and all enlightenment, do nothing more than change the name of that Being, and put another in His place. Far from destroying His indestructible existence, they prove His reality and all the powers which belong to Him. For if the Atheist and the Materialist find it repugnant to believe in a God Who is pictured as being in their soul, what do they do, when they substitute Him with matter, but simply transfer the True Principle's attributes into that matter, whose essence makes them forever inseparable? So, that idol they present us with is still a God.

Moreover, by raising matter up in this way, indeed it isn't so much the rule of matter but their own that they are claiming to establish. For the reasoning they use to support their theories, the enthusiasm which drives them, all their declarations: aren't these all being used to persuade us that they possess the truth? Now, given the intimate connection we feel exists between God and truth, could being the possessor of truth be anything other than being God?

Therefore, the Atheist confesses, despite himself, the existence of that Supreme Being, because he cannot undertake to prove that there is no God without appearing to be a God himself.

How indeed could he not point to the existence of the Supreme Principle, for, since all Beings of Nature are the visible expression of the creative abilities of that Principle, man must come both from His creative abilities and His thinking abilities. The Atheist, therefore, cannot escape the Law which is common to everything contained within the temporal realm. We will go into this subject in some detail. Don't let its depth frighten you, for it is important to go into this, and the outcome will be fruitful.

Before temporal things have an existence which makes them physical to us, original and intermediary elements are needed between them and the creative abilities from which they are descended, because these temporal things and the abilities from which they descended are of too different a nature for them to be able to exist together without a space; which is physically represented to us in Sulfur and Gold, and in Mercury and Earth, which can only unite by means of the same Law of an intermediate substance.[27]

These elements, which are unknown to the senses, but whose necessary existence is confirmed by the intellect, are determined and fixed in their essence and number, like all the Laws and all the means that Wisdom uses in order to accomplish its purposes. Finally, they can be regarded as the first signs of the superior abilities to which they are immediately connected.

Consequently, everything that exists in physical Nature, all forms, the smallest traces, are and can only be the unions, combinations or divisions of those primitive signs, and nothing can appear as a physical thing which isn't written in them, which doesn't descend from them and which isn't a part of them, just as all figures possible in Geometry are always composed of points, lines, circles, or triangles.

Man himself, in his material works, which are only secondary works compared to the works of Nature, is limited, as are all other Beings, to these primitive signs. There is nothing he can build, draw or construct; there is truly no form he can imagine, nor can he execute a single voluntary or involuntary movement which doesn't result from these exclusive models, of which everything that moves and everything that lives in Nature is their creation and their representation. If he could do otherwise, then man would be the creator of a different Nature and a different Order of things, which would not belong to the Creative Principle and the model of everything that physically exists for us.

So, the admirable creations of the Arts, those wonderful monuments to human industry, reveal at every step man's dependence and his destiny. They only present compilations, or pieces reassembled from other monuments, which themselves were various combinations of basic elements, which we have said were the original signs of the creative abilities of Divinity. Therefore, there is nothing in corporeal man or his

---

[27] Presumably a catalyst of some kind.

creations which is not, although in a very second-hand manner, an expression of the universal creative action which all corporeal Beings represent, since they exist and act.

Let us raise ourselves above material forms and apply these principles to speech and writing, both of which are signs of thinking abilities, since they are for us its first physical expression.

It is certain that alphabetical *sounds and characters, which serve as the basic instruments for all the words we use to express our thoughts, must stem from the original signs and sounds which serve as their basis; and this deep truth is shown to us from antiquity in the fragment of Sanchuniathon*[28]*, which depicts Thoth drawing the portrait of the Gods in order to make of them the sacred characters of the letters; a sublime emblem of immense fruitfulness, because it is taken from the very source from which man should always draw.*

In accepting these original signs as being the physical expression of our thoughts, we shouldn't find pause in the infinite variety of those which are in use among the different Nations on Earth: for that variety only proves our ignorance. For if the Law which serves as the organ of Supreme Wisdom established order and regularity throughout in order to express the thought He sends us, He must have established invariable signs, just as He established them for the production of His material things; and if we were not buried in the deepest darkness, or if we were more concerned with following the instructive and enlightening path of *the simplicity of Beings*, who knows if we wouldn't come to understand both the form and the number of those primitive signs, that is to say, to finalize our alphabet?

But whatever our deprivation in this respect, since these original signs exist, all those which we use, although following our particular conventions, are necessarily derived from them: and thus, all the words we might want to compose, imagine and manufacture will always be assemblages drawn from those original characters, since, being unable to

---

[28] Sanchuniathon was allegedly a Phonecian author whose writings only survive in three fragments and are only found quoted by Eusebius in his attempts to discredit pagan creation stories. Because of this, many scholars now believe the excerpts are either apocryphal and invented by Eusebius, Emperor Constantine's biographer, or by Philo of Byblos, who Eusebius claims translated and transcribed the original texts. However, it appears that in Saint-Martin's time the authenticity of both the fragments and the existence of the author were widely accepted. It is in one of the fragments, the *Cosmogony of Taautus*, that we find the story of Thoth's creation of the alphabet.

depart from the Law which has produced them, nothing can ever be found outside of them, and which aren't, so to speak, they themselves.

These original sounds and characters being the true physical signs of our thoughts, must also be the physical signs of the unity of thought, because there is only one single idea, just as there is only one Principle of all things.

Thus, even the most disfigured creations we can produce in speech and writing will always bear the indirect imprint of those primitive signs, and consequently the imprint that unique idea or unity of thought: so, man cannot utter a single word or draw a single character which doesn't manifest the thinking ability of the Supreme Agent; just as he cannot produce a single physical action or movement without manifesting His creative abilities.

Even the most insane, the most prideful, the most corrupt use he may make of these original instruments of thought, in his language or in his writing, don't destroy the point we're making. Since there are absolutely no materials other than those primitive characters available: man is forced to use them, even when he wishes to raise barriers against the unity they represent and declare them to be the enemy.

Indeed, it is with the weapons of this very unity that he wishes to combat it; it is with the strength of this very unity that he wishes to prove its weakness; finally, it is with the very signs of his own existence that he wishes to claim that it doesn't exist and that it is a phantom. If the Atheist wants to attack, in whatever manner he may, the First Principle of everything that exists, let him therefore refrain from using any action, any word, and let his Being even descend into nothingness: for every time he shows himself, writes anything, says anything, or even moves, he proves that it is he himself that he would like to destroy.

We are therefore justified in saying that man is meant to be the sign and the clear expression of the abilities of the Universal Supreme Principle from Whom he is *emanated*; as all individuals Beings, each according to their Order, are the visible sign of the particular Principle which has communicated life to them.

This word, *emanated*, can help to shed new light on our nature and our origin; because if the idea of emanation is hard to think about, it is only because men have allowed it to symbolize their whole Being. In emanation they only see the separation of a substance, as in the way a fragrant body evaporates, or how a river divides into several streams – all examples taken from matter, in which the total mass is actually reduced when some constituent parts are removed from it.

When they wish to carry the idea of emanation across to objects which are livelier and more active such as Fire, which seems to produce a multitude of Fires identical to it while remaining the same as it, they believe they had achieved their goal. But this example is still foreign to the true notion we should form about immaterial emanation, and it is our duty to point out that error to those who would take it further.

Since material Fire is only visible to us through consuming substances, it can only be known to us so long as it remains upon the base it devours, whereas Divine Fire vivifies everything. In the second place, when it appears that this material Fire produces other Fires, it doesn't bring them forth from itself at all, like Divine Fire; it only reacts on the seeds of Fire innate in the body that it comes close to and brings about the explosion. We have evidence of this, in that it is impossible for Fire to ignite ashes because the Fire *Principle* has disappeared.[29]

These differences are too striking for a wise man not to cease making such abusive comparisons.

All Beings of material Nature, which only show physical things and act by means of the physical senses, only indicate the physical Principle alive in those Beings and causing them to move. They don't indicate a Holy and Divine Principle sufficiently clearly to prove its direct existence. In addition, evidence taken from matter is quite insufficient to prove God, and consequently, for us to demonstrate man's emanation out of the bosom of Divinity.

But since we have already discovered in man the evidence of the Principle which made him, and which is in man himself, it is in man's spirit that we should find the Laws which presided over his origin. Finally, since man is a real Being, we should never judge him by comparing him, as we can physical Beings whose qualities are related to him.

What does he tell us, then, when considered from this viewpoint? He shows us through his own actions, that he can be emanated from Divine

---

[29] Saint-Martin extensively covered the prevailing theory of *phlogiston* in his first book *Of Errors & Truth*. Prior to an understanding of the element oxygen, a popular theory was that all flammable substances contained an element called 'phlogiston', and it was this which ignited when a flame was held close to the substance. When the 'phlogiston' was exhausted the flame went out, which was why ashes could not be ignited. Similarly, since air could only absorb a limited amount of 'phlogiston', if a glass was placed over a burning object, it went out because the air rapidly became saturated with 'phlogiston', and then could not support further reaction. See also Footnote 57.

abilities, without those Divine abilities showing any separation or division, or any alteration in their essence.

For when I externalize any intellectual act, when I communicate my most profound thoughts to one of my fellow men, the impulse I transmit to his Being which will impel him to act, and perhaps give him a *virtue*; that thought, I tell you, although it comes from me, although it is, as it were, extracted from myself and my own image, does not in any way deprive me of the right to produce similar thoughts. I still have the same source of thoughts within me, the same will, the same action; yet however, in some way I have given new life to that person by communicating a thought to him, a Power which meant nothing to him before I performed a kind of emanation which I was able to produce for him. Ever bearing in mind, however, that there is only one sole Author and Creator of all things, we can see why I can only communicate fleeting images, whereas that Universal Author communicates existence itself, and imperishable life.

But, if in considering that action which is common to all men, we evidently know that emanating my thoughts, will and actions[30] doesn't change my essence in any way, this is all the more reason that divine life can be communicated through emanations: He can produce innumerable and endless signs and expressions of Himself, and never cease to be the Source of life.

If man is emanated from the Divinity, it is therefore an absurd and impious doctrine to say he is drawn from nothingness and created like matter, for then it would also be necessary to regard Divinity Himself as nothingness, He who is the living and uncreated source of all realities and all existences. As a result, which is just as natural, man drawn from nothingness must necessarily return to nothingness. But nothingness is a void and empty word, which no man can have any concept of, and nobody could take the time to consider it without being repelled.

Therefore, let us distance ourselves from the criminal and foolish notion of nothingness, to which blind men teach us we owe our origin.

---

[30] Thought, will and action are how Pasqually described the process of creation by the Divinity in his *Treatise on the Reintegration of Beings*. Sometimes he refers to the process as intention, will and word, where the Word is the active action of creation (a concept beautifully explored by David Cooper in his book 'God Is A Verb'). Since man is the fruit of this operation, he must also contain these three Principles within himself, though in muted form. Saint-Martin comes back to this process regularly in this book. We will see this idea revisited often in this book.

Let us not demean our Being: it is made for a sublime destiny, but it cannot be greater than its Principle, since, according to simple physical Laws, Beings can only be elevated to the level from whence they have descended. Yet such Laws would cease to be true and universal if man's Principle was nothingness. But everything clearly shows us our relationship with the very center, the Producer of the immaterial Universe and the physical Universe, since all our efforts continually lead us to adapt both to our use, and to take hold of all the powers around us.

Let us also observe that this doctrine concerning the emanation of man's intellectual Being is consistent with that which teaches us that all our discoveries are, in some way, actually reminiscences. One can even say that these two doctrines are mutually supportive, for if we are emanated from a Universal Source of truth, no truth should appear to us to be new; and similarly, if no truth appears to us to be new, but rather we perceive in it only as a memory or the representation of something which was hidden within us, we must have had our birth in the Universal Source of truth.

We see in the simple, physical Laws of bodies, a physical image of this Principle, of which man is but a Being with faint recollections.

When physical seeds produce their fruit, they are simply manifesting visibly the abilities or properties which they had received through the constituent Laws of their essence. When these seeds – an acorn for example – accomplishes its individual existence suspended from the branch of the oak which had produced it, it has, as it were, participated in everything that worked upon it in the atmosphere, since it received the influences of the air, since it existed in the midst of all living corporeal Beings, since it was observed by the Sun, the stars, the animals, the plants, men: that is to say, everything in the temporal sphere.

It is true that it was only passively present among all these things because it only had an inactive existence, linked to that of the oak, and not having any life separate from that of its Principle it lived the life of that Principle, but without power to do anything itself.

When this acorn reaches maturity and falls on the ground or is placed in the soil by man's hand and produces a tree, and produces its own fruit, it is only repeating what had already been carried out by the very tree from which it came. It has simply risen up, through its own abilities, to the place from which it descended, and been reborn in the area that it had previously occupied, that is to say, it has reproduced itself among the same things, the same Beings, the same phenomena by which it had already been surrounded.

But there is an important difference in that, in this secondary state, it now exists in an active manner, being itself an Agent, whereas in the first state it was only passive and had no action distinct from that of its Principle.

We can think the same thing about intellectual man. Because of his original existence, he had, according to the universal Law of Beings, been attached to his generative tree. He was, as it were, the witness of everything which existed in his atmosphere, and as this atmosphere was so far above the one we inhabit, so the intellectual was above the material, and thus the things in which man was involved were incomparably superior to the things of the Elemental Order. And the difference between them is the same as that between the reality of Beings who have a true and ineffaceable existence, and the appearance of those who have only a dependent and secondary life. Thus, since man is linked to the *truth*, he participated, albeit passively, in all the things appertaining to *truth*.

Having been detached from the *universal tree* which was the tree which gave him birth, and man finding himself precipitated into a lower region to experience intellectual vegetation, if he succeeds in acquiring enlightenment and manifests the powers and abilities analogous to his true nature, he must himself accomplish and represent what his Principle had already shown him; he must recover sight of at least some of the things that had previous been in his presence, and must reunite with the Beings he had previously lived with; and finally, he must discover once again, in a more intuitive and active manner, those things which had already existed for him, in him and around him.

That is why we can say that all Beings created and emanated in the temporal region, and therefore man as well, are working towards the same end, which is to recover their resemblance to their Principle: that is, to grow without cease until they come to the point of producing their own fruit, as their Principle had produced its seed in them. That is also why, since man has a memory of light and truth, this proves that he is descended from the realm of light and truth.

Let us return to our subject and say once more that man is born to be the universal figure, the living sign and the true image of an infinite Being. He is born, I say, to prove to all Beings that there is a God Who is necessary, bright, good, just, holy, powerful, eternal, strong, always ready to revivify those who love Him, and always terrible towards those who want to fight Him or disown Him. Happy is the man, if he has only ever represented this God by *manifesting* His Powers, and not by *usurping* them!

And let us not be at all surprised to see man bear such an imprint. The abilities of the Necessary Being are as endless as He is, and since He has placed the expression of His number upon us, it must be that we have within us the seal of His universality.

As for the fear of disparaging that Supreme Principle by attributing our origin to Him, let us remember that we have in our very emanation only what we are able to preserve of Him: for all creations are inferior to their generating Principle, and we are simply the expression of the Divine abilities and the *Divine Number*, and not of the same the nature as those abilities and that *Number* which is the personal and distinctive characteristic of the Divinity.

That should reassure anyone as to the greatness exclusive to the Supreme Principle and to His glory. However high we raise ourselves up, He will be eternally and infinitely above us, as He is above all Beings. *It is as much to honor Him as to ennoble our own essence thus, because we cannot raise ourselves up a single degree without elevating Him fourfold at the same time, since any action, like any movement, any progression is quaternary* [31] *and we cannot move except in accordance with the immutability of His Laws. Finally, if we are descended from the Divinity, if He is the Immediate Principle of our existence, the more we come closer to Him the more we elevate Him in the eyes of all Beings, since then we bring out the refulgence of His powers and His superiority all the more clearly.*

We might even believe that we would render an important service to men if we could bring them to see such sublime truths. Contemplating such things is the true means to abase ourselves, since by comparing their strength and grandeur to ourselves, we are compelled to remain in a state of profound humility. That is why it is a good idea to fix our sight continually on knowledge, in order to convince ourselves that we know nothing; on justice, so as not to believe that we are irreproachable; on all

---

[31] Saint-Martin wrote at length about Quaternary Progression in his first book, *Of Errors and Truth*. God, or the First Principle, being everything in Himself, bears the number '1', while man in his state of perfection, is '4'. He implies through this that, reciprocally, any action taken by man will be reflected fourfold in the immutable region.

the *virtues*, so as not to think that we possess them: for generally speaking man only lives in peace and is content in himself when he thinks about the things which are above, and if we wish to preserve ourselves from all illusion, and particularly from the allure of that pride by which man is so often seduced, we should never take men, but always *God* to be our point of comparison.

Heh (ה) - The Fall, Loss of the Light

In raising ourselves up to that Supreme Principle, without which Truth itself would not be, we will see that all his *abilities* must be real, fixed and positive; that is to say, constituted by their own essence; which preserves them forever against destruction, since their entire Law resides in them alone, as well as the path which leads to the Sanctuary of their existence.

Indeed, since this First Being is the original source of all Powers, how could one conceive of a Power which wouldn't be Him? By what or by whom could He be defeated or changed if all Beings have come from Him either indirectly or directly, and if they have no real abilities or powers other than those that He has given them? For then one must suppose that He would be attacking Himself.

Other evidence shows us that no Being can, or could ever, do anything against God; for if anything were to declare themselves to be His enemy, in order to defeat them He would only need to leave them in their own darkness; those who wished to attack Him would become blind from the very thing they wished to attack. Thus, for the same reason, all their efforts would fail, and all their powers would become null and void, since they could no longer see where they were going.

But so that the first man could manifest this Majestic and Invincible Being, so that he could serve as a sign of the Supreme Divinity, he had to have the freedom to see and consider the true, fixed and positive rights which are in Him, and he had to have a title which gave him entry into His Temple, so that he might rejoice in the spectacle of all His greatness.

Without that, how could he represent the least trace of Him with any accuracy; and if he were only able to represent Him imperfectly, how could those who had lost the image of the Supreme Being be found guilty of continuing to misunderstand Him?

But if it is possible for man, as a free Being, to have stopped presenting himself at the Temple with the humility of the Levite, and to have decided to put the Victim in the place of the Priest, and the Priest in the place of the God he served, the entrance of the Temple must be closed to him, since he came there to seek a light other than the one which alone fills the great immensity. That would be enough for him to lose both knowledge and sight of the beautes of the Temple, since he would only be able to see them in their own habitation, and he had been forbidden to enter.

He believed himself able to find the light elsewhere than in the Being which is his Sanctuary and his Home, and Who alone could allow him to enter there. He believed that he could obtain the light by another path, and believed, in a word, that those true, fixed and positive abilities could exist in two Beings at once. He ceased focusing on Him in which they existed in all their power and brilliance in order to focus on another *Being*, from whom he dared to believe he would receive the same support.

This error, or rather this insane crime, instead of assuring man of an abode of peace and light, precipitated him into the abyss of confusion and darkness, without the Eternal Principle of Life even needing to make the least use of His Powers to add to that disaster. Being felicity by His very essence and the Sole Source of happiness in all Beings, He would be acting against His own Law if He were to distance them from any resource necessary for their happiness. Finally, being only goodness, peace and enjoyment by His very nature, if He Himself sent forth ills, disorder and deprivation, He would be producing things that the Perfect Being should not know, which shows us that He isn't, nor could He ever be the Author of our suffering.[32]

On the contrary, we will see later on in this book, that not one of the *Powers* of this Beneficent Hand have been used or are being used to bring

---

[32] This intriguing retelling of Pasqually's story of the Prevarication and Fall of man shows us how Saint-Martin has developed his understanding of it in the ten years since he could talk directly with his Master about the *Treatise*, and although he clearly had his own handwritten copy, we can see how he has now both embellished the outline provided in the *Treatise* and slanted it more towards a Biblical – and frankly Masonic – setting. In this he has also provided an immensely useful tool to Jean-Baptiste Willermoz, who in the same year that this book was published was steering the Masonic heads of mainland Europe towards a unified system based on the Rite of Strict Observance but containing the teachings of Pasqually, which was to be called the Scottish Rectified Rite, or Knights Beneficent of the Holy City of Jerusalem. Here, Saint-Martin introduces the idea of the heavenly (i.e. not made with human hands) and spiritual Temple in the New Jerusalem, and introduces man as having been the Levites (i.e. Élus Cohen) who had permanent access to the Sanctuary, or Holy of Holies. The Translator believes that in this passage, we can find a key source for the imagery used by Willermoz in his new Rite. It is also interesting to note, in his development of Pasqually's teachings, and as we also saw in his first book, that Saint-Martin has substituted a single Principle of Evil (the 'another *Being*' in the text) for the several prevaricating spirits which had been imprisoned on Earth for their sins, and who collectively tempted Adam into an act of creation without the cooperation of Divinity, for which act he was himself cast down to Earth.

Heh (ה) - The Fall, Loss of the Light

us anything but relief. We will indeed learn to understand that if the powers of this Supreme Agent have constantly done battle since the origin of things, it has been on our behalf, and not against us.

We will see what the difference is between this Being and us, since when we do evil it is we who are its authors, and sometimes we have even had the injustice to blame Him; whereas, when we do good it is He who makes this happen in us and for us, and after doing this in us and for us He rewards us again, as if we did it ourselves.

Finally, we will see that if man paid the same attention to satisfying his true needs that he gives to satisfying his imaginary needs, he would achieve the object of his desires far more quickly; and if I am permitted to say why, it is because both *Good* and *Evil* pursue us towards the truth, but the first pursues us with *four powers*, and the second pursues us with only *two*. Now, since man also has four *powers*, we can see how, if he moved without stopping towards the one with the *same number*, how quickly they would unite.[33]

Since the Divine Being is the sole Principle of light and truth, since He alone possesses the fixed and positive *abilities* in which true life and essence exclusively reside; when man seeks these *abilities* in another Being, he must necessarily lose sight of the true ones, and discover there what is but a mere semblance of all those powers.

Thus, since man has ceased to read in the truth, he could only find uncertainty and error around him. Having abandoned the only abode which is fixed and real, he had to enter a new realm which, with its illusions and its nothingness, was totally opposite to the one he had just left. This new realm, through the multiplicity of its Laws and actions, presented him with the appearance of a unity different to that of the Simple Being, and truths different from His. Finally, that new Being on which he now relied had to show him a fictitious image of all the abilities and all the properties it claimed to possess, when in fact it had none.

And here we find an explanation for the numbers *four* and *nine*, which I have already covered in my previous book. Man has strayed by going from *four* to *nine*, which is to say that he has left the center of fixed and positive truths which are found in the number *four*, being the source

---

[33] The number '2' is seen as 'evil' or 'confusion', since it reflects the division of Evil from Good to form two poles; while as we saw earlier, the number '4' is considered the number of the spirit, perfection, or man's immortal part. For a more detailed understanding consult Saint-Martin's *Of Errors & Truth*, and Pasqually's *Treatise on the Reintegration of Beings*.

and correspondence of everything which exists; moreover being, even in our degradation, the universal number of our measures and the path of the stars; a divine truth of which men of prior Centuries have made the most positive use in order to determine the Laws of celestial movements, although they were only driven to that immortal discovery solely by the certainty of their observations and by the torch of the Natural Sciences. That is to say, then, that man is joined to the number *nine* of fleeting and physical things, whose nothingness and emptiness are set down in the form of the circle, or nonary, assigned to them, and holds man fast as if beneath a spell.[34]

Here, then are those rights which today all the things in this temporal realm have over man. As each of the Beings which compose it is complete and entire within its species, the gaze of this unfortunate man remains fixed on objects which indeed represent unity, but which only represent it through false and very defective images, since they are all formed from compounds; for as they can as seen by our material eyes, they are necessarily composites, seeing that our material eyes are themselves composites and because there can only be a relationship between Beings of the same nature.

By remaining in this temporal realm, man is therefore reduced to seeing only apparent unities, that is to say that now he can only know relative weights, measures and numbers, instead of the absolute weights, measures and numbers he employed in his birthplace. And he has proof of this in the most common experiments, for it would be impossible for him to determine whether a proportion of matter were equal in weight, number and measure to another proportion, since he would have to know the former's absolute weight, number and measure: yet he has left the domain of everything that is fixed.

However, these physical things which are only apparent and of no account to man's spirit, do have a reality which is similar to his physical and material Being. Wisdom is so fertile that He establishes proportions in *virtues* and in *realities* in relation to each Order of His creations.

---

[34] Much of Chapter 6 in Saint-Martin's book *Of Errors & Truth* is taken up with this comparison between the numbers '4' and '9', indicating how man strayed from the center where he was in possession of his full powers, and should have been forever happy ('4', being the intersection of two straight lines of equal length), and ended up moving aimlessly around the circumference (represented by the number '9'), drawing an analogy to that of the Masonic conundrum of 'squaring the circle', by needing to return from '9' to '4'.

That is why there is a propriety – and even an insurmountable Law – connected with physical things, without which their action, being fleeting and temporal, would never have the slightest effect. So, it is quite true when considering the body, that bodies exist, that they feed, that they come into contact, that they touch, that they communicate with one another, and that there is a necessary commerce between all the substances of material Nature.

But this is only true for the body, because all material actions, having no connection with the true nature of man, are or can in some way be foreign to him, when he wants to make use of his powers to draw closer to his natural element. Finally, matter is real for matter, yet never will be for spirit. This is an important distinction, which would have long since ended the arguments between those who have claimed that matter is only apparent and those who have claimed that it is real.

Since corporeal and physical things mean nothing to man's intellectual Being, we can see how it would judge what we call death, and the impression it would produce in intellectual man who in no way identifies with the illusion of those corruptible substances. Man's body, though real to other physical bodies, has no reality for the intellect, which barely notices when it separates from the body. Indeed, when the intellect leaves the body, it is simply leaving an appearance or, to state this more strongly, it is leaving nothing.[35]

On the contrary, everything tells us that the intellect must win rather than lose, because, with a little thought, we can only be filled with respect for those whose Law delivers them from these corporeal shackles, since then there will be less coming between them and the *truth*. In the absence of this useful reflection, men believe that it is death which frightens them, whereas it isn't that, but rather *life* they fear.

If the allure of temporal things were still not enough for us to show the difference between man's current state and his primitive state, we should look at man himself, because as much as it is true that the study of man has allowed us to discover relationships with the First of All Principles within us and the traces of a glorious origin, it also allows us to perceive his horrible degradation. To be convinced, we have only to

---

[35] To clarify this comment, in his first book Saint-Martin distinguishes between physical man and intellectual man, meaning the material body, and the imperishable soul which leaves the composite body on death; while the composite body now decomposes into its constituent parts – whereas the soul or mind of man is 'simple' and not composite.

compare ourselves to the Principle whose *abilities* and *virtues* we should, by our nature, represent. We should see what there is in us which can justify His TITLES. We should see if we reflect the Being from whom we are descended, and Who has expressed in us the image of His Wisdom and Knowledge, so that we might give Him honor.

We seek and He posesses, we study and He knows, we hope and He rejoices, we doubt and He is Himself the evidence, we tremble from fear and He has no other concern than that of love, by which He is even more enflamed for man than man is for his own thoughts and essence. One is great, multiplying His images in all Beings and in man, the other often uses his glory to annihilate and destroy them. Not only has the Author of Things brought into existence for us and for our needs all those Elements and all those Agents of Nature, who use we pervert; He has even produced in us those abilities which should be the sign of His greatness which we use to attack and combat Him, so that men who should be the *satellites* of truth, are instead its persecutors; and to judge man today, huddled in reprobation, crime and error, he who had been emanated simply to show that there is a God, would seem more suited to show that there isn't one at all.

For when, by repeating his original crime man so often usurps the rights of Divinity on Earth, he only profanes His name and debases Him through yet more acts of prostitution. Using that Sacred Name, he decides, he strays, he errs, he tyrannizes, he slaughters, he massacres. Hmm! Over whom does this strange 'God' exercise his even stranger rights? It is over man, over his colleagues, over a Being of his species who, as a result, has the same right as him to the title of 'God'.

And so, by performing contradictory actions which instead accord with his pride, man erases that glorious title within him, even as he desires to clothe himself in it. Thus, he takes the surest path to destroy any idea of the true God around him, showing himself to be only a Being of lies, fury and devastation, a Being who only acts to denature everything, to corrupt everything, and who only expresses the superiority of his power through the superiority of his mad injustices, crimes and atrocities.

One could therefore exclaim with reason: Man, it was through you that the *ungodly* should have learned justice, and you can barely answer when you are asked what justice is. It was through you that they should have been led in the paths of illumination, and you use all your efforts to obscure that light and corrupt its paths. It was through you that the truth

Heh (ה) - The Fall, Loss of the Light

was meant to appear, and you offer only lies. How will justice, illumination and truth become known if the Being appointed to express them not only hasn't retained any notion of them, but even strives to destroy any trace of them which were written within him and on the whole of Nature? How will anyone know that the important Principle is *Holy* and *Eternal* if you profess the worship and doctrine of matter? How will anyone know that He is only concerned with forgiveness and that He burns with love for mankind if you only breathe hatred and pay back His beneficence with blasphemies? And finally, how will anyone believe in *order* and *life*, if all you show in you is *confusion* and *death*?

Although we cannot compare our titles with the ignominy with which we are covered without bending toward the Earth and seeking to bury ourselves in its depths, yet there is a desire to convince ourselves that we are happy; as if one could destroy that universal truth that happiness only comes to a Being so long as he is within his Law.

Some fickle men, having themselves become blind, have tried to communicate their falsehoods to us. They have begun by closing their eyes to their infirmities, then, having us close our eyes to them too, they tried to convince us that they didn't exist, and that our condition was proper to our own true nature.

What do such doctrines produce? They charm our ills but don't heal them. They give rise to a false calmness in us and, as a result of this calmness, corruption makes much faster progress since no balm is applied on the wound to correct the malignancy.

They weaken the *Principle* of *life* in man, they corrupt it even in its *seed*, they ensure that the man who seeks truth and who has only taken a single step to obtain it, extinguishes this precious impulse within him, this *virgin* and *sacred* instinct, which he would normally seek to be his sole support; finally, once even the Sage has been shaken, the Universe runs the risk of no longer containing a single virtuous man within it; and that is the deplorable evil produced by those false doctrines which harden man against the Law of his Being and against the deprivation in which he lives as his true home.

Let us leave these dangerous Masters to feed off their illusions and lies; even the briefest glance at our current condition will suffice to convince us of their deceptions.

Pain, ignorance and fear: that is what we face at every step in our dark enclosure, that is what is represented by all the points of the narrow circle within which a power we cannot overcome holds us captive.

All the Elements are unleashed against us: barely have they produced our corporeal form when they work to dissolve it, continually calling back to them the principles of life they have just given us. We only exist to defend ourselves against their assaults, and we are like the infirm, abandoned to ourselves and reduced to continually dressing our wounds. What are our buildings, our clothes, our servants and our food, if not further indications of our weakness and our impotence? Finally, for our bodies there are only two states: decay or death. If they are not deteriorating, they are annihilated.

Of all the men who have been called to corporeal life, some wander like spectres upon this surface, endlessly delivered over to their needs and to infirmity; the rest are no longer here. They have been as their descendants will be, dragged along in the torrent of the Centuries, their accumulated sediments now forming the ground of almost all the Earth; where one cannot take a single step without trampling the humiliating vestiges of their destruction underfoot. Here Man is therefore like those criminals who, among some Nations the Law requires to be attached alive to corpses.[36]

Let us now focus on invisible man. Uncertain about the times which preceded our existence, about those which must follow it and about our Being itself, so long as we sense no connections we are left to wander in the middle of a somber desert, whose entrance and exit both seem to flee before us. If bright yet fleeting flashes sometimes shine forth in our shadows, they only serve to be more terrifying still, or disparage us all the more, leaving us to realize what we have lost; and then, if they reach us, it is only when surrounded by *nebulous* and *uncertain vapors*, because our senses would be unable to handle the flashes if they revealed themselves

---

[36] While there is only one passing reference to this gruesome practice available online, it does appear this was a punishment which the Romans, at least, prescribed for certain forms of murder. Once the criminal who was forced to carry the body died, which one imagines wouldn't be long, since it would be hard to find food or lodging while carrying such a grotesque burden, then the newly-dead criminal's body would itself be used as a punishment. The use of a criminal's body makes sense, since the family of the murdered victim would surely prefer to bury their relative with honors, rather than having their corpse attached to the very person who murdered them, particularly given the importance of ritual burial in those days, as now.

unprotected. Finally, compared to these impressions of the superior life, man is like a worm that cannot breathe the air in our atmosphere.[37]

I tell you: that *ferocious animals* surround us in the midst of these shadows, exhausting us with their *irregular* and *lugubrious cries*, they *throw themselves* suddenly upon us, and devour us before we have *perceived* them. *Burning sulfur thunders down* on our heads, and with their imposing thunderclaps seem to pronounce a thousand times the judgment of death. Even the *Earth* is always ready to tremble beneath our *feet*, and we never know if in the next instant it will open up and *swallow us up* in its *depths*.

Could this place, then, be man's true residence, this Being who corresponds to the center of all knowledge and all felicity; could he who, through his thoughts, through the sublime actions which emanate from him and by the perfect proportions of his corporeal form, present himself as the representative of the Living God? Would he be at home in a place which is only covered in lepers and corpses, in a place where ignorance and *night* alone can live, and, in a place where this unfortunate man cannot even find a place to *lay his head*?

No, in man's present state, even the vilest of insects are above him. They at least take their rank in the harmony of Nature; they are in their place, while man is certainly not in his.

All the Beings of the Universe are in continuous activity. They enjoy without interruption the portion of that right which is conferred upon each of them, depending on the course and the Laws of their existence. As they only exist through movement, so long as they exist, the movement never stops for them. And the plants and animals too, all the powers of Nature are in an activity which never ceases, because if it stopped for a moment all of Nature would be destroyed.

Now, among these Beings who are always happy and alive, a Being who is incomparably more noble, man, man's thought, his mind, are

---

[37] The vivid description is very like the passage of 'La Chose' in the theurgical rituals of the Élus Cohen, where the Initiates are meant to perform rituals to invoke the evil powers in order to banish them, and this being accomplished, to watch for signs which come in the form of flashes of light, sudden loud sounds and similar manifestations, so show that the Operation had been successful. This passage suggests that such experiences would be terrifying for those who were not prepared both to look for these signs, and to protect themselves from the influences of the evil forces. The next paragraph is even more terrifying and leads one to wonder if Saint-Martin might be sharing some of his personal experiences of performing these Operations.

subject to pauses, to rests, to suspensions, that is, to inaction and nothingness.

Let us therefore stop believing that man belongs here below. *He is connected to the Earth as was Prometheus, to be torn like him by the vulture.* Even his time of rest isn't something to be enjoyed, for it is only an interval between tortures.

Vav (ו) - Temporal Life

This would be the place to shine a light on man's original crime. We could even note in this connection that man only brought to the world regrets and not remorse, and even those regrets are still ignored by the greatest number; for one can only feel pain for the crimes one knows, for we can only understand or experience these original crimes through much work, and most men have done none of this. This is what makes the truth of this crime so uncertain in their eyes, even though its effects are so obvious.

I might add that in the Social Order, when a man has failed to be honorable he is sent back to the Order of those who have no honor; thus, in observing here below what the main attribute lacking in the Beings with whom we are confused is, it should be easy to understand the nature of the original crime.

But, without discussing the many opinions which have been offered on this subject, we can believe that man's crime was to have abused the knowledge he had of the union of the Principle of the Universe with the Universe. Also, we cannot doubt that deprivation of this knowledge is the true punishment for his crime, since we all suffer this irrevocable punishment through ignorance, where we are in shackles which bind our intellectual Being to matter.

The clear evidence that this knowledge cannot be perfectly understood by us during our sojourn on the Earth, is that, only being in this base World to suffer the deprivation of that light which we have allowed to escape, if we were able to fully recover that light we would no longer be in privation, and, consequently, we would no longer be in this base World.

Indeed, the simplest observations of elemental light shows us to what degree we should raise ourselves up to reach intellectual light, because the Laws of these two kinds of light are similar. In addition to the need for a primordial and generative Principle, both of them require a basis, a reaction and an Order of Beings capable of being witnesses and to participate in its effects, which shows that both physical and intellectual light can only act, proceed and manifest itself by means of a quaternary. And it isn't without reason that elemental light ranks as the most admirable phenomenon of material Nature, since it cannot be complete in its actions and effects without exercising and acting on the four cardinal points of universal Creation.[38]

In just considering these effects in relation to the three terrestrial Kingdoms, we will note that minerals, being buried in the earth, are totally deprived of that light; that plants are not at all deprived of it, but they receive it without seeing it and enjoying it; that animals see and enjoy it, but they can neither contemplate it nor enter into an understanding of its Laws; and finally, that this last privilege is reserve to man alone, or to any endowed like him with the abilities of intelligence.

It is there that we'll learn to understand everything we lack in not possessing intellectual light. There are intelligent Beings who are totally separated from that light; there are those who are not at all separated, but that only participate externally in its effects; there are those who receive its rays internally, but who are in complete ignorance of the paths by which it is spread. Therefore, it is only those who are admitted to its counsel, or to the same knowledge as Him from Whom everything descends, who can recover this primitive knowledge, because it is only then that they can both receive the light, see, enjoy and understand it. Finally, this is where all the powers of the great quaternary are employed with superior efficiency, because in this Supreme Order resides all kinds of the four cardinal points of the elemental World.

Man hasn't been able to preserve this sublime enjoyment which was once his prerogative, for he wanted to transpose the order of those four fundamental points of all light and truth; however, by transposing them he confused them, and in confusing them he lost them and was deprived of them.

It is for this reason that man is now swallowed up in the Inferior Orders, where not only does he no longer comprehend that intellectual light which, despite all our crimes, eternally retains its splendour, but he can still glimpse it slightly on occasion, when it is often little more than similar to the minerals' relation to elemental light.

It is however in the heart of this privation that careless men let themselves conceive ideas which are so hazardous to their nature, and

---

[38] Given that the word 'light' works identically in French and English to mean both physical and spiritual illumination, it isn't difficult to follow the analogy beyween physical or visible light, and invisible light or enlightenment, which sheds its beneficent rays in all directions, or in Saint-Martin's terminology, in a quaternary – or perfect – manner.

build blind systems upon the chains which we retain in our slavery; even persuading us that by suicide we can break them.

If God alone knew the chains which bind our intellectual Being to the temporal region, then He alone, without doubt, would have the power to bring about their rupture. But we are not afraid to say that He has no such intention, for then He would be acting against His own justice.

Man, on the contrary, may well have the desire to deliver himself from these fetters which are foreign to his own nature, but he doesn't have the power, because those unfortunates who give themselves over to death believe in vain that they are escaping from evil and suffering. Yet they can neither destroy nor avoid a Law which condemns the unjust man to suffer.

And indeed, impure men can be separated from their body without being separated from their physical soul, since, according to the preceding Principles, if their body, though real to other bodies, is only apparent to their intellectual Being, they must be, after they have been delivered from this body, what they were during the time that they were enclosed in it.

If it was therefore weakness which made the pain unbearable, if it was the poison of vices and the *vapors* of crime with which made corporeal life unbearable, the death of the body will change nothing of their intellectual situation. They are still consumed by the same poisons, they still have the same *vapors* to breathe, the same infirmities to suffer; in a word, they are like fruits which have barely matured and are already spoiled, whose unhealthy quality doesn't change even when they remove their skin, and which, then receiving the action of *Air* more directly, corrupt even more.

Moreover, since man can be defiled by many crimes during his life and identify himself with a multitude of objects contrary to his being, he must, after death, successively experience all the impressions relating to those events. He must still feed off the experiences and tastes which appeared most innocent to him during his life, but which, having nothing to offer him of a sound and true purpose, left his Being in inaction and inertia.

It is all those foreign *substances* which inspire the torment of the suicide, like any other guilty person deprived of life. *And perhaps we might find in this some explanation of the system of metempsychosis*[39],

---

[39] The transfer to another body – or even another species – after death.

where men, after their death, continue to be linked to various elemental objects, and are even transformed into plants and lowly animals, expressions which are simply the image of the tastes, vices, and objects which man had made of his idols on Earth; for who are those whose Being, after death, will be assailed by the torments and illusions of their physical soul? Finally, who will they be whose Beings will live on physically, though separated from their bodies? They will be those here below who lived separated from their Being.

According to what we have just seen, the imprudent man who, through suicide, precipitates himself into a new realm before his appointed time, even though he only committed this single crime, is clearly exposed to sufferings even more frightful than those he would have faced with the powers acquired in the visible realm by his constancy in cultivating the abilities he could have used to fight them. It is like a prisoner who, in order to recover his freedom demolished his prison by the foundations and had it fall in on him. Thus, any action on our part which doesn't have the consent of Nature and order, further increases the ills and sufferings attached to the condition of our unfortunate posterity.

According to these Principles, we can already recognize the wisdom and goodness of the Divine Being, all of Whose Decrees bear the imprint of love. He doesn't demand men to follow what would bring them closer to Him, and He doesn't forbid them from doing those things which would distance themselves from Him. And if all the Laws of Nature and reason are against suicide, it is because it deceives man instead of making him happier.

I could demonstrate that this wisdom and goodness are similarly manifested by man's birth into earthly life, since it is to bring him relief, through his struggles and efforts, from some of the ills which the first crime incurred on Earth; for the secret and the work of the Divinity Himself is entrusted to him, to allow him to cooperate in his particular sphere, in repairing the disorders of the human species. Finally, however rigorous the evils which await us here below, it is sufficient to believe it possible for man not to be totally destroyed by them; for him to understand that it is his errors and weaknesses which give them the greatest weight; that therefore they should be meaningless and only apparent for him; and finally, that perhaps it is man himself who gives them all their power. But, to understand such truths, it is necessary for man to raise himself up to a sublimity which is quite foreign him, who has trouble even forming true and constant thoughts – even the very simplest ones – on the subject of material justice; and so I will not explore this point further.

Man, in uniting himself, as a result of the corruption of his intention, with the composite things of an apparent and relative realm, is subject to the actions of the various *Principles* which constitute it, and those of the various Agents established to sustain them and to preside over the defense of their Law. And since those composite things, in their combinations, only produce temporal, slow and successive phenomena, it follows that time is the main instrument of man's suffering and the potent obstacle which keeps him distanced from his Principle. Time is the venom which gnaws at him, whereas it was man who was to purify and dissolve time. And time, or the realm which serves as man's prison, is like water which has the power to dissolve everything and change the form of all bodies at varying speeds, and into which we cannot plunge *Gold* without it being deprived of *nine-tenths of its weight*, a phenomenon[40] which, according to sound calculations, reflects our true degradation in the real world.

Indeed, time is simply the interval between two actions, it is only a contraction, a suspension in the action a Being's abilities. Also, every year, every month, every week, every day, every hour and every moment, the Superior Principle removes and gives back powers to Beings, and it is this alternation which creates time. I can add, in passing, that area also expresses this alternating, and that it is subject to the same progressions as time: so that time and space are similar to one another.

Finally, let us consider time as the space contained between two lines forming an angle. The more Beings are removed from the summit of the angle, the more they are obliged to subdivide their action to fill it or to move across the space from one line to the other. On the other hand, the closer they come to the summit, the more their action becomes simpler. Consider from this what must be the simplicity of action in the Principle Being Who is Himself the apex of the angle. Since that Being only has to navigate the unity of His own essence to attain the wholeness of all of His actions and powers, time is absolutely meaningless to Him.

On the other hand, the whole weight of time makes itself felt in man who, born to unite actions, finds himself at the extremity of the two lines.

---

[40] This refers to buoyancy, as in Archimedes' discovery of how to verify the purity of gold in a crown, and doesn't of course imply that gold actually loses weight in water. Here Saint-Martin is making the point that, in being thrown down to Earth, man has lost ninety percent of his primitive rights and glory.

That is why, of all physical Beings, man is the one who has the worst of it, for being the one whose natural action is now the furthest from his Principle, and as the only Being whose action is foreign to this terrestrial realm, this action is perpetually interrupted and disunited in him.

There can be no doubt that man's true action wasn't made to be subject to the physical realm, since the light moves to communicate with him to the extent that physical action abandons him and he strips himself of it; and since, far that him having to wait for all his senses to work, he learns nothing until they are quiet and in a state of passivity with regard to his mind.

For it would be an error to assume he was subject to the physical, just because his soul generally follows the growth and deterioration of the body. This may be true in childhood, when everyone has to suffer the initial effects of their degradation, and exhibits an example of total servitude, and complete dependence on the actions of temporal Beings.

This can also be true of a more advanced age, if man has not used his will and his judgment to evaluate the effects of his physical actions. But, although the physical body can harm the mind and suspend its actions, we should not conclude that man's intellectual abilities are the result of his senses and the creation of the material Principles which act within him, because not to kill or to give life are two very different things. And one can never say that a thick veil is the Principle of my sight, because I can distinguish nothing when it covers my eyes.[41]

Besides, haven't we recognized that rather than learning we can only remember, as it were, what we already knew, and perceive that which had never ceased to be before us; and thus, since physical objects provide us with nothing but on the contrary distract us, our task while remaining among them isn't so much to acquire them than to lose nothing?

Indeed, if the Laws of Beings are that they manifest all their abilities without mixing them with any foreign substance, if all physical Beings follow these Laws precisely, each according to their Order, when they are not impeded in their actions, why would man alone be deprived of that power?

Seeing so much beauty in the creations of physical Beings whose Law hasn't been disturbed, we can therefore form an idea of the wonders

---

[41] That is, blindness or cataracts in old age are neither a punishment nor a Principle, since they don't add to man's learning, but are instead simply physical conditions.

that man would have blossom in him if he followed the Law of his true nature, and as the image of the Hand which has formed him worked in every circumstance of his life, to be greater than what he created.

His intellectual Being would come to the final point of its temporal career with the same purity it had when it began it. We would see old age unite the fruit of experience with the innocence of his first age. All the steps of his life would have made him find illumination, knowledge, simplicity and candor within him, because all these things are in his essence. Finally, the seed which animated him would be prolonged without being altered, and he would return, with the calm that *virtue* brings, back to the Hand that formed him, since being manifested in Him with no change in the character or seal that he had received, He would always recognize His imprint, and see His image there.

We can say that if most men are so far from such calm at the time of that important separation, it is because they haven't been ingenious or proud enough during their life to see their greatness and preserve it, so that, being confused with composite and temporal things, they believe that they will cease to be when they abandon them.

The number of times man must suffer to accomplish his work is proportional to the number of degrees he has fallen, since the higher the point from which power has fallen, the more time and effort it needs to climb back up.[42]

But for man to acquire illumination on that object, he must enumerate the powers, abilities and rights he is missing. It is on that number that the measure of his level of regeneration resides, as well as the weight or result which should come from it. Now, man can see at a glance the abyss into which he has descended, since he lacks as many *virtues* as there are *stars* above his head.

In addition, the action of time on man is proportional to the greatness of the *virtues* inherent in the degrees he must travel through, because the more powerful and necessary they are to man, the more their deprivation must be long, painful and miserable for him. It is that which makes his state so cruel and so distressing, because if those degrees are the

---

[42] This is perhaps the most overt statement Saint-Martin makes demonstrating his break with orthodox Catholicism, since this is clearly a bold statement in favor of reincarnation. St. Paul's letter to the Hebrews, 9:27 states: "And as it is appointed unto men once to die, but after this the judgment", and this has been used by all churches since to claim that there is no doctrine of reincarnation in the Christian faith.

expression and the strength of the Divine *Virtues*, if they are animated by rays of life itself, if they carry within them a primitive Fire so necessary to the existence of all Beings, it follows that since man is separated from them, his deprivation is complete and absolute.[43]

While man would be happy enough, during his sojourn on Earth, to assemble a mass of enlightenment and knowledge which embraced a kind of *unity*, he still couldn't expect to enjoy them completely, since they are superior to the Terrestrial Order. He would only have a shadow and image of that true enlightenment, for since everything here is relative, so to speak, he can possess nothing which is real and truly fixed.

Let the intelligent man meditate on the Laws of the Lunar body which represents our privation under a thousand faces and let him examine why it is only visible to us during its days of substance, and why we lose sight of it on the twenty-eighth day of its course, even though it still rises on our horizon.

Everything comes together to prove to man that after traveling laboriously across this surface, he must reach degrees which are more fixed and more positive, which are more analogous to simple and fundamental truths whose seed is in his nature. Finally, at death, he should obtain knowledge of the objects which here below he has only been able to see in appearance.

I can agree that this superior knowledge consists in the understanding and use of two languages above common and everyday languages, since they are connected to man's original estate. The first is for Divine things and only has four Letters for its entire alphabet; the second has twenty-two and applies to the creations, be they intellectual or temporal, of the Great Principle. The same crime deprived man of these two languages. If there was a new prevarication, it would create for him a third language which would have eighty-eight Letters, which would push him even further away from the end of his imprisonment.[44]

---

[43] This is another passage which seems to allude to the Degree or Grade system of the Élus Cohen. While the statement is made in an authoritative manner, there appears to be an undertone of self-doubt, again asking if all the accoutrements of the Degree rituals and practices were truly necessary to 'know God', as Saint-Martin asked of his Master, Martinez de Pasqually.

[44] The four letters refer to *Yod-Heh-Vav-Heh* (יהוה) or the name of God (commonly written at Yahweh) by whose utterance tradition states He performed the act of Creation. The alphabet of 22 letters refers to the Hebrew alphabet, which enumerate the chapter in this book. The alphabet of 88 letters represents 4 x 22, which shows man's further distancing from his Primitive Estate. Remember, too, that the French for language is *langue*, or 'tongue', to remind us that the name of

I would add that there are false languages which are opposed to the three I just mentioned. One which corresponds to the divine language has an alphabet of two letters; that which corresponds to the second has five; finally, if there were a new prevarication, the false language which would accompany it would have one hundred and ten *letters in its alphabet.* [45]

Knowledge of the two pure languages which man acquires at his separation from terrestrial objects must produce more satisfactory effects in him than everything we can experience down here: they should extend his pleasure since they have actions which are more vivifying than the objects of visible Nature. But also, if he must still experience impediments in his progress, these obstacles become increasingly more painful for him, because the closer a force comes to its center, its inclination increases and the shock of resistance becomes more violent.

However, it is inevitable for man to experience impediments while travelling through the new levels of his rehabilitation, because they are only a continuation of that terrible barrier which separates him from the great light, and because the Earth is only the first of all these levels. Now, if there is a space between man's prison and the place of his birth, it is essential that he crosses it and that he successively experiences all of its actions.

If an agile and adventurous traveller comes to the foot of a group of mountains piled up on one another, and wants to stand upon upon the summit of the highest one hidden in the clouds, it would be necessary for him, after climbing the first of these mountains, to discontinue his climb and to go horizontally in order to arrive at the foot of the second to

---

God is a word of power to be spoken; and the Hebrew alphabet contains many corollaries, including number, value, correspondence, and so forth.

[45] After seeing the two perfect languages in the name of God and the Hebrew alphabet, the name of God is contrasted by the number '2', which to Pasqually was the 'evil number', representing the splitting of unity or Divinity, as well as the 'number of confusion'; while '5' to him was the 'diabolical spirit', which he further describes in his *Treatise* as: "...the one the demons use for operating the counteraction against the purely divine spiritual action." Thus, the perfect tongue is subjected to confusion, as in the Tower of Babel; while the language of the Angels is countered by the demonic language. Finally, the product of 2 x 5 x 11 gives us 110, the number of the 'false language'. The number 11 is referred to by Pasqually in his discussion of the measurement of Noah's Ark as follows: "the number 11 is a number which signifies the opposition of the corporal form of man, which is analogous to the terrestrial body and all that proceeds therefrom." In Saint-Martin's work *Des Nombres*, published posthumously in 1861, he says in Stanza 50 concerning the number 11: "In the present state of things, 11 is formed by 2 and 9 which, both of them, are the powers of 5 and 6. In the future 11 will exist through 6 and 5, which are the Agents of the two powers above. This is why the suffering will be so harsh and why there will be gnashing of teeth."

conquer it in its turn, and so on until he arrives at his goal. This is a physical image of man's regeneration, in which we can clearly see beneficent Wisdom accompanying his steps while he submits to the Laws of justice, because, even when due to various impediments our success appears to be delayed, it is only to conserve our strength and give us time to renew and increase it.

Man cannot cross the fixed and real regions of purification without acquiring an existence which is more active, more extended and more free; that is without *breathing purer Air* and discovering a broader *horizon* as he approaches the desired summit. We see that the more the Principles of his body become simpler the more they acquire powers, and as the coarse Air delivered to material substances fills such an enormous space compared to that which it occupied in his body, it is almost terrifying to contemplate.

Moreover, as the fixed and real truths which man can acquire at his death belong to the Intellectual Order, which is the only true one, it is not surprising that, so long as we are immersed in matter which is relative and apparent, we cannot always see those works of other men who were already separated from their bodies, though the singular light of intelligence has clearly shown us the need for this; and the same example of the traveler can still serve as an analogy of that idea, since those who remain at the foot of the mountain lose sight of him above a certain height, but don't doubt his elevation and his existence even though their physical eyes can no longer follow him on his climb.

It is that which makes our judgments so unsure concerning men's fate after the separation of their intellectual Being and their body, since we can't justify our judgments unless we can base them on a fixed and resolute foundation, whereas the foundation we have is only apparent and relative; *for that Intellectual and Invisible Order is like simple elemental Physics: all Nature is volatile and tends towards evaporation. She would do that in an instant if the fixed which contains her belonged to her, but this fixed sustance does not, for it is outside of her, though acting violently upon her, and it never forms a mixture with her which isn't started with dissolution. Now, like these two Orders, Physical and Intellectual, there are several degrees of dissolution, as there are also several degrees of combinations and compositions.*

Vav (ו) - Temporal Life

All we can allow ourselves to say about things of such importance is to draw a few inferences from some faithful observations on the Law of bodies.

So, like the globules of Air and Fire which escape from dissolving bodily substances and which are given off at varying speeds, depending on the degree of their purity and the extent of their action, we cannot doubt that, on their death, men who haven't allowed their own essence to *combine* with their terrestrial habitation, rapidly return to their native region, there to shine, like the stars, in brilliant splendor[46]; while those who have to some extent mixed themselves with the illusions of this dark abode, cross the space which separates them from the realm of life more slowly; and those who identified themselves with the stains with which we are surrounded remain there, buried in shadows and obscurity until the last of these corrupted substances has been dissolved, taking with them that corruption which cannot end until they are themselves dissolved.

And to give more weight to these truths, I would say that after death, criminals remain under their own justice, whereas wise men are under the justice of God, and the *reconciled* are under His mercy.

But what doesn't permit us to pass a verdict on how these various actions or various periods of time work, is that justice never acts alone and there are other powers which, combined with it, never cease to direct its action toward the greatest good of Beings, which for them is to return to the light.

---

[46] This phrase was used by Papus in his system of Martinist initiations.

Zayin (ז) – The Works of Man

Without concerning ourselves further with these future actions to which man has delivered his posterity, let us consider those to which he has been condemned on Earth as a result of his material incorporisation[47].

Man only received physical Being in order to exercise his action on the universality of temporal things, and he only wanted to exercise that on a part of it. He should be acting for the intellectual against the physical, yet he wants to act for the physical against the intellectual. Finally, he should be ruling the Universe, but instead of watching over the preservation of his empire he has debased himself, and the Universe has collapsed upon the powerful Being who was meant to administer and sustain it.

As a result of that fall, all the physical powers of the Universe which should be acting in a manner subordinate to man within the temporal circumference, have acted confusedly upon him and have repressed him with all their strength and all their power. Thus, all the intellectual powers with which he should act in concert, and which should provide him with unity of action are found to be divided for him, separated from him, and are each enclosed within their own sphere and in their own realm; so that what had been simple and one for him have become multiplied and subdivided; and what was now subdivided and multiplied has become agglomerated and crushes him with its weight; so that, for him, the sensual has taken the place of the intellectual, and vice versa.

Unequivocal information indeed tells us that all the physical powers of Nature served as barriers to unfortunate man at the moment of his fall. And just as the body we have which enslaves us is an extract of all the fluids, fires, liquors and other substances of the corporeal individual that generated it, so the chains binding the first guilty man were composed of an extract of all the parts of *Humanity*, so that, alongside it, we can consider our body to be an image of this material Universe, too[48].

By becoming a slave to matter, not only has man become separated from the intellectual and superior *virtues* with which he cooperated

---

[47] This is possibly a word made up by Saint-Martin, and means becoming flesh.
[48] That is, man is the microcosm.

because of his power, but he has even allowed his own *virtues* to become mixed and amalgamated with all the parts of his prison, and we have a sign of this mixture and of the material origin of the first man in the particular act of generation by which present day man obtains life.

Before his creation as an individual Being, man's body is spread throughout the father's form; he is united with all the powers which are in his father's generative Principle. When the moment of conception arrives, the physical seed spread abroad in the universal form of the father is concentrated and gathers into a single point. Then it is exiled and buried in the dark womb of the woman where, mixed with impure fluids and surrounded by a thousand barriers, he cannot even enjoy the Air, his most perfect organs are without function, and he only receives life and the support of the Elements by means of a single passive point, whereas man's destiny was to relate actively with all of Nature.

Such is the image of the first corporeal state of the body of culpable man who, banished from his universal sphere, was thrown ignominiously into the form or the material prison of men; who, experiencing there nothing but universal opposition to his true action, was reduced to the most complete privation, and now shows only a shameful mixture of his own powers with all the heterogeneous substances which form his dark home.

In this state, what should have been the first action of man? It should have been to extricate himself from these foreign masses which assailed him; it should have been to laboriously separate his own powers from all those impure materials with which they had become confused; and finally, it should have been to use all his powers to climb out from beneath the ruins of the Universe.

But since active Laws prevent a Being from being able to join with what is contrary to it without bearing the imprint and the signs of his amalgamation, it was impossible for the first man to come out of his sewer[49] with the same purity and the same agility that he had prior to

---

[49] This is a complex word. On the one hand, in French *cloaque* means sewer, and is named from the great sewer running through ancient Rome. However, in most vertebrates (though not mammals) the *cloaca* is a posterior cavity through which both excretory waste and genitory fluids are released. It would appear that Saint-Martin is drawing attention to the fact that the organs of generation and birth are also closely tied to those of excretion and 'impure' fluids and is of course referring to the act of birth. Still, this is a somewhat harsh word to use for the birth canal. Also, it is worth noting that the later term 'being precipitated there' reflects the contemporary belief that

being precipitated there. And that is why individual man, after sojourning in the woman's womb, and undertaking the actions which would make him capable of separating his physical embryo from all the links and barriers which enclose him, comes into the light contained in a form which is more opaque than the subtle fluid which enveloped his embryo.

After primitive man had overcome that obstacle, there remained to him a very considerable step to make: which was to unite himself successively with the powers of the various *Elements* which act in his atmosphere. This is still the task of individual man, who, having been brought to elemental light, still languishes for some time before accustoming his eyes to its brightness, his body to the impressions of Air, and his organs to the various Laws established for corporeal forms.

For man, up to now we have only seen corporeal and physical works. All these things take place in the Elemental Order, and by causes which are not free, and one cannot distinguish any real signs of the work of intellectual man, but one can at least see their Law and their need; and just as by being born man is supposed to have gathered within him his physical and specific *powers*, with which he can participate in the *universal powers* of the atmosphere which he left and which are external to him, so intellectual man, delivered from his first prison and admitted with his material form onto the Earth, must work to successively recover his own strength and his own intellectual powers, with which he can work to recover those he has been separated from because of his crime.

But what physical man does in a passive and blind manner in the physical body, intellectual man must do so by the constant and liberal efforts of his will. This is how he can free himself from the death to which he has condemned himself by focusing on a specific action. For bodies themselves are destroyed when their activity brings them to a single point and abandons the other parts of the form. Now, just as bodies affected by disease cannot escape death unless the action concentrated in them becomes general again, so intellectual man, who is voluntarily reduced to an Inferior and limited Order, must generalize his whole Being and extend his powers to the extremities of his particular bounds, if he wishes to reach up to that universal and sacred precinct from which he is banned.[50]

---

the baby was created from the father, while the mother had no role to play other than providing the matrix in which the father's seed took refuge and grew.

[50] This appears to be how illness was regarded at the end of the 18th Century. Cholera, smallpox and typhus were rampant, especially in cities, and everyone know people who had died, not least

Finally, the will being in a way the *blood* of intellectual man and all free Beings, being the Agent by which alone they can erase in themselves and around them the signs of error and crime, the revivification of will is the principal task of all criminal Beings; and truly, it is such a Great Work that all the powers have worked on this since the beginning of things, yet still without being able to work in general.

This would be the time to present new and precise correlations between the material incorporisation of individual man and man in general and, by following the Laws of generation to their conclusion, we can educate ourselves usefully on the punishment of the original guilty man, on the time he spent his first prison, and the exact moment he left it. *There one could discover the very origin of the Universe and the action of the Agents in all Orders, and seeing all the* numbers *operating. There we would learn the difference between the regular division of the circle and its irregular division, why the size of the placenta is in inverse proportion to the increase in the size of the fetus; why the movements of that fetus never take place prior to the third month, nor later than the sixth; why he first takes on a spherical form in his mother's womb; why, later in a more advanced term he is positioned with his head at the top and his face forward; why, toward the end of the eighth month, he is bowed down and is ready to come crawling out on the earth; and finally, why he has such an inclination to sleep following his birth.*

But, to connect these facts with their symbols one must be used to kinds of observations which are not well known to most Readers, and whose results they would not understand since they don't not possess the necessary background.

Therefore, let us confine ourselves to noting that the first work that intellectual man must do, after painfully separating and disengaging his own powers buried beneath the ruins of his throne, it is to unite himself to those of the Being which is closest to him or to those of the *Earth*. And just as the physical child is obliged for a period to draw his sustenance from a woman's milk, so intellectual man is obliged to begin with the *Earth*, in order to recover the light he has lost and which is now

---

because a significant number of children didn't live to see the age of two. Since there were few remedies available at that time, the most common approach was to wait for the fever to 'break', which is probably what Saint-Martin is referring to when he says that the generalization of a focused disease is an indication of recovery.

fragmented across all the realms; for the *Earth* is the *mother* and the *root* of the Universe.

All the physical and intellectual Laws which we just discussed concerning the necessary progress of degraded man are so natural to him that, even in the Human Order, temporal man puts them into action every day and constantly exhibits that activity which is essential to our Being, although he is so often mistaken as to what its purpose should be.

When the ambitious and greedy man seeks so hard to distinguish himself from his fellow man, when privileged men and sovereigns extend the limits of their domains and their empires, and would like to extend them to the ends of the World, they are only following – albeit in a false manner – the Law of their nature which despises limits and barriers; that is to say that they are demonstrating what true man should do, by pushing back to the limits of his domain those physical and material boundaries which should always keep their natural distance with regard to him. Indeed, it is this indelible Law which, operating in full force in children, gives them that tumultuous activity, that destructive impulse that when seen in impulsive men find them accused of vice and mischievousness, whereas it is simply the outcome of that necessary opposition which all true and universal Beings should feel towards all the false and constricting objects by which they are imprisoned.

When, on the other hand, the curious and industrious man seeks to amass around him the precious things of Nature, he need not fear traveling to the most distant places in order to bring back rareties of every kind and bring them together; when the experienced Naturalist lets his mind wander to all climates, and when he makes all kinds of discoveries and thereby imposes a kind of universal tribute upon terrestrial Nature[51]; when again, by destroying the envelopes of bodies, the Chemist seeks to penetrate the *Principles* to which they owe their existence, all of these works are but an image of what man should do here below, and teaches him that he is meant to assemble all parts of his empire around him.

It is therefore true that having received a coarse envelope in a dark realm, and having mustered in himself those intellectual powers which belong to him, man still has to augment those very powers. By uniting them with those which are outside of him, he must harvest the powers of

---

[51] 'Tribute' in the sense of payment to a ruler; in this example making Nature offer up its finest examples for the Naturalist's collection.

Zayin (ז) – The Works of Man

all the *Terrestrial Kingdoms*, distinguish all the *species* in each *Kingdom*, and even the *specific characteristics* of each *individual*. Finally, he must investigate the very *bowels* of the *Earth*, learning there to understand the disorders which are the horror and shame of our sad domain, which are shown to us both in the metals that have no *oil*,[52] in the fury of *volcanoes*, and in the great number of *injurious* and *venomous insects* and *animals* which are banned from the Earth's surface and hide in its pits, as through the light of day were forbidden to them.

And it is here that the works of man in his terrestrial sojourn are painted in all their bleakness, because, by recalling the temporal example of greedy, ambitious, curious, industrious man, addicted to vulgar knowledge, one can see the enormous obstacles that he must encounter daily before being able to satisfy his desires.

Seas to be crossed, chasms to be traversed, entire Nations to be subdued, intemperate weather of all kinds to be experienced, foul realms to cross, deprivation and *slowness* to suffer due to *delays* and the *vagaries of the seasons*, this is the daily experience of intellectual man, of whom temporal man is the image.

What makes these tasks so imposing is that, if man lets the time allowed to complete them slip away in vain, he will need a second period of time which is longer and more painful than the first, seeing that he will then have both the first and the second activities to perform. If, during this second period of time, this unfortunate man doesn't better complete the tasks he hadn't fulfilled in the first, there must necessarily be a third period of time which is still more trying than the other two, and so on, ascribing yet more periods to his ills than those which he himself set by sacrificing all the powers which are within him.

If he removes a part of the sacrifice, he who receives it also retains a part of the reward, until he submits himself to pay unreservedly a tribute he cannot do effectively and completely except by contributing his whole Being towards it.

However, man only has the period of his terrestrial life to offer that tribute, that sacrifice, that work; for terrestrial life is the womb of the man to come. And just as corporeal Beings on this Earth bear and maintain the

---

[52] Extracting 'oil' from metal was an Alchemical process which resulted in a healing tincture, so commenting on metals which don't produce oil is making the point that they are useless and even harmful to mankind, adding them to the list of the terrible things which exist on and beneath the Earth.

form, sex and other signs they drew from their mother's womb, so man will carry to another *Earth* the *plan*, the *structure*, the manner of being which he himself took on during his time here below.

If he crosses the gap uselessly, far from being revivified, he will only render himself disqualified from ever knowing *life*, like those thin and corrupted plants which not only find the Sun's rays falling on them in vain, but which are also dessicated by its heat, so that they lose what little sap they had to grow and become fertile.

Such are the dangers which have threatened us since the corruption and the fall of the first criminal, and such is man's state in his dark sojourn, where not only does he not know his own *name*, but also where, pressed down by the weight of all the *spheres* and all the *actions* to which he is subject, he will be forced down by them if he doesn't usefully employ all the efforts of his will and the benevolent aid he is still offered to endure their violence and direct their effects to his advantage. For the action of these formidable powers is all the more painful for him so long as he is left to himself; and not enjoying their light, he doesn't know where to flee to avoid shock and pursuit. Finally, placed between the abyss and the imposing powers which are crushing him, he is constantly exposed to being hurt, tortured or falling into the precipices which are always open beneath his feet.

In this awful degradation, no longer perceiving the fixed and simple properties of unity, he is reduced to wandering around outside the Temple which contains them, and to which he is himself denied access. If through perseverance he might occasionally reach the foot of that august chamber and hear from afar the canticles which pure voices sing with words of Fire, those voices, no longer finding the same purity in him, cannot permit him to join his voice with theirs, nor come together with them in concert. And that is the outcome of man's first crime concerning all his posterity.

These disastrous results are not limited to man, for they extend over all physical Beings and over all the parts of the Universe, since there is nothing inside of time which can avoid suffering, given the definition we have given of time.

Indeed, man, chosen by Supreme Wisdom to be the sign of His Justice and Power, should confine Evil within His bounds and work tirelessly to bring peace to the Universe. And his sublime destiny clearly indicates what his *virtues* should be, since he alone should possess all the powers shared between all the rebellious Beings.

But, if he has let his virtuous[53] activity become corrupted, if instead of subjugating disorder, he has made an alliance with it, that disorder would grow and become stronger instead of being erased, and that universal enclosure which had served as a limit to *Evil* would instead be all the more exposed to its attacks and its activity. That should lead us to understand how all the Beings of the physical realm are now suffering even greater hardship that they were before man's crime.

One must nevertheless agree that the natural sufferings of those physical Beings cannot be compared to those of man, because man, having a Principle in addition to theirs, is exposed to pains and pleasures which are completely unknown to them.

It would also assume that there are differences between the sufferings of Beings which compose the Material Order. If a plant were to suffer, it would be less than for an animal; if a mineral were to suffer, it would be less than for the plant and the animal, given the difference between the Principles which constitute those three Kingdoms. But, so as not to slow down our progress, under the definition of physical, corporeal Beings, we'll include everything which is in Nature, and everything which is a material body, leaving it to the Reader's intelligence to make the specific distinctions that the immensity of details may require.

One might wonder how it can be that the physical and corporeal Beings of Nature which aren't free can suffer the effects of disorder without it being unjust.

The physical, corporeal Beings of Nature are Beings of action. As such, they are not capable of good or evil by themselves, and we cannot apply any of the Laws of morality to them. All that these natural notions can help us understand is that the Supreme Principle doesn't force them to perform actions more powerful than they have been accorded. So, to the degree that this action takes place, as it cannot exceed their powers, Wisdom is protected from injustice. For all the existing Powers coming from Him are subject to His rights and usage, when the Law of His council asks it to employ them.

Besides, this Wisdom measures and disposes all the forces and all the Powers on the rule of His own glory. Thus, it would go directly against

---

[53] The actual word used is *virtuelle*, which means 'virtual'; however, it would make more sense, given the preceding sentence, to assume the intended word was 'virtuous', pertaining to 'virtue'.

His interests to allow these powers to extend beyond their bounds, since that would dissolve and destroy them.

The suffering of physical Beings no longer appears to us to offend justice, since these Beings are but the instruments of Wisdom and the temporal means He uses to stop the progress of Evil. For their particular and essential Law – founded on the ineffable basis of all Laws – is completely contrary to any rebellious and disordered action which constantly tends to disturb this order in them. Also, they are never changed in their Principle, although they often experience the results and the effects of that Principle.

In this sense, when physical Beings are in pain, the temporal decree of justice is in the strength of its accomplishment, because their Law fights more vigorously against the opposing force which seeks to destroy them and send disorder into the Principle of their action.

One sees from that how the sufferings of material Beings turn to the advantage and maintenance of the Law which constitutes them, and how they fulfill the decrees of Divine justice over the enemy powers, which in these fights and in their results experience only contrariness and inexpressible torment. For what greater ordeal can we conceive than to persevere in strenuous but powerless efforts which, the more they are continued the more they turn to shame and rage towards those who have abandoned them?

If imprudent men, observing the sufferings of sentient Beings, have dared to condemn the ways of God and accuse Him of injustice, it is because they've never paid attention to the fact that since man is meant to represent Divinity in his actions, he also represents Him in the means by which these actions occur. Although all of the Orders have descended, nowadays these connections can almost only be discovered as material, which is nevertheless sufficient to raise the issue.

Now, if a father sees his son attacked by criminals or threatened by some great danger, that kind father will no doubt rush to his assistance, and in order to save him he won't hold back from using all the powers and organs of his own corporeal, physical form. However, the arms and legs of that kind father are not excluded from the attacks against whom they are used, and although they can be mistreated and even wounded we see no injustice in it, because they are only subordinates Beings and because the paternal love which commands them justifies all the actions he requires of them.

Let us accept for a moment, that universal physical Beings are with regard to the Divinity what material bodies are in the example quoted, and we will no longer be surprised that He uses them to come to man's aid, although those Beings or those physical organs would never have cooperated in crimes which have exposed man to death.

But as the use of physical Beings in the Great Work of Divine Wisdom rests on Laws and higher knowledge, this subject is beyond the scope of the majority to hope that with further reflection, it would be generally understood.

Besides, irrespective of the suffering attached to all sentient Beings by the Laws of Nature, they also experience substantial suffering which seems to come from causes other than those Laws. Such are the sufferings which come as a result of man's rule over the animals and the use he makes of them, either in religious sacrifices, or for his alimentary needs, or for various services and uses, or even just for his amusement.

If, to justify this new form of suffering which Religion, need, cruelty and the depravity of Society can add to the natural suffering of animals, I might again emphasize man's rights by recalling the extent of his authority, nevertheless the abuse he metes out to physical Beings doesn't appear any more excusable, or the animals any less innocent.

Nevertheless, such is the immensity of his powers through which he subjects to his action everything destined to be their object, and just as he takes it upon himself to *justify* the least acts of his power, so too, he can render them worthless, criminal and pernicious.

But to allay all the difficulties of this profound truth, we will add here that the *Superior Virtues* which never participated in man's crime do participate in the laborious results that this crime drags behind it. And if man was able to bring the pitiful influences of his disorder to the free Agents[54] and the Ministers of Divine Wisdom, it isn't surprising that he could also extend them over simple passive objects, over objects of dependence and servitude.

Now, what we have said concerning the various sufferings of corporeal Beings because of the various Principles which constitute them, we can also say of Beings which are superior to the Elemental Order and above man. We can show the nature of their suffering, or rather the

---

[54] The Papus edition of the book uses the word *Anges*, maning 'angels', but it seems clear that Saint-Martin wrote 'Agents', since the term 'angel' is used nowhere in his writings, except when quoting the Bible or other sources.

liveliness of their zeal and ardor for the reestablishment of order since they communicate with all the *Principles* and all the *Powers*. We could say that the closer a Being is to the *Truth*, the more it suffers at the hands of those who deny it and fight it.

Indeed, such a Being sees a first cause of suffering and affliction when it perceives that Beings which take all their power and even their slightest movement from it, are mad enough to claim they can destroy its powers and its very existence.

Secondly, that Being feels, in the midst of its continual enjoyment and gentleness, a new cause of suffering and affliction when it sees Beings who are *Divine* in origin distancing themselves from the source of their life, and wishing, so to speak, to force themselves to separate from it and tear themselves away.

From this, one can imagine how much sorrow can be produced out of the interest and love in those Beings which touch *Truth* Himself and which are even united and mingled with Him; and yet, though they are intended to contemplate order, harmony and peace, are forced to avert their eyes from that delightful spectacle in order to bring them to bear on disorder and confusion.

What crime, therefore, can equal man's, if there is nothing in material and immaterial Nature which isn't influenced by it, and if the entire chain of its Beings is torn apart by it?

Heth (ח) – The Universal Law of Reaction

Let the veil fall over that abyss of disorder and pain and let us rather focus our attention on the help that surrounds us, in order to discover how much hope remains to us. The Universal Law of reaction, serving as a guide on that sublime path, will convince us of the extent of the wonders of Him from Whom we have our origin, and of His extreme love for His creations.

In the order of generations, the Agents of action and reaction need to be distinguished by their powers, but they must be of the same essence and the same nature for their work to be physical.

It is for that reason that the generation of plants isn't physical for them because they work through the reaction of Water, or those other terrestrial saps which are so inferior to and so different from them.

It is for that reason that the reproduction of the majority of animals is indeed done with great physicality, because their Agents of reaction are Beings of their species.

It is for that reason that the fruits of thought and the actions of intelligence are so seductive to man, because those things work on him by means of *Agents* of his own nature and similar to him, even though he is in fact separate from them.

One may conceive, then, what must be the activity and the delight of the existence of God, Who never ceases to produce from within the immense number of Beings and Who, in order to produce them, uses only His own abilities and His own essence; that is, not only Agents of reaction which are relative to Him, but also those which are equal to Him, who are joined with him, which are Him. Thus, producing works above all that the senses and thought can offer us, and reuniting all the Agents and all their joys in Him alone, He becomes to our eyes the Supreme Focus of all happiness, and the universal center reflecting the ardor of all the affections of *life*.

This incontestable relationship necessarily affects the connections which unite temporal productions to their generative Principle, connections which are more physical when the work itself is more considerable, since these links barely exist, as it were, between a tree and its fruit, by comparison to those found between animals and their offspring, and they appear even lower still when compared to those which exist between our intellectual Being and his creations.

What must those which connect God to man be like, then? What must be the strength of His love for us, seeing that, since man is the most sublime creation and God the most sublime of all generating Principles, all the connections of love and union that our highest thoughts can allow us to conceive must exist between these two Beings?

Here there would be an infinity of other relationships to explain concerning the Laws of the conception of Beings, on their simplicity to the extent that they raise themselves up to come closer to the First Source, and on the subdivisions to which they are subjected in proportion to how far they are descended from Him. We would see the reason, why outside of time, all abilities are in the same Being; whereas, for Beings inside of time, those abilities require many separate Agents. We would understand the final cause of that great and magnificent Law by which perfect animals are born looking like their generative Principle, whereas imperfect animals, such as insects, experience several physical mutations in their forms before achieving that resemblance.[55] We would observe that our body, passing through all the revolutions of matter, is in a way like an insect when compared to our intellectual Being, which, from the moment of its emanation, received the fulness of its existence. They would finally take note that our intellectual Being itself, in its current state, is a kind of insect when compared to Beings to which corruption and time are unknown.

For, although he received the fulness of his existence at the time of his emanation, since his fall he has been subjected to a continual transmutation of different successive states before coming to an end; while the First Author of all that exists was and will always be what He is and what He should be. But these details would lead us down paths which are without number and without limits.

---

[55] In this instance he is talking about instars, or the steps throught which many insects mature to adulthood, such as a larva, to a pupa, to an imago. Indeed, it is likely he had caterpillars in mind, since this would have been the most transformative insect he would be acquainted with; and indeed, he may even have been thinking of silkworms, given Willermoz' profession as a trader in silks.

It is enough for us to remember here that man carries within himself an invisible, incorruptible seed, from which he has the right to expect fruits similar to his own essence, just as when we sow vegetable seeds we get fruits similar to the Principles from which they have come. It is enough to point out that if we wish to see our work crowned by success, we must, for example, after sowing flowers, cultivate them with the most careful attention and when the term of their growth is reached, it is then that, compensating us for our care, they give us the sweetness of all the properties within them as tribute. They delight our eyes with their colors and our sense of smell with their scents, and they can even bring joy and well-being to our whole person through the sap and the health-giving balms that flow from them.

These images should help us understand that since the good or evil state of Beings almost always depend upon the kind of reaction they receive, we are placed here below to protect ourselves from evil reactions and to procure advantageous ones; and if it wasn't the hand of Wisdom which cultivated His own seed, and which activated the sacred seed which was placed within us, in vain could we claim to produce fruit similar to the tree which has produced us; in vain could we ever hope to see brought forth those active powers of which all Beings are the custodian, each according to their Order; those powers which, continually circulating from the Supreme Principle to His creations and from those creations to their Principle, form that living and uninterrupted chain, where all is action, all is power, all is joy.

But, irrespective of the need we have for that superior reaction, we see the impossibility for that reaction not taking place in us, though so often we neglect its effects.

And truly, if man's original and essential nature had called him to be the image and expression of the powers of the Great Principle, and if the nature of Beings is indestructible, although their actions and their properties can change or be destroyed, man is unable to erase the Law and the convention by which he is constituted. Therefore, he always retains the means to work to accomplish them, and despite the dark abyss into which man has fallen, the divine essence never stops causing the streams of his glory to flow into him.

Indeed, since the Supreme Wisdom is the sole source of all that truly exists, if nothing can exist which doesn't come from Him and which doesn't result from Him, when a true Being exists it must necessarily be in His image. Now, since this Universal Source never interrupts the action by which He reproduces Himself, as a result He never ceases to reproduce His own images universally. Where, then could man go where he wouldn't encounter them, and wouldn't be surrounded by them? To what exile could he be banned which didn't bear some impression of them?

We should also say the same about the Principle of Evil whose existence is attested to by the distressing counter-action that it works upon our thoughts. The active rays of light undoubtedly reach it; for if we observe that fresh water isn't limited to making the soil fertile by subdividing into a thousand streams over its surface, but continuing on to reach the sea and, along with other natural causes, contributes to tempering its bitterness and prevents it from becoming a useless mass of salt, surely this shows us that, in a similar manner, the superior *power*, having vivified and filled the heart of man which is their natural reservoir, overflows so to speak, and descend into the abode of corruption, to soften the bitterness and prevent the ardor of its unclean fire from desiccating the seed of crime so much that it can no longer either dissolve or decompose.

However, when Beings become criminal, they are truly separated from the Divine Master by being deprived of exercising their abilities, and although the Creator's *Virtue* is communicated to them, if it isn't returned from them to Him because of the corruption of their desire, they remain in darkness and in the death destined for all Beings of falsehood and error.

For it is a very great truth that the relationships of Beings must be judged by going back up from them to their Principle and not by descending from their Principle to them; because it is from this Principle that they have their source and all their value; whereas this Principle, having all these things within Himself, has no need to seek them in any other Being.

Finally, we can say that if God still sustains the *life* and the *powers* of guilty Beings, it is because He maintains the *Word* in *futile* man and thus, in both examples, the signs of degradation are clear.

Although there is an immeasurable distance between degraded men and the Creator, we should recognize that this distance is only in relation to them alone, and in no way threatens the indivisible universality of the Eternal One. It has always belonged to them by right of their intellectual nature, and the common Father of all Beings will never lose sight of the least of His creations; otherwise His love should be extinguished, and if love were extinguished there would be no more God.

We will allow ourselves a comparison taken from the Physical Order of things. When a man is physically awake he experiences elemental light, and he physically knows that it exists and is close to him. If he goes to sleep he no longer perceives it, but those who remain awake around him and who see it cannot deny that it reflects on that sleeping body.

It is the same with mental light. When we draw near it, it warms us and we clearly know it exists; but if we close our eyes to its brightness, we no longer see that light and we are in darkness; and yet for those who remain *awake* it is very clear that it is still there, and that in our quality as free and everlasting Beings we still have the power to open our eyes to its rays. Thus, whether we were to die or live mentally, we are still beneath the rays of the great light, and we can never be inaccessible to the eye of the Universal Being.

Here let us place the principal column of our edifice and examine the paths which Wisdom never ceases to use in order to bring this superior power to man, without which all the fruits of his nature would be stifled at birth.

If man, having been expelled from the place where the light resides, can now no longer contemplate the highest thought, will and action in their unity or their individuality [56], he can still recognize them in a subdivision relative to him alone, that is, in the multitude of images of all

---

[56] In Jean-Baptiste Willermoz' letter to to Baron von Turkheim, dated August 18, 1821, we read: "Adam, tempted and seduced by the Demon, sinned grievously in Thought, Will and Action. At the same instant the innumerable multitude of his Order acquired knowledge and sinned to the extent that they were capable of doing so. Some rejected the Thought with all their Will; others supported it to some extent; still others embraced it wholeheartedly. Surely, we can see in the first the Righteous or the Predestined or the Blessed of my Father; in the second the swamp of humans ensnared by the pleasures and seductions of the World; and in the third the greatest scoundrels and villains across the ages?

"Thus, each Order is tarnished by man's prevarication, and the most righteous remain encumbered because of their great interdependence with the most guilty, and all of them must settle their portion with a more of less prolonged sojourn in material incorporization and in the mortal death they must suffer, as well as the expiatory and purifying pains which Mercy has in store for them after death. Now, is this portion equal for all men? Reply: No! It is different for some than others, and almost nothing for yet others."

It is interesting to note how Pasqually's original view of man's prevarication has by now, in Willermoz' mind, transformed into an almost straightforward concept of original sin (eating of the Tree of Knowledge) and we even see an allusion to Purgatory in the second paragraph: all very traditional Catholic teachings.

kinds which surround him, whose purpose is to cause a response in him and make him open his eyes to the truth because, without this response, man wouldn't be guilty at all of remaining in darkness and of not regaining the concept of his abilities.

Indeed, if among material Beings there are none who can manifest what is within it without a reaction, there is similarly a reaction for man's spirit, since like them he has a generating Principle.

And man cannot gaze around himself without seeing the most expressive images of all those truths he needs.

The Supreme Principle primarily manifests the existence of His creative abilities through the existence of matter, since any material individual is and can only be a result of this. He also manifests the progressive Law of action of these abilities by means of the successive generative actions of the Elements. And here is their Order.

There is an invisible and irrepressible Principle of Fire, from which come all the specific substances which constitute the body. This Fire Principle is indicated by the phlogiston[57] exhaled from matter during dissolution. It produces three physical actions.

Through the first it causes material, visible Fire, which in animals is represented by the blood, and this coarse fire is threefold in that it contains within it both Water and Earth; but this triplicity is simple, because there is still no degree of separation.

The second operation separates an aqueous fluid from this material, visible Fire which is much coarser, represented by the animal seed, which is extracted from the blood, or the universal principle spread throughout the body. This aqueous fluid, this seed, this Water is dual, in that it is joined with Earth, and because it is produced by the second action.

The third action separates from this Water the Earth, the solid or the body. This body appears simple or single to us; but this simplicity is threefold in its dimensions and its level of emanation, and because it is the opposite of Fire, whose triplicity is simple.

---

[57] In Saint-Martin's time, there was a belief in a fiery principle, called *phlogiston*, which was contained in combustible bodies, and released during burning. It was an attempt to explain such observed phenomena as combustion and rusting. This theory was initially proposed by Johann Joachim Becher in 1667 and refined by Georg Ernst Stahl, most clearly published in his Chemical Treatise, *Fundamenta chymiae*, in 1723, and popularized by his successors. Indeed, this belief continued until the latter part of the 1780s (after this book was written), when the involvement of oxygen in the combustion process was proved by Antoine-Laurent Lavoisier and others.

This, then is the Progressive and Numerical Law of the physical, general and specific actions of the Universal Creative abilities. We can see how things become physical and gross as they descend, and one can see here the source of the Philosophers' arguments, which have claimed, on the one hand, that everything came from Water, and on the other, from Fire, or again, from Mercury or Earth. All of them are right, and everything depends on the degree of progression at which they stopped.

There is also an ascending Law, by which the emanations of these abilities rise back up to their Generating Principle, and this Law is the inverse of the first. But while the one and the other act in a circular manner, they succed one another without harm, and they work in concert, following the dual sense which constitutes time.

Through this ascending Law, the solid and earthly body disappears, liquefying or becoming Water; the Water volatilizes and disappears, devoured by the elemental Fire; the elemental Fire disappears, returning to its Fire *Principle*, whose voracious but invisible action is indicated by that of elemental Fire itself, which before our eyes consumes all the objects it has produced.

As the descending and ascending forces of the Universal Creative abilities are constantly in motion before us, we can therefore always discover the source from whence all things came, and to which they must return: for each of the degrees we have just observed is like a lamp which illuminates the points above and below it, between which it is placed in the circular progression.

But let us consider these elemental objects in the Terrestrial Order. Although we're unable to reach their Generating Principle, we can at least see and admire the Laws which govern them.

Indeed, if we consider the body and the Elements in their facts and in their temporal terrestrial actions, we will be able to discern an image of the continuous activity of these Universal Creative abilities in them, in that perpetual state of exhalation and inspiration, both of which are visible in Beings of all Orders in our realm.

We'll see that among the three Elements, Fire rises, Earth descends, and Water follows a horizontal line, which teaches us that the action of the superior abilities, for which the elements are the organs, fills and encompasses the breadth of the universal circumference.

If we consider the properties of the Three Kingdoms, there we'll find the sign of hidden *powers* of which they are the emblem and the expression.

Gold, by its astonishing malleability, shows us the prodigious extension of the powers of Nature which, through infinite efforts, transmits its *Virtues* to the most distant Beings, and through this establishes a universal connection.

The plants absorb all the impure vapors of the atmosphere and, combining them with their scent, dissolve them and return them to us with less harmful qualities, to teach us once again, and physically, that the existence of all the Beings of Nature are meant to ameliorate ills and disorders.

If plants produce different effects during the night, or even during the day when not exposed to the Sun's rays, it is because, since it has the same rank among the Three Kingdoms as Water has among the three Elements, they are, like Water, especially a dual type and they can manifest both the advantageous results effected by an Agent associated with its Principle of reaction, and the dire results to which one who is separated from it is reduced.

With respect to the Animal Kingdom, we see an active representation of the speed with which the life of the Great Being is communicated to the whole chain of His creations in that rapid movement which conveys both the action of blood in all the arteries, and which requires no progression or interval to move from the center to the farthest extremities.

Finally, the Air[58], that Being separate from the other Elements, that physical symbol of *invisible* life, whose purpose is to cleanse the Earth as its action is more well-ordered and constant, depending on whether the climate in which it works is exposed to corrupting exhalations to a greater or lesser extent. That Air, then, being the image of the superior action, works on the body's overall response, penetrating right into the heart of every seed, thereby becoming a universal motivator for all Beings to find what should play a part either in their existence, or in their health. For there is an Air for Earth, an Air for Water and an Air for Fire.

---

[58] It should be noted that Saint-Martin didn't consider Air to be a true Element, indeed being superior to Earth, Water and Fire from which the World was formed. The reason for this may be found in detail in his book *Of Errors & Truth*. Note earlier that he envisages Fire as being an ascending force, Earth as descending and Water as being a horizontal line, which is quite different to the symbols usually employed for the Ancient Elements.

It is true, therefore, that however dark our current domain is, we cannot take a single step in it without being surrounded by visible signs of these living, creative motivators which are unknown to us.

Heavenly Nature presents us with the same truth. Though we can't see the Principle which moves the stars, and while we are an immense distance from them, we enjoy their light and receive the emanation of their fire. We can even form bold and insightful hypotheses about the orders they received at their origin, and the true purpose for their existence: up to now wise men have thought that all the Laws regarding physical Beings are written upon that vast and beautiful Tableau[59], and that the Divine Hand enveloped the Earth with it, as it were, so that those who inhabit it might continually read the signs and characters of truth there.

Thus, the whole of the material Universe paints for us the majesty of its supreme Powers in a magnificent statement. There we see the brilliant stars dispense their light to the World, the physical heavens stamp the Laws and the patterns of Beings on the atmospheric Air which carries these plans to the Earth, and the Earth execute them with ceaseless zeal and activity.

It is therefore true that Universal Nature is, for man, like a great tree which he can gaze at and enjoy its fruits, as a consolation for not being able to discover its *seeds* and its *roots*.

In these Tables, not only does Nature present man with symbols of what he had been able to study at his origin, it also teaches him to fix his gaze on that Original Table and the steps he must take to reaquire its use. Indeed, the Laws of Beings in the physical realm provide man with many

---

[59] The title of this book is *Tableau Naturel*, and it is really this passage which explains the meaning of the title. In the Foreword, the reason why the title 'Natural Table' was selected over 'Natural Image', 'Natural Portrait' or other possible titles was explained. To expand on the reason set forth there, we would also point out that the word 'tableau' has many meanings in French. Among these is the idea of a stage set when the curtain goes up; a picture; an image; and, perhaps most significantly for our case, the Tracing Board in a Masonic Lodge. All of these are images which affect the mind through the eye, presenting symbols and concepts to be interpreted. In a Masonic Lodge a Tracing Board is similarly covered with symbols, and at a point in the ceremony there will be a lecture to explain the symbols and tie them into the points of the ritual just experienced. While Saint-Martin is suggesting that the vast canopy of heaven with its stars is a great picture which man can study, he also introduces the idea that all is set by a Divine Hand, all is in motion, and by studying its Laws we can better understand ourselves. This both reflects the concept of the heavens as a macrocosm and man as the microcosm, and perhaps also suggests that Saint-Martin still had some affection for Astrology. Therefore, the word *Tableau* will be translated as 'Table', 'image', 'picture' or 'portrait' depending upon the context.

clear instructions about what he must do each day to recover his former splendor and glory.

All bodies in Nature tend to shed their coarse external layer, to reflect the radiance they carries within them back to the Principle which animates them. The Fire which is particular to each of these Bodies ceaselessly cooperates in that Great Work, continually purifying the substances on which they feed.

Our own blood is intended to fulfill this important function without respite. It must work on our drink and food to separate the pure from the impure and employ its action to keep at a distance everything they contain which is harmful and too material.[60]

No doubt this is to teach man how to use the two key Agents within him: his *intellect* and his *will*. He must exercise their *fire* on the intellectual substances which are offered to him and separate out everything that isn't in harmony with his thinking Being, in order only to permit pure, invigorating juices to enter him, with which he can enter into that union, that harmony, that unity which is both the object and the goal of all actions and all Beings of Nature.

With regard to Fire in general, it teaches men how great their pleasure and their knowledge would be if they persevered in exercising the abilities they possess, and if they directed their action to the level which their species allows them to strive for. Fire has the power of destroying bodies completely, that is, to purge them of their dross and their outward appearance, so that their core Principle achieves to some extent its purity and its natural simplicity.

Through this, those bodies whose opacity makes them impenetrable to our sight and block our view of other objects, those bodies truly acquire a visible clarity, a transparency whose effect no longer leaves any limits to our desires and our knowledge.

They give man the means to enjoy the light of the stars without experiencing the rigors of the atmosphere, and to exist amidst the storms of this terrestrial realm without suffering their effects, as if, in fact, they presented an instructive – if gross – image of another kind of light and

---

[60] It is clear from this paragraph that Saint-Martin was familiar with the *Emerald Tablet*, admired by Alchemists and Hermeticists throughout this and preceding Centuries – so much so that Sir Isaac Netwon was inspired to translate it a Century earlier. As well as the references to the *Emerald Tablet*, the description is heavily influenced by alchemical processes.

another kind of confidence that man might also obtain for himself in the midst of the *tempests* which rumble in this stormy abode.

Those bodies give him the means to penetrate, as it were, the mysteries of Nature, to perceive, on the one hand, the wonders that the smallness of some objects would seem to have forever excluded from his knowledge; and on the other hand, to direct his eyes upwards to the most elevated region of the stars. They make it possible for him to measure their dimensions, calculate all their movements and to openly read the Laws of these great mobiles from which he is separated by a distance so prodigious that, since so many are beyond his sight, he would not have even been able to suspect their existence.

All these facts are so many signs to man to show him that if he had the courage to bring his will to its rightful period of purification, it would give his intellectual Being a clarity, a *transparency* similar to his Order; it would provide him with a level of *purification* which would not only let him discover the procession of invisible Beings which surround him, but even help him rise up to the highest Intellectual Order above him, up to that living Order in which he drew his origin, but from which he now so distanced that he regards it as being inaccessible to his sight. For in the physical and in the intellectual, it is certain that it is grossness and impurity which created the shadows, the remoteness and distance around man; and that everything is clear, everything is near to him when all is pure within him.

In spite of all the beauty written into temporal Creation, we must agree that we only see Laws of rigor and violence in it, things which aren't free; and which don't even show intelligence in the Agents which work within it, although there must necessarily be such outside of those Agents who controls all their actions, since those actions are executed with order and regularity.

It is in vain, then, that we would seek in matter any true and enduring image of the Principle of Life from which we are unfortunately separated. And if man didn't have signs in addition to material objects to help him recover knowledge of that Principle, Divine Justice would have little to ask of him.

We have already noted that, in man, corrupt as he may be, we may still find traces of powers and abilities unrelated to all material Nature. We have seen that, across all the Centuries, in all Nations, the ideas of justice and beneficence have been known, though so often they have been distorted, and their respectable names applied to criminal purposes.

Further, when considering his corporeal form, man can prove that he possesses *virtues* which are even more active that those powers of which we have just spoken.

We can say that he carries the living signs of all the Worlds and all the Universes[61], and if one intellectually considers three of the main organs found within his head, we'll see why the organs of hearing are completely passive, receiving impressions and communicating nothing; why the eyes are active and passive, expressing internal feelings to the outside and communicating impressions of external objects to the interior; finally, why the tongue is a completely active organ, having the dual power to paint with the same ease the operations of thought or reason and the transports or passions of the soul.

We can even bring our intellectual observations to bear upon the invisible center which animates these three organs, that hidden domain of thought which has its home in the inside of the head, just as the Supreme Divinity has placed His own within an impenetrable sanctuary, though His attributes manifest His existence and actions to all Beings.

In this invisible man we will find the number of the three abilities of the Divine Principle that form the basis of all Beings. Even though they now only act in us in slow and painful succession, they are absolutely indivisible as they are in the Divinity. They must clearly have the same function, and if man has the terrible right to stray using the sole power of his will, *it is because* he doesn't recognize how he differs from his archetype.

Independently of the objects in Nature which surround man and which express his Principle to him, he therefore has an even more useful and accurate means to recognize it in himself and in his fellow man. It's clear that since God is Himself illustrated in all of Nature's works, and

---

[61] While this comment is made in passing, it is very intriguing. The words used are *les Univers*, which clearly means the plural. While it could be argued that Saint-Martin is simply employing hyperbole, although Newton had tangentially alluded to their possibility, it was not until the end of the 20th Century that the idea of there being more than one Universe was put forward in any seriousness. So, in his comments about what we now call the multiverse theory and in his earlier statement about the existence of stars and more which humans had never seen, which clearly went beyond the teachings of the Church at that time, was he only exaggerating to sound impressive, or did this suggest teachings of another Order of which he was a member? We will probably never know.

more particularly in man, there is nothing in our dark abode which does not bear His sign, and an immense number of God's images. This is a resplendant truth which should serve as a sure guide to discover all those which can fulfill man's desires.

In the union of man with the Universe, how can we not see an active image of divine harmony, in which the First Being reveals Himself to us as dominating every intelligence, and receiving from them the tribute and homage they owe to His greatness? Indeed, what rank does man occupy on Earth? All the Beings of Nature are in motion around him, and all work for him: air, fire, stars, winds, seas, Elements, everything acts and contributes to his well-being; everything contributes to sustain his existence. He alone, in the midst of this vast empire, has the privilege of being above this temporal activity. He can, if he so wishes and has the courage, have no other pursuit than that of taking ownership of all the gifts and all the powers of the Universe.

The only tribute that Wisdom requires of man while giving him the use of these benefits, is that he gives Him glory and that he recognizes Him as being the Sovereign Arbiter of everything that exists; that it is He that restores to his abilities the same Law, the same Order, the same regularity by which he sees that all Beings in Nature are governed; that is, in a word, that instead of acting in his own name, as he constantly does, he should always act, like those Beings, in the name of the Living God who alone created him.

That, then, is the Great Work, or that change of will by which, as we have said before, all the *Powers* of Nature have been employed since the beginning of things without yet being able to make it happen.

But this superiority of man over Nature is shown in a more active way through the simple manipulations he can perform on matter, which should give us an even greater idea of the extent of his rights.

There is no material body, however hard, however crystallized as it might be, from which one couldn't extract the Principles which are used to generate all the bodies of the three Kingdoms. To accomplish this, it is sufficient to go in the opposite direction to that which the hard body followed to achieve its state of solidity. One must therefore commence by working on its dissolution.

Although man has little knowledge of how to perform those types of dissolution, it is no less true that they are possible, because Nature, through its secondary operations provides us with the evidence and the means every day. For, in the absence of knowledge, one can at least avail oneself of the examples of Nature, which is always ready to make up for our weakness and ignorance. But it must be remembered that the results of our operations will always be inferior to those which Nature herself works, which alone deserve the Names attached to their Kingdom, as they bear their key characteristics.

Without losing sight of this cautious observation, let us pulverize the densest salt, or the hardest marble or granite. Let us expose this powder, which cannot be ground too finely if one wants to succeed, to the free air of the atmosphere; but without water, covered and sheltered as much as possible from rain, dust and the foreign bodies we have already identified. Little by little the acid in the air will act on this pulverized salt. It will extract substances which are similar to it, and leave behind the rest which, over the course of time, will be completely converted to vegetal earth.

As soon as one is in possession of this vegetal earth, all the discoveries are complete: the air's humidity joins with it and brings about the birth of small plants.

These plants, coming to maturity, undergo a new operation, or a dissolution more natural than that of gross infusion, and we will see the birth of insects and even kinds of metals, if one knows how to do this, and this will be a complete demonstration that the Universal Principle of life exists in all bodies.

Do not think that I am contradicting here what has been previously put forward concerning the fixed characters of Beings, which can never rise to a higher grade than what has been assigned to them by Nature. In the processes we are discussing the transmutations only take place because the different seeds innate in each Body are separate from one another and can act freely depending on their Law, but none of them can depart from their Kingdom. We should also note that the results of such transmutations always tend towards degeneration and that, the more we repeat this process on the same substances, the more their results are weakened, which makes them increasingly inferior to the primary creations of Nature.

Nevertheless, we can admire man's rights, since, by the use that he is free to make of all material substances, he has the power to transmute, so to speak, everything he finds in his bounds, to convert soils into minerals, plants into insects, and those into a new earth from which new combinations will come forth, since, ultimately, by a single process he can transform animals and plants into minerals and salts, the hardest rocks into organic and living Bodies, and in some way change the appearance of everything around him.

Let us not hesitate to apply these observations to intangible objects. To him, they are either separate from, or entangled in material substances and envelopes which appear to impede their action. But as he himself is a universal solvent, *he could to some extent, if he enjoyed the rights of his intelligence, accomplish in the Order of intellectual things that which he can accomplish with the body by means of physical and corporeal Agents.*

All this leads us to believe that man, restored to his rights, could act as much on immaterial and corrupt Beings as on the pure Beings from which he is presently separated by formidable barriers. Being the image of the Supreme Agent, he would have the power to dissolve and decompose envelopes, in order to discover the Principles which are contained and concentrated therein, and furnish them with the means to produce the fruits and all the Kingdoms which are theirs, to recreate those which are simple, to maintain the inactivity of those which are harmful, that is to say to replace stertility with abundance, darkness with light, death with life, and so to transfigure everything that surrounds him, that his dwelling would resemble that of Truth itself.[62]

---

[62] This is perhaps the only section in italics which gives any indication of having been written by a person separate to the author. However, even then the style is similar enough to make it hard to be certain of this. Despite its length, it reads like the other, shorter passages in italics, in that it serves to give an example of the philosophy being advanced. Indeed, given that this passage focuses on dubious science such as Spontanous Generation, it might have been better if this section had been omitted entirely!

Teth (ט) – Rehabilitation: Thought, Will, Action

We should not deceive ourselves: the marvelous spectacle of the continual action of corporeal Beings, *and even that of the superiority that man should have over them through the practice and application he can make of their Law* is without doubt only a very weak and inferior representation of that divine harmony which links the three *primary powers*[63] to all intelligent Beings.

In that Divine Order all is holy, all is true, and all works together towards a single purpose. The Divine Master at the center of His pure emanations, pouring out the sweetness of His existence and His Powers into their breasts, uniting them to Him by all the rights of love and felicity.

There, the subjects can never raise themselves up above their Sovereign, and if some of them were misguided enough to revolt against His laws, they could never carry out their attacks against Him, since the moment they conceived that terrible thought they would lose sight of His presence. Moreover, regardless of the nature of the crimes, the clemency of the Master never departs from the guilty. He tempers His justice rather than being inflamed by it, and He seeks to win over the criminals rather than subjugate them; He envelopes them, so to speak, in the power of His love, to spare them the terror of His Name, and to show them that He is more desirous to reign over them through love than through power.

This isn't the case in the Temporal Order: the subject and the master are almost always confused. All those corporeal Beings, all those Agents of Nature intended to serve man are continually at war with him, and when he is abandoned to himself, far from regarding him as the king of the Universe, instead they take him to be an exile or the lowly slave of those he should command, and even when he utilizes his rights, and his empire appears well-ordered, it only offers us glimpses of that true empire of which we can only draw a feeble image. The power and extent of his abilities are neither constant, nor unalterable, and if he indeed exhibits a

---

[63] Although it is explained at length later on in the text, note that the three Divine Powers referred to are Thought, Will and Action.

representation of the three divine powers, one can say that it is only a very unrecognizable outline.

Not only is his thought not his, not only is his will not constantly pure, but his very actions are unsure, and have neither the assurance nor the authority of the Master and Sovereign, so that one can barely recognize in them any of the living traits of the third Divine Power which Action should represent.

However, it is through our resemblance to this third power that we should begin to correct the deformities which disfigure us. Since the Law by which the First Principle allows us see His image here below is linked to a temporal and successive order, we must work to manifest the rights and lives of Divine *Action*, before claiming to manifest the two abilities which precede it, since in any ascending progress, one must pass through the inferior levels before going on to the superior ones.

However, these words 'superior' and 'inferior' should only be used in reference to the boundaries which presently contain our intelligence. In God[64], nothing is superior, nothing is inferior; everything is indivisible, everything is identical, everything is equal in unity.

But man's successive mistakes have not just caused the subdivision of the temporal powers of the Beings of Creation, they've also persuaded the Divinity to only reveal the powers of His own essence to that guilty Being in successive steps, and that is another new proof of the love that He has for him; for as man no longer has the strength necessary to contemplate the Divine Unity without peril to himself, He divided Himself up, as it were, for his benefit, so that he always has some means to recognize it, and yet it doesn't dazzle him, which would happen if He were to reveal Himself to him in all His splendor.

So, in this form of subdivision, which is with respect to man alone, the third Divine Power, or *Action*, is the one which we must consider first, since its number places it after the other two and, consequently, closer to us.

---

[64] In this chapter in particular, it is surprising how Saint-Martin harks back to his first book, in using a dizzying list of euphemisms for God, including Supreme Wisdom, Divine Master, the Divinity, First Principle, Great Principle, Supreme Thought, Universal Principle and others. It is this endless use of different terms for the same concept which can make his work difficult at times. Similarly, in this chapter in particular the Translator has translated the French word *virtue* as 'power' more frequently than in other chapters, since in this chapter in particular the 'powers' being focused on are thought, will and action, and these are neither Theological nor Cardinal Virtues: and so, the word 'powers' makes for a clearer reading experience.

If one finds too many difficulties understanding these words, *action, will, thought*, which I present as being distinct from one another, though these three powers are essentially one, it will suffice, to better understand what I am writing, to keep in mind the general idea that, because of his crime, man lost sight of the unity of the Divine Powers, and can no longer contemplate them except separately, and these powers, in communicating themselves to him, can only reveal themselves by means of an innumerable host of facts, signs and emblems, under a complication of Agents and means, which makes man feel his deprivation from this unity and this source and abode of delight.

If in the human species, when we consider it in terms of the Physical Order, we see men who are remarkable in their beauty and the proportions of their bodies, by their strength, agility and various advantages of form and limbs, we should consider that it is the same with intellectual abilities and that, if the vast majority are in fact reduced to the most common and basest thoughts, it must have been that throughout time there were those who were distinguished from their fellow men, and who were closer to the light than them: differences which one may still observe each day with reference to what is commonly called: the *Sciences*.[65]

Although all men on Earth are meant to manifest, even here below, some rays of divine abilities, we can therefore believe that a few among them are called to this Work with a more positive determination than other men, and they have to work with facts which are more extensive and more substantial.

Most of mankind, charged solely with their own regeneration have only, so to speak, to ponder the Table of Relief which Supreme Wisdom shows them and try to apply its teachings. The others, who are destined to spread this relief abroad, must have greater strength and more extensive gifts.

To focus our thoughts on this subject, we will regard all the men on Earth as Elect but divided into two Orders: those who are the *Particular Elect* and those who are the *General Elect*.[66]

---

[65] Or 'Knowledge'.

[66] The name 'Elect' or *Élu* comes from Pasqually's 'Order of Elect Cohens of the Universe', more commonly referred to as *Élus Cohen* or *Élus coëns*. This Masonic and Theurgical Order taught that man could effect his Reintegration – and that of all mankind – through a series of Theurgical Operations both on his behalf and for that of the world in general. However, Saint-Martin has focused the application of these terms on a narrower field than Pasqually did, for in his *Treatise* he talks of General and Particular Creation, referring to the creation of the Earth as 'general' and

Teth (ט) – Rehabilitation: Thought, Will, Action

We would add that the General Elect may only with difficulty descend to the rank of the Particular Elect, but that it is possible for any of the latter to raise himself up to the level of the former through courage and sustained efforts of will; for it is harder for a man accomplished in knowledge to forget what he knows than for an ignorant man to acquire knowledge.

This compels us to consider for a moment the alleged system of fate which is connected to man's destiny.

The difficulties raised by this subject come from the fact that we attribute to the Particular Elect what is said concerning the General Elect alone.

It is clear that the latter, given the immensity of their advantages, can consider themselves to be predestined according the vulgar notion. But since, in the human race, there would be a few privileged Beings intended for greater Works, should we not conclude from this that all men are capable of being such, since it is clear that the majority continue to be Agents of their free will and also Agents of their actions, and consequently of the outcomes which must result? It would be wrong, then, to make all the Elect like one another, and conclude the universality of men from a small number.

This cannot be correct, and one will ask why such a man has been chosen in preference to all the others and elevated to the rank of Privileged or General Elect.

To get to the core of this difficulty, we must ascend to the simple but universal Laws of Divine Wisdom Who, having placed His mark on all His works, has engraved them upon the human species as He has on His other creations. Let us add that human Nature, being the universal figurative image of Divinity, as well as of His *Virtues* and *Powers*, should see all these patterns repeated in the various individuals of its own species.

That is why there must be men tasked with manifesting Divine things; others intellectual things; yet others physical and natural things; without speaking of another kind of manifestation whose need is also essential among men, but which it wouldn't be prudent to reveal to the multitude.[67]

---

of man as 'particular', meaning individual. Here, the term 'General' is used for those who work not only on their own reintegration but that of all humanity; while the lesser term 'Particular' is reserved for those who only work on their own reintegration.

[67] Although Saint-Martin does this less in this book than in his previous one, he is still not above hinting that he possesses secrets not known to the general public. This either stems from his

The Law which directs these kinds of decisions is similar to the Law which constitutes Divinity Himself: it is based on the sacred property of the abilities of the First Principle, and the numerical order acting on all Beings which must represent them, a property coeternal with the Supreme Essence, for which there can be no other purpose than that of His existence, since this purpose and His existence are one and the same thing. And it is by that sole knowledge that we can understand what we have called *liberty* in that Great Being.

Thus, one wouldn't know why some men have such and such traits to exhibit in preference to other men without first knowing the numerical Law which the Supreme Wisdom has given to their origin. Or rather, one would have to know why the Divine Powers[68] are themselves diverse, albeit intimately united and forever inseparable; and finally, why thought isn't will, will isn't action and action is neither thought nor will. But if, in a strict sense, these questions aren't above man's intellect, they are at least unnecessary and often very dangerous for him, especially when he doesn't pursue them on the true path, which is action. For if this *action* is the essential seed for our rehabilitation, this seed is required first for us to obtain that knowledge and enlightenment which are its true fruit. Thus, by remaining faithful to this *action*, we will recognize that it is the only means to confirm all the truths explained up till now and to dispel any confusion.

Let us return to our topic and discover the physical and intellectual paths by which the General or Privileged Elect have been admitted to this sublime title.

If they had only had that natural and human assistance of the Table which we have gone through earlier, and even if they had only had the assistance of other Privileged men like them, they would still have only seen the secondary and inferior types, by which they wouldn't have discovered why man exists.[69] And having no knowledge at all of the effective *Powers* of the Great Principle, it would have been impossible for

---

membership in the Élus Cohen, which would make sense here as he is referring to them; or some have conjectured – without concrete proof – that he belonged to another secret organization which supplemented his understanding of how the universe works.

[68] That is, of Thought, Will and Action.

[69] That is, if even the brightest of men had only the stars and the wonders of Nature to contemplate, as well as the guidance of even the most intelligent fellow men, they would still only be seeing the results – the reflection, as it were – of the work of the First Principle; and if they were not privileged to know of His existence, then man's purpose on Earth would still be hidden to them.

them to return to the sublime rank from which they had descended, and God would have issued a decree for man which could never have been accomplished.

Therefore, it must be, according to the Order of Divine Immutability, that Supreme Wisdom has presented those Privileged Elect with *active*, *striking* and *direct signs* of those powers and abilities by which man should begin the path of his Regeneration.

Finally, it is essential that the very Powers of Divine Wisdom are brought to those Privileged men, that they are touched, so to speak, by His very substance, to provide them with the means to manifest their activities and to begin to fulfill the task for which they had received their temporal existence.

We will have no doubt about these truths when we reflect that the Divine Powers, radiating in all directions like Solar Fire, are in continual activity which makes them progress at the same time in every direction to infinity; and because of this, they must of necessity encounter man in their journey and that, the more that man is like them, the more they will tend to unite with him because of the essential similarities of their natures.

And that is the reaction which, irrespective of the universality of the Divine Action, shows itself in each of us, since man, having no thought within him, nevertheless receives thoughts which are both vivid and luminous every day. For if a person complains that he hasn't received anything like this, that lack isn't a flaw in his nature, but rather a result of his negligence in taking hold of those rays which were offered to him in his earliest age, and which were shown to him to be guides which could lead him to the habitual enjoyment of a Greater Light.

When we say that the Powers of God are necessarily communicated to men, we are talking about a necessity applied to the Fundamental Laws which God imprints upon Beings, and on the immutability of His decrees. So, this shouldn't weaken the greatness of His love in our eyes, and even less make us believe that we are excused from cooperating on the Work with Him, as if He had to work alone and without the cooperation of our free will.[70]

---

[70] This also works the other way around: not only does man need to cooperate on the Great Work with God; he must voluntarily involve God in all his works as well. Indeed, it was man's arrogance in the first place, by attempting an act of creation on his own without seeking the cooperation of God, which resulted in him being cast down to earth in a material body.

By creating a Order apart of *General Elect* which, being constantly united with the Great Principle Himself, leaves us no point of distinction to make between His Divine Action and their free will, tells us that this is done out of love as well as justice: for both are simply supports offered to us to help us climb out of the abyss: though we are usually given absolute freedom either to make use of them, or to run from them and leave them alone.

Although the aid which the Supreme Wisdom offers man is a necessary result of the love which constitutes Him, man must still ask Him for the strength to make *use* of it, he must use all the *powers* of his Being so that this aid isn't given to man in vain. For this Wisdom, always requiring labor from man, places a condition on His mercies, and then it is up to man's will to determine how effective he is. Finally, like those beams of colored light which continue on when they find themselves in an environment which is too thin and weak for them to find a surface to reflect them, the supreme rays shine uselessly upon man and pass right by him when he has no foundation within him on which to fix them.

If men could act according to their true Law without God's help, or if God had to act in them without their cooperation, the Theologians and Philosophers would be justified in raising many questions about free will and the effects of Divine grace, which is nothing other than love. But as good use of free will attracts that grace or that love, and as that love reciprocally governs and purifies free will, it is clear that they can never be separated. It is clear that love and liberty continually support each other and that those two actions, while separate, are always linked through an intimate and respective relationship.

However, we shouldn't believe that human will can ignore the decrees of the manifestation of the Supreme Power which must take place in man's body; for if man is filled with the purpose of His emanation, it is that Power which shows it to him. And those who are its object can never fail to have it present before them, either to their advantage or to their annoyance. Let us continue with our subject.

It isn't enough for the Divine Powers, in subdividing, to supply man with the *Powers* which constitute them, for there is also a need for each of them do this in a manner appropriate to the dark realm he inhabits. They must use, so to speak, the same means they used to descend here, passing along the same paths, covering themselves with the same colors as him and following the Laws of the same appearance which surrounds him, and using the connections which I will shortly explain between man's body, the origin of languages and the characters of writing.

Without this, his feeble sight wouldn't be able to bear the radiance of those *Powers*, or, not seeing in them any similarity with himself, they would have appeared strange, or too far above him, and he would have become suspicious; and turning aside he would have lost the sole and unique means he could have used to remind himself of his original estate.

And then the Fire of the stars would dazzle us or consume us if it could cross the space which separates us without having to traverse the atmospheric fluids, which by their moist and dense nature moderate its activity and its splendor at the same time.

Then those fluids themselves, being too subtle and too rarefied for our realm, would be useless and even harmful to the earth if they could descend upon its surface without condensing further into dew, rain or snow, and without coming together into physical globules, like the very things which they come to fertilize.

Finally, man's thoughts would be meaningless to his fellow man if he didn't use intermediary physical forms or characters to communicate them. However, those means which man must use in his current state are only images of what is really happening to him in a broader and more elevated Order, since everything must be physical here below: a truth which will be developed further later on.

In a word, it is a constant and invariable Law that, depending on the Orders into which they penetrate, all *powers*, all *actions* and all *abilities* are proportional, and change depending on the channels through which they pass and the objects they must identify with themselves. And such is the violent state of temporal things that all the *Principles* which descend here can only do so through the physical channels which conserve them, whereas in their true nature they would communicate without any intermediaries. And being obliged to produce those preserving envelopes themselves, the effort they need to expend on that undertaking is always at the expense of their true action.

Here we therefore already see the need appearing among men for visible *signs*, substantial *Agents* and real Beings, clothed like us in physical forms, but at the same time Beings who are depositories of those original *powers* which man had lost and which he endlessly seeks around him, but the evidence of which he only sees in the weakest and most impotent form in everything which surrounds him and which, although subdivided, should show themselves to man in their original character.

It might even be possible that, among those signs and Agents there are some which have existed, and which still exist in the very midst of men, without the ignorant or corrupt perceiving them. Their action and progress could only be detected by those pure enough to see them, and they are almost always invisible to the rest; in the same way that all my intellectual actions are unknown to the matter from which my body is formed, because there is nothing in them which isn't foreign to it: and it is that which casts so much doubt, uncertainty and obscurity on the existence of these *signs* and *Agents*.

Let us examine a third Law which is also essential: that is, if, due to the sublime destiny on which man's origin was founded, not only was it necessary that even after his crime the *Powers* of Wisdom must visibly reach him and recall his origin to him, it was also necessary for the Depository of those gifts to instruct him on the paths by which he could be regenerated into his primitive estate. It was necessary, too, for those *Agents* to fulfill their destiny by means of physical actions, since they lived in service of a physical Being and were therefore obscured by his matter. Finally, they had to send that man abroad in the world to practice and transmit to his fellow men those gifts and knowledge which he had received from them, as much for the instruction and benefit of other men as for his own, which leads us to recognize the need for a physical form of worship on Earth, and to show us at the same time the purpose for which there are Elect who have been so privileged.[71]

In its true definition, worship is simply the act by which a Being who seeks to gain possession of the things he needs joins with Beings whose similarity attract him, and avoids those who are different to him. In this way the act of worship is based on a primary and evident truth, that is, on

---

[71] This is a powerful paragraph, which is an eloquent summary of religion. If man has fallen, it is necessary for God not only to find a way to inform man of his original state of glory, but what he must do in order to return to it. Since He does not interfere directly in man's existence, He sends intermediary Agents to teach certain capable Privileged – or General – Elect what to do, and they in their turn go out into the world to teach their fellow man. This would be accomplished through the establishment of a Religion in which the Privileged Elect were the Priests. But we must remember that all men are Particular Elect, and therefore everyone can be a Priest, that is, have a personal relationship with God and follow their own personal Path of Reintegration. The task of the Privileged or General Elect, then, is to show them the way. The structure is orthodox Catholic – but the message is clearly not!

the Law which necessarily follows from the state of Beings and their respective relationships.

In the state of things here below, there is no Being who does not have needs, for as all are separated and divided here, they all seek to unite and rally their *disparate action*, and they are all driven by the impulse of their mutual similarity which compels them continually toward each other according to the Laws and desires of their nature.

From this, even if we cannot precisely bestow the word worship on the Laws of physical Beings who are not free, at least we should recognize that all those Beings of whatever Order they are, that our blood, that our bodies placed alongside all the creations of this Universe have actions to perform, and an order to follow to accomplish the purpose of their existence, and to heal or protect themselves from the various diseases to which the elemental influences continuously expose them.

However, what is that Law based on if not on the similarity which is found, for example, between our bodies and food, or the remedies whose action and *virtues* come to revive and renew our strength, and give us health?[72]

So, the similarity between our intellectual Being and the other Powers of the Divinity having been recognized, proving moreover that there exists outside of us a source of false and disordered thoughts which obsess us and which ensures that, in a way, man's soul is exposed to as many ailments as his physical body, it follows that our natural connections with the Divine Powers place us in the same dependent relationship and the same need that our bodies have for food. It follows that, with regard to those Divine Powers, we are also subject to a worship or a Law which can obtain from them the *relief* we are hoping for. Finally, it follows that since we must heal or protect our Being from intellectual influences harmful to us, just as we protect our body from harmful physical influences, we should – since we clearly need to – seek similar *aid* for that intellectual need and use it *actively* when we've found it.

It could be the lack of such reflections over time which has led men of most Religions to become indifferent to such things, and has led them

---

[72] Here we see a correlation with the Laws of the Pentateuch, which concern themselves as much with preserving health and life as with the worship of God. Would Saint-Martin not have made the point that, while these both constitute the Laws they followed, he would have expected them to distinguish between those Laws ordained by God and those created by man for the purpose of self-preservation?

not only to neglect the content, times and kinds which should be in their forms of worship; but even prayer itself under the pretext that the First Being has no need of it, and that it is sufficient for men simply not to do what they call evil: yet in truth prayer is to their intellectual Being what respiration is to their body.

Perhaps they would be right if their own thought could read the Supreme Thought, as He can theirs, because then their pleasure being total and guaranteed, they would have no other business other than to enjoy and celebrate peace without having to fight to obtain it. But in man's present state, between the Supreme Thought and him, there is an *action* which prevents them from uniting, and he can only demolish and destroy that *barrier* by a means similar to it, that is, by an *action*.

Finally, we see in physical Nature itself the evidence that all Beings should pay homage to the Principle of *Life* if they wish to receive His assistance and favors. For the land to produce, the steam must rise up out of its breast to go and unite with the celestial *powers*, and then descend again upon its surface to moisten it with that fertile dew without which it can grow nothing. Surely a living lesson, which teaches man that he has a Law to follow if he wishes to learn about the rights and the pleasantness of his existence.

The time may come when his zeal for truth will cause him to reject all excessive desires; and when those wishes and movements which are creative rise up from every faculty of his Being and ascend to the source of the Light; and, having received the holy and salutary unction, they will bring back to him those vivifying influences which must make the treasures of Wisdom and Truth germinate inside him.

But by having man's Religion derive from his needs and the importance of combatting the obstacles which serve as a barrier to him, I might appear to be admitting to an innumerable number of different faiths, for since man is generally exposed to very different needs, both in his intellectual Being and his physical Being, wishing to prescribe a uniform Law for those various types of needs would appear to be going contrary to order and reason. A few words will suffice to remove this difficulty.

If the unity of a Religion is an undeniable truth and based on the unity of the One who should be its Subject, that unity does not exclude the multiplicity of ways that the infinite variety of our needs requires us to use. Then that Religion could be given innumerable elaborations in the details, and for all that not cease to be perfectly simple and always *one* in its purpose, which is to reconcile what we lack in our Being and what is necessary to its existence.

And who are man's Gods in his childhood and his youth? They are objects which are natural and physical, they are those who reveal their beauty to him, they are his father and mother, they are those who guide and support him in all his steps and become for him the visible Agents of Divinity because, not yet having the intelligence to be open to great truths, he can only receive ideas from through signs and Agents who are physical like him.

At a mature age the wise man, having a clearer idea of Divinity, isn't slow to recognize that those who were the Gods of his youth are, like him, infirm and impure, that they are also dependent on an Intelligent and Invisible Being which reveals Himself to him through thought, and Who makes him understand that he has only received life and intelligence to manifest in his turn the titles of his true Author.

He then realizes that, being charged to do His Work, it is up to him to perform it, up to his own intelligence to direct it; that since the Supreme Being is pure and without stain, He must have pure and incorruptible Ministers in whom man can put his confidence without risk or concern.

But although in these successive states we see man's worship diversify, or rather extend and grow according to how he best determines the scope and nature of his true needs, that Religion, so long as it conforms to the Natural Order, is always one, since it tends continually towards the same end, which is to provide for man's needs according to the several states through which he passes, and to do so by means which are the most real and natural to what he is able to understand.

For the paths of Wisdom are so abundant that they transform at every moment to accommodate all our situations. And if, in the fullness of His abilities He embraces all Beings, all time, all space, in any position in which we find ourselves, He can never exhaust the source of His gifts, and however multiplied they become, they all have the same unity for their Principle and their end.

From this, whatever superiority a particular form of worship may present, it would be imprudent to proscribe those which, not yet having yet reached that level, display it less perfectly: because not only are the Laws of man's Rehabilitation, combined with the Laws of physical things subject to time and a successive order; but also, we cannot be certain that there might not be hidden true light and secret *powers* beneath its unimposing appearance.

Finally, man isn't the judge of prayer: he is only its generator and its organ. And just as *emanations* from terrestrial bodies, rising up into the air, disappear from our material eyes and leave us in uncertainty both as to their progress and the place which awaits them in the immensity of Nature's reservoirs; so the prayers of men, not remaining on Earth become inaccessible to our view and our senses, and we can determine neither their value nor the course that they follow in approaching the Light, nor the rank that the First Principle will assign them about His throne.

Despite the superiority of one Religion over others, perhaps the entire Earth participates in the rights which distinguish the perfect Religion; perhaps, among all the Nations and all the Religious Institutions there are men who have access to the True Wisdom; and, far from wishing to reduce the number of true Temples of the Eternal One, we might believe that according to the universal gifts that He has spread over our domain, there is no man on Earth who couldn't, if he wanted, serve as a Temple to that Great Being. For, wherever man goes, however isolated he may be, *there are* always *three together*, and that number is sufficient to constitute a Temple.[73]

So, let us refrain from judging the paths of Divine Wisdom and trying to draw boundaries to His *Powers*. Let us believe that men are all equally dear to Him; that if He has filled some with His most precious and freely-given favors, it is one more reason for them to imitate His example by showing his fellow man the same indulgence. Finally, let us know that this indulgence, which is nothing other than Divine Love, is gentle, kind and never proscribes, even though He leaves Beings in privation.

Well! How could this *Virtue* proscribe? Wisdom[74] is alive in Himself and He can only multiply to infinity that order and life which are in Him.

---

[73] This of course refers to the famous line in Matthew 18:20: "For where two or three are gathered together in my name, there am I in the midst of them." With regard to the reference to a Temple, the reference is also a Masonic one, to the need of three Master Masons together in order to open a Master Mason's Lodge. The Reader is left to contemplate the meaning of Saint-Martin's comment: "For, wherever man goes, however isolated he may be, there are always three together." Martinists will probably have a head start.

[74] Perhaps it is worth noting at this point, now that the phrase has been employed many times by Saint-Martin, that 'Wisdom' or 'Divine Wisdom' is masculine, being used simply as another name, another attribute for God. Although the text of Pasqually's *Treatise* can be read through a Gnostic lens, it isn't a Gnostic source text, but rather an unorthodox exegesis on the Bible, and one must remember that even Christianity, in referring to *Hagia Sophia* (Ἁγία Σοφία), or 'Holy Wisdom',

Teth (ט) – Rehabilitation: Thought, Will, Action

He alone is the means by which man can acquire a true and intimate notion of his Being, both in its present state and in its state to come. He alone extends all of man's abilities at the same time. Finally, perhaps it is through man alone that the First Principle can understand Himself and be assured of all His grandeur.

From the point we have now reached, the Reader can see spread out the Table of the relationships which exist between God, Man and the Universe, since the true Religion and the Agents appointed to impart it have had the one goal of restoring harmony between these three Beings, to show man the use of all the things in Nature and their properties in order to visibly paint for him those that are within him and which, combined with all the other natural powers, should be the complete image and expression of the Great Being from Whom everything has descended.[75]

Indeed, we cannot ignore that immense chain which binds together the Beings of all Orders and which distributes to each of them the *powers* they need.[76]

In the Physical Order, we see the creative abilities of the Great Principle produce and vivify the bodies of Nature, and they retrace the activity of their models up to the final subdivisions of the physical, celestial and terrestrial Universe.

In the Superior and the Physical Order, we see the sentient *powers* of that same Universal Principle reposing in intellectual Agents, from whom they are passed on to privileged men and to all the offspring of man's posterity.

---

used it to refer to the Logos or Christ, and not as a feminine part of the godhead. The idea of Sophia as a separate, feminine, entity would come until much later with the discovery of Gnostic source texts. In 1782 Christianity was still very much a masculine Religion.

[75] Here, then is the full title of the book, and the reason for it. This tells us that, far from being a true *Tableau*, which would suggest an image frozen in time, such as the opening scene of operas of Saint-Martin's time, this is rather a very dynamic image, with constant activity taking place through intermediaries between the three categories of Beings.

[76] It is noteworthy that in these writings the chain is always successive, which is a motif often used in both Martinism and Freemasonry (and for that matter the Church), to refer both to the chain of initiation and to the link between the Past Masters or Elect and present-day initiates.

Finally, man himself represents this dual activity in Nature, for he is a living *Tableau*[77] of those two fruitful Laws which serve to give substance[78] to all Beings.

From the inside of his head there flows incessantly a powerful, physical fluid which, descending successively into the various regions of his animal schema, communicates its strength and its action into the slenderest fibers and those most distant from their root source.

From the inside of the same organ, the pure and wise man senses the birth of bright and profound toughts; and expressing them to the outside world by his speech, he may, through them, invigorate the men who surround him and with successive steps bring his own light to all the points of the circle he inhabits.

It is therefore clear that man exhibits a complete imprint of his Principle, and that he is His expression both in the physical Universe and the intellectual Universe.[79]

We also find what is Wisdom's purpose in distributing His beneficial gifts, and the purpose of His constant and continuous action. In the same way that the unhealthy exhalations of the Earth are constantly ameliorated by superior physical influences, so the false and criminal thoughts of men and those of corrupt Beings which sojourn with him are contained and purified by the active imprints of *life*, or by those *virtual Agents* which we should regard as the primary and necessary organs of worship and the physical means granted to man to help him to continue to fulfill the Supreme decrees.

We must not hide the fact that this worship and these physical means, transmitted to man by pure Agents, require very vigilant attention, constant steadfastness and very shrewd judgement on his part, so that he doesn't confuse the true *actions* which should animate his worship with the false *actions* which continually try to distort it, and which are always

---

[77] *Tableau* or 'table' is the word used here. Since Saint-Martin earlier used the word to denote the relationship between God, Man and the Universe, here it is being used to indicate man the *microcosm*, as opposed to the *macrocosm* of the Universe.

[78] The word used in French is *substancier*. Although this did not appear in any dictionary consulted, it may therefore be an invented word – or simply one which is no longer in use – and the Translator has guessed its meaning to be 'to make substantial' or 'to give substance to'.

[79] These are very graphic examples of the control of the mind over the body and over thought from an 18th Century perspective, and given what we now know of the sympathetic and parasympathetic nervous systems, the analogy of a fluid spreading throughout the body and controlling all its functions isn't that outlandish an image.

ready to mislead man, either visibly or invisibly. For in the intellectual as in the physical, many *unhealthy exhalations* steal from the *pure action* which combats them, often rising up over the region where they should remain buried, and it is that which, in both Orders, gives rise to storms and tempests.

If you ask how you can recognize the good or bad quality of *intellectual actions*, I would suggest you undertake a careful study of those different impressions, either of thought or feelings, to which we are daily exposed and from which, by their variety, we suffer so much uncertainty.

By doing that you will discover that, when man is limited to sensory material impressions or false intellectual impressions, he cannot be sure of anything because these two Orders of impressions, being exposed to several relative actions without anything being invariable, open up Beings under attack to being unable to distinguish anything positive, leading thme to make only confused judgments or remaining in the deepest doubt.

But when man receives a good intellectual impression he cannot fall into the same errors, because the action of the pure intellectual Being, being simple, it carries with it the proof of its simplicity, its unity, and consequently of its reality. He would therefore see that this reality can only be found in pure and true Beings which is its Agent: it is in it alone and by it alone that we can learn to know it.

We can also see that, when such impressions are working, man is immune to all uncertainty and misunderstanding, for impure eyes are subject to being deceived, seeing that they can only see mixed and compound outcomes: but the pure eyes of intelligence are never wrong, since they see *Principles* which are simple.

Finally, we know that, because it is one of those gifts which have been granted to man in his miserable existence to serve him as guide, false intellectual impressions are subject to Laws similar to those of the Physical and Material Order and that, like the body, after presenting a graceful and regular appearance, finally become hideous and malformed, just as in the Intellectual Order: for even the most seductive false images[80] are not slow to decompose and betray their illegitimacy. That is all I can say on this subject.

Let us summarize in a few words all the truths we have just explained.

---

[80] *Tableaux impurs*.

They teach us that, as a result of the love that Wisdom has for man, He must, even when man turns his eyes from His light for the first time, maintain His rays in him in proportion with the weakness of his sight, and that, however far his crime has caused him to fall, he can only fall into the hands of his God.

And, since he was not constrained, like us, by the false ideas and dark veils that his unfortunate posterity never ceases to add to his original degradation, criminal as he was, first man was still much closer to that God which has formed us than we are. He could better perceive the Pure Source from which he had just been separated, and he didn't languish as we do in nothingness and the cruelty of the ills which devour us. Finally, as much as it is true that we have only regret regarding the estate of our primitive existence, the first guilty man had both regret and remorse.

To the extent that man's posterity has multiplied and time has passed, the Greatness and Goodness of Supreme Wisdom has had to manifest Himself more and more by placing living images of Himself near him, or *Agents* which were *virtuous* enough to help him recover His image.

Those *Agents* have had to initiate actions by themselves, since those actions were only instituted for him, to help him separate from himself what was contrary to his true nature and to attract what was lacking in perfection and the life of his Being; finally to give him a glimpse of his powers, which he had been able to contemplate in their unity when in his glorious estate, and work towards expressing them in their purity, and by that to fulfill both his destiny and the decree which the First Principle had pronounced on him when He gave him existence.

It is there that we recognize the foundations and the paths which are shown to man's will in order to accomplish his Work. For just as those foundations are useless if man's will doesn't use them to his benefit, so man's will, though being the main motivator of his labor, would remain ineffective if it had no foundation on which to exercise its action. It is that which led some of the Ancients to say that *the sacred prayers have been given to us by the Gods*. But there is a type of prayer intended to allow us to procure those precious gifts: those are prayers of suffering, and those cannot come to us from the superior and supreme center, where there is no suffering at all. *Infinite Wisdom has, however, taken care to ensure our weakness and our negligence doesn't prevent us from satisfying the need we have to pray, and some believe that Wisdom put an animal on the Earth which only sings at specific and regular hours to warn men to attend to that beneficial occupation.*

Such is the Table of Laws and Truths which we have firmly established by applying them to the relationships and the nature of Beings. Let us seek to confirm that evidence in the universality of signs, and the visible traces they show us among all the Nations of the Earth.

Yod (') – Religions and Myths: Natural Human Needs

Man's sublime origin, his fall, the horror of his present deprivation, the absolute need for visible Agents to bring superior relief to Earth, and the fact that they use physical means to make these powers effective, here we find so many of the truths engraved in man, that all the peoples in the Universe[81] have celebrated them and have left us traditions which confirm them.

All historical, allegorical and fabulous[82] stories contained within those Traditions tell us about the first state of man in his purity, and the crimes and punishment of guilty and debased man. They outline with equal clarity the kindnesses extended by Divinities towards him to assuage his pains and to deliver him from his darkness.

It was not sufficient for him to deify virtuous men who had given their fellow men examples of justice and charity and who, by their actions, had indicated some vestiges of our First Law; and so, they were not afraid to have the Divinities themselves descend to Earth to bring man the *superior relief* which mortal Heros could not, in order to help him understand and to help him become like them, as the sole means to felicity.

At the same time, those who had the duty of transmitting such stories to us were in agreement in representing those beneficial Divinities to us in physical form, and appropriate to the region in which we live; for without that their aid would to some extent have been lost on Beings as grossly material as us.

Finally, among all the Nations, the assistance of those benevolent Divinities has been celebrated by means of Religions. Who would dare claim that all laws, customs, all social, civil, political, military and

---

[81] Saint-Martin uses the term *Univers*, but it is clear he is simply broadening the definition to help us keep in mind the Myths and Histories of the Gods of Ancient Traditions, since in most cases the Gods were associated with the planets.

[82] In its true sense of being from Fable or Myth. This also means that it is derived from commonly held beliefs, is the following definitional sense: 'a usually traditional story of ostensibly historical events that serves to unfold part of the world view of a people or explain a practice, belief, or natural phenomenon' (*Merriam-Webster*), rather than meaning a purely invented story.

religious conventions we see established on Earth are not expressive traces of those original Institutions, that they are not emanations, alterations or deteriorations of those original gifts given to man following his fall, in order to lead him back to his Principle? For we shouldn't forget that men can change everything, that they can corrupt everything, but that they cannot invent anything.

And so, we see we have yet another means to read and recognize in all of man's works that Law which concerns him and on which he should focus; seeing that, despite the infinite differences which the forms of those human Institutions present to us in all the places on Earth, they all have the same purpose and the same aim, and that this objective pierces through all his envelopes.[83]

One must nevertheless agree that those allegorical and fabulous Traditions, in attempting to assimilate the Gods with man, have often ascribed to them his passions and vices, and have made them like the most corrupt Beings; and that debasing them this way has to some extent has made them lose all their rights to our belief.

But we should not feel that when Mythology talks about them having ridiculous moods, such as fury or jealousy and that sensual intensity which appears to be almost the only motivation of Gods and Heroes, it is because, being a Universal Table, it must present the bad with the good, order along with disorder, the vices along with the *virtues* which circulate in the sphere of man. Besides, the abuse of words and the ignorance of their true meaning have given those emblematic stories a host of ambiguous and strained meanings which they didn't originally have, when they describe things as being so correct, so heroic, so respectable that those emblems appear nowadays to be imperfect, ridiculous and worthy of contempt.

---

[83] The concept of *envelopes*, or barriers which are both physical and metaphysical protecting the body, has a long and distinguished career. Mention of them may be found in Papus' book *Elementary Treatise on Practical Magic* (1895), where he performs experiments on the *envelopes* of hypnotized patients. These envelopes are sometimes referred to as '*psychic envelopes*'. Envelopes are also invoked for healing purposes, such as the references in the *Rose Croix d'Orient* rituals of using one's *envelopes* to send out healing rays. A more modern approach may be read in a paper on the site *Frontiers in Psychology*, originally published in French in 2014 and titled, appropriately enough: "The psychic envelopes in psychoanalytic theories of infancy" by Denis Mellier, at the following website:
www.frontiersin.org/articles/10.3389/fpsyg.2014.00734/full/

That is how we can explain in part the contradictions that Mythology presents. Ignorance of the real meaning of names has led to assigning to one Being, Hero or Divinity those facts and actions which belonged to other Beings. So, we shouldn't be surprised to see the same character sometimes exhibit the pride and ambition of guilty Beings in his actions, or even the excesses of the most shameful debauchery, yet sometimes the *virtues* of Heros and Gods. We shouldn't be surprised at all to see Jupiter as Master of the Heavens, Chief of the terrestrial Gods his brothers, and also Jupiter given over to the vilest passions; to see Saturn as both father of the Gods, and eating his own children; and to see Venus as Urania, and Venus as the Goddess of prostitution. So, although we find every concept and every archetype brought together in Mythology, though it shows us many contradictory images under the same names, the intellect should be able to distinguish their true appearances and their true subjects.

Moreover, I will shortly outline an insightful viewpoint on this important subject, by which we will discover most satisfactory conclusions, because we shall see the true source of all Mythologies coming from man himself; for we should not seek the natural origin of all the facts submitted to his speculation anywhere else but in him.

If we reflect on the diverse range of opinions that Nations have concerning the visible manifestations of Divine Powers, the evidence we have presented about the need of those manifestations to accomplish the Supreme decrees, and those impressions which endure in all the various Institutions established on Earth, we should find it easy to believe that those manifestations indeed arose from among men.

We can confirm this thought if we appreciate the fact that similar Traditions are found among Nations separated from our continent by considerable distances and immense oceans, Nations which breathe the same air as us and have enjoyed the same sun for many Centuries without us knowing them or them knowing us.

The various Nations in America had similar views about the Creation of the Universe and on the *number* which governed its origin. Like the ancient Nations, they believed in a host of benevolent and malevolent Gods which populate the Universe, and to whom they offered many victims as sacrifices. They were in agreement with all Nations on the perfection of man's previous estate, on his degradation, and on the future destinies of those who were good and those who did evil. They had Temples, Priests, Altars, a Sacred Fire maintained by Vestal Virgins who were subject to severe laws, as they were among the Romans. The Peruvians had physical leaders who, like Orpheus, claimed to be children of the Sun, and received the tributes of their realms. They had an idol whose name, according to interpreters, means *three in one*. The Mexicans had a person whom they all regarded as a God, who was incorporealized for their Nation. So, it appears we have only to change the names to find the same theogony and the same Traditions among those Nations as was a part of every Nation in the Ancient World.[84]

If a conviction of the visible manifestations of Divine Powers and their necessity wasn't a fundamental feeling in man and analogous to his own nature, such opinions would only have been communicated by Tradition from relative to relative. They would never have existed at all among those Nations if they hadn't been connected to them by some link, or else they'd have been erased from their memories because of the length of time since our separation, even if we had originally been associated with them.

We don't claim at all, by this alternative view, to support the uncertainties and doubt which have been entertained regarding the diversity of origin of all those Nations. Nowadays we no longer doubt that Northern Asia communicates very closely with North America; that the Strait which separates those continents is filled with islands which make

---

[84] To put this in context, the United States was coming to the end of the Revolutionary War in 1782, which means the indigenous Peoples were still mostly independent tribes who had not yet succumbed to the territorial invasions which were to follow. Nevertheless, stories of the Native American Indians were well known in Europe. Benjamin Franklin was no stranger to Paris, and he had stayed with upstate New York tribes for extended periods; and a number of American notives – not least Pocohontas – had made the journey to Europe. Mexico was still part of the Spanish Empire, and it wouldn't earn its independence until after a protracted war which ended in 1821 with the Treaty of Córdoba. Archaeology was largely an amateur and haphazard process at the time. It wouldn't become systematic until the Nationalism of the late 18th and 19th Centuries, with the establishment of National Museums and the impetus to record a country's heritage and to display the grandeur of its past. In Mexico this didn't begin to happen until the last decade of the 18th Century, largely because it was not in the Roman Church's interest to draw attention to the indigenous cultures, since that would focus a spotlight on what they had done to them. For all these reasons, Saint-Martin's understanding of early native American and Latin American cultures would have been sketchy at best. For example, the Translator has been unable to find a single reference to a Peruvian idol which has any connection to '*three-in-one*'. In an age which believed in Spontaneous Generation and sea monsters, it isn't unlikely that Saint-Martin either heard this as an old wives' tale or even invented it himself.

communication easier; and that their inhabitants trade with one another and that there are even American tribes in Northern Asia.[85]

Independent of this channel of communication between the two continents, we can believe that in the interval which has elapsed since the first Centuries a number of sailors, either from the East or the West, have been thrown onto those unknown shores where, producing different tribes in different places, they would have transmitted to them those vices and *virtues*, ignorance and illumination which they had brought with them.

Because, if we consider the diversity of the Nations which inhabit America, the extreme variation in their habits, their customs, their languages and even their physical traits, if we consider that most of these Nations or families were unknown to one another and showed no indication that there had ever been any relations between them, we will be able to show without fear of contradiction that they owe their existence to the various shipwrecks or migrations from the old continent, and that their fathers had been thrown on those shores at different times in distant Centuries.[86]

Without spending any more time on this question, and regardless of the manner in which that population developed, we cannot avoid recognizing a unity in the early origins of Nations whose diverse species have developed like us; of Nations among which we can find traces of the truths we have discussed on the need for the abilities and powers of the Divine Being to manifest in this Universe and to men; finally, of Nations

---

[85] Again, this is an extraordinary claim given the lack of knowledge of this region in those times. The Translator can find to reference to an 'American tribe' ever being found living in Russia (modern theory has the migration going in the other direction). Once more, the existence of conditions, such as the Bering Strait, which facilitate trade and communication is no guarantee that is actually took place. Vitus Bering entered the Strait in 1728, and in 1732 Mikhail Gvozdev crossed it for the first time. Credible theories about a possible land bridge and migration didn't exist until the 20th Century.

[86] While Saint-Martin actually gets the part about migration correct, according to modern theory, the idea that many tribes arose through shipwrecks is both insulting and clever! On the one hand it seems ridiculous to claim that Tribes and Nations were formed as a result of shipwrecks – yet on the other hand archaeologists such as Thor Heyerdahl have demonstrated that this may have occurred in a limited form; and if we discount shipwrecks, there's no doubt that most of America was later settled by a deliberate migration of nations from the Europe, and later Asia, to the New World; something which had already been taking place for centuries at the time of Saint-Martin. However, since his point was to demonstrate the spontaneity with which diverse and separated groups develop similar belief systems, by introducing mass migrations he is weakening – rather than strengthening – that argument. The impression is that Saint-Martin is trying to have his cake and eat it: either Nations spontaneously reach the same conclusions concerning Divinity; or the sparks taken from the earliest societies and Religions are spread throughout the world by sailors.

who are completely like us in their nature, their fundamental ideas and their traditions.

Let us go further: when even their primitive origin isn't common to ours, since they resemble us they must participate in the same benefits. Finally, if they are men, if they are in privation like us, and need the Superior and Universal Being Who created them, this Being is connected to them as He is to all His creations. So, when they could never have had any communication with our continent, that Being would still have been able to send them the proofs and manifestations of His love and His wisdom.

As to how long ago it was when manifestations of these Superior Powers began to appear among men, the Traditions of most of the ancient Nations still offer us the most certain indications.

The origin of those Nations is almost always enveloped by a marvelous and holy veil. Almost all of them say they are protected by and even descended from some Divinity who presided over their birth, Who founded their country, and Who supports them with an invisible power.

Does this not tell us how long Wisdom's eye has watched over man, despite his crime? Does this not tell us that, from the moment that man became guilty and unfortunate, the Light was eager to come to him to share Himself, so to speak, to come down to him, and since then has never ceased to impart the same benefits on all His posterity?

It would not be so easy to determine from the Traditionals the number of solemn acts of manifestation which the Divine Powers have made among men since that First Age.

The ancient doctrines, being unable to agree on this point, have given rise to doubts concerning most of the Agents they tell us about, so that people have been reduced to thinking that there could be some whose memory Tradition hasn't transmitted to us; and that many of those who have been introduced as the true Agents of these supreme abilities never existed, or were perhaps even imposters.

Careful observation, based on knowledge of the true Laws of Beings, could no doubt guide us in *enumerating* these events and identifying their periods in history, for according to the most natural notions they should be equal and related to the number of *abilities* and *powers* which man had abandoned, that is, the same as man's true nature of which, depending on the number, they must provide the *complement appropriate* to him.[87] But the present generation isn't yet at that point: the false ideas it has about man and about his destiny still bar the roads which lead to the Sanctuary of Truth.

For the same reasons we shouldn't be surprised if the sublime lessons glimpsed in the Mythological Traditions of the ancient Nations seem imaginary to most men. They have lost so much knowledge of their Being and their Principle, that they no longer know any of the bonds which eternally bind them together.

Indeed, in Mythological stories the common man only sees the play of the writers' imaginations, or a corruption of historical Tradition, or perhaps the effects of idolatry, or fear, or a Nation's proclivity for fantastical ideas. And so, save a few ingenious allegories, everything in these Fables appears to him to be bizarre, ridiculous and extravagant.

Renowned men, considered to be scholars, have used their vast erudition to establish theories which make more sense than common opinion. But, since they haven't thoroughly examined the true nature of things, their doctrines, imposing though they may be, fall short of the Traditions they have tried to interpret.

Indeed, one might pronounce the same judgement on those who have limited the meaning of all the Mythological Traditions to one inferior and isolated purpose alone, who are compelled to see in all of them proof of the one specific theory they embrace, and are unable to see that those Traditions, as they don't all have the same nature, can't all have the same meaning; that one, coming from distant antiquity, contains the emblems of the most profound truths; while others, much more modern, only owe their existence to the superstition and ignorance of Nations which, unable to understand the original Traditions, changed and confused them with later Traditions which were individual to each Nation; and that the mixing of those Traditions, the prejudices of Historians and the fruits of the Poets' imagination have only increased their unintelligiblity. And so, far from desiring to concentrate all of Mythology into one, specific purpose, we

---

[87] That is, to the extent that man has forgotten or abandoned certain virtues and skills, those are the ones which must the Agents must bring back to his knowledge. Saint-Martin appears to be implying that these 'interventions' in man's history are often indicated in the early sacred texts and histories, including Mythologies, as times when God, a messenger or angel came to earth to communicate knowledge or to perform an action; and that if all of those events were documented and tallied, we could ascertain how many times this has happened, and by means of that, the nature of these interventions and therefore what powers man had lost through his prevarication.

should agree instead that it portrays things which have no similarity with one another.

Finally, if all the Observers are allowed to seek connections between these stories and the Orders of things which are known to them, reason forbids them from being so blind as to see nothing beyond this and reduce those emblems which could have a broad and elevated purpose to an inferior and limited role. Further, reason would oppose any attempt to give those Traditions and symbols meanings and allusions which they were never meant to convey.

These are the false and limited applications which we intend to dispel, in order to direct man's thought towards interpretations which are more correct, more real and more beneficial.

However, so as not to stray from our argument, to which these remarks are only incidental, we will limit ourselves to considering the two principal theories about Mythology, which will suffice to emphasize the opinion we should have of all the rest.

The first of these theories suggests that all the ancient Fables provide us with symbols of rural activities, the signs of time and the seasons specific to Agriculture; and all the Laws which terrestrial and celestial Nature are required to follow for the growth, maintenance and life of vegetative production.

Once this theory had been conceived by the Observers they made astonishing efforts to justify it and to find connections with every detail in Mythology. But to see its error, only the briefest attention will be necessary.

At no period of history and among no Nations have we seen more beautiful and noble images used than those employed in Mythology. Would it not upset all the notions we have of the progress of man's soul to claim that he has used superior emblems to denote inferior things, and that he invented symbols and hieroglyphs more sublime and more spiritual than the things he wanted to denote?

Isn't it evident that, on the contrary, the true purpose of an *emblem* is to veil a truth from the eyes of the common man, whose abuse or profanation is to be feared if it were to be revealed, to make it difficult for a person unworthy of that truth to discover it or to attain that truth by contemplating the emblem; whereas those more fortunately disposed will see at a glance all the correspondences it contains?

Isn't it also certain that *symbols* and *hieroglyphs* are pictures or signs intended to make the greatest number of truths and useful knowledge intelligible, and to make them understandable to those whose limited minds could not perceive them, nor conserve their memory without the aid of these coarse signs?

These simple definitions clearly show that emblems, pictures and symbols can be neither superior nor even equal to what they represent, for then the copy would be elevated above its model or confused with it, which would make it pointless and unnecessary.

All we need to do, then, is to compare the majority of Mythological symbols to the subject the interpreters wished them to represent, in order to determine, depending upon the inferiority of these subjects, whether their application was accurate.

Let us consider, then, which appears nobler and more ingenious: the coarse and mechanical details of plowing, or those vivid paintings in which we see all the passions at play, and which personify all the vices and virtues.

Let us consider, too, if we can regard the purpose of Mythology to be to describe the celestial constellations and their influences on the terrestrial body for the purpose of studying vegetation. This theory shows a similar inferiority of subject to its symbol, and for the same reason makes it unacceptable.

Concerning the common Astronomical signs, which we would like to focus on for a moment, we will say that through ignorance man has based almost all of them on imaginary divisions, on the arbitrary names of animals, people and other physical objects, whose connections they present, being imaginary and traditional themselves, do not provide the idea of a true image, but rather the vaguest of figures, a long way from the *true* Astronomical *signs* and the *powers* which serve to move them.

That should be enough to open the eyes of anyone who, looking at only one isolated object in the Fables of Tradition, believed that the entire Mythology of the Ancients owed its origin to Agriculture and Astronomy. The error comes from the fact that, later in time, some of the symbols of those two Sciences became confused with the original symbolic Traditions. Because of that, men found themselves even more distanced from the simple and important truths which were the true subject of those Traditions.

So, without claiming to deny the small number of symbols which Agriculture and Astronomy have provided to Mythology, we can best serve our fellow man by warning him that those Traditions, such as we have received them from the Ancients, contain an infinite number of other emblems for which it is completely impossible to claim the same meaning and the same relationships, because their subjects can be found neither on the earth, nor in the stars, nor in any corporeal Being.

Those who have provided these interpretations of Mythology have also debased the art of writing and painting, using them above all to transmit the visible signs of Laws and facts whose memory and understanding the Nations wished to perpetuate. Using this same principle, they explained all the emblems of idolatry, claiming that the hieroglyphic images it used were the symbolic representation of material objects of worship.

They believed they had found evidence in the Traditions of the Hebrews, where a Prophet spoke about sacrilegious paintings which he saw on the walls of the Temple of Jerusalem, and before which the Elders of Israel and the High Priest himself, taking censers in their hands, appeared to offer criminal sacrifices. All we can say about this interpretation, is that one might hope that it was as true as it is ingenious.[88]

Even before me, some Observers have also refuted the theory I have just criticized concerning Agriculture; but having disposed of it, they didn't replace it with anything. For telling people that Mythology simply wanted to paint the living fire of Nature, and that its sole purpose must have been to prepare them to repair their strength and to conserve their bodily form, is to give men a wonderful image, it is true: but that doesn't give them the whole truth, since men have a still more elevated destiny. And this brings us to the case of the Hermetic Philosophers, whose dogmas and doctrine we will now review.[89]

---

[88] Ezekiel 8:10-11. "So I went in and saw; and behold every form of creeping things, and abominable beasts, and all the idols of the house of Israel, pourtrayed upon the wall round about. And there stood before them seventy men of the ancients of the house of Israel, and in the midst of them stood Jaazaniah the son of Shaphan, with every man his censer in his hand; and a thick cloud of incense went up." However, from his last comment Saint-Martin clearly thinks it was more a case of creative invention than reality.

[89] Saint-Martin isn't very fair to the Hermetic Philosophers, describing them as little more than 'puffers', or materialistic Alchemists attempting to turn base material into gold and searching for the Elixir of Life. This is strange, since he often refers to the *Great Work* in his book, and clearly sees it as an image of what we now call *Spiritual Alchemy*, or the process which applies the symbols of Alchemy to our own being, to purify ourselves and bring us to a higher level of spiritual

The rule which requires subjects to be superior to their images, symbols and hieroglyphs, also applies to the opinion of those who only see in the Ancient Traditions the processes of the Hermetic Art, and who only perceive in the Divinities of Mythology the emblems of the primary materials or substances, on which they claim to work.

The purpose of the Hermetic Art, the one most widely known, never raises itself above matter. It is ordinarily confined to two objectives: the acquisition of wealth; and preservation, and the curing of disease which, in the minds of its disciples, removes all boundaries to man's desires and powers, and allows him to hope for jolly days of indefinite duration.

In vain, some followers of this seductive Art claim that by this means they obtain a still more noble Science, which elevates them as far above material adepts as they are above the common man. These men, while most praiseworthy in their ambitions, cease to be quite so noble when we consider the path they seek to fulfill them. For any substance can only produce fruits according to its nature, and most certainly the fruits for which they seem to long are of a nature which is quite different from the materials they submit to their manipulations.

If the material Hermetic Art doesn't go beyond material objects, then this so-called Art is in an Order no more elevated than Agriculture. It is therefore obvious that the emblems and symbols of Mythology are equally foreign to it, since they present the language of the intellect, and because they give life and activity to abilities which are unknown to matter.

Those who have believed they saw so many connections between things which are completely different were not so much confused, but rather allowed themselves to be seduced by the similarity of the Laws which are common to them. One needs to observe time, degrees, measures, weight and quantities to engage in the Hermetic process. One similarly needs *weight*, *number*, and *measure* to direct us in accordance with the Laws of our intelligent Nature. There is a need to be precise and extremely accurate in all Hermetic operations. There is still greater need to follow a fixed and regular order on the *intellectual path*.[90]

---

awareness. Later, he will become a disciple of the writings of Jakob Böhme, who was not averse to using Alchemical symbolism. Why he doesn't extend the courtesy of believing Hermeticists capable of seeing Alchemy as symbolic, and representative of the human spiritual evolutionary process, seems a little unfair.

[90] Saint-Martin makes a good point. In his first book, *Of Errors & Truth*, we were introduced to the critical importance of the Biblical phrase "Thou hast ordered all things in measure, and number, and weight" (*Wisdom 11:21*), describing the First Principle's act of Creation. This concept is of a

These are the apparent similarities which have confused the Observers. They have attributed to completely material processes a host of Principles which could only relate to superior objects by their action and by all the properties inherent in them. In doing this we can be certain that they have debased the ancient symbols, rather than explaining them to us.

Our scorn for the followers of the Hermetic Science therefore comes from the fact that, both in their doctrine and in their work, they continually confuse two perfectly distinct Sciences.

The love of the Supreme Principle had introduced men to the Laws of material Nature to help them recognize impressions of the Living Model they had lost sight of. On the contrary, the Hermetic Philosophers avail themselves of the similarity between the subject and its image to confuse them and to create one single Being.

Deceived by this rash notion, the Hermetic Philosophers have not seen that the simple material Physics to which they have applied all their efforts isn't at all worthy of all those mysteries nor of that enigmatic and confusing language in which they present the ancient emblems. They have not seen that, if there was one science worthy of man's study and tribute, it was the one which gave evidence of his greatness by providing instructions on his origin and on the breadth of his natural and intellectual abilities.

So, one can say that, even if their goal isn't chimerical in all possible senses, the path they follow is at least very foreign to man's true function, and completely opposed to that of the Truth they all claim to honor.

In the first instance, they attack Truth by claiming to equal Him in their work, and by seeking to create the same things as Him, without His Order, although they defend themselves against that charge by saying – and with good reason – that they aren't creating anything.

Secondly, they attack that Truth in the most intemperate manner, seeking to do Hits work by means of a path opposed to the one He has followed in all His creations. And so, not acting according to the *path of virtue*, they have certainly procured the vague outlines of Nature, yet derived nothing but silent and dumb fruits, without life, without intelligence, before which they abase themselves, as if they had received

---

wholly different order to that required in Alchemy, where exact amounts of various substances must be mixed together in precise quantities and heated for exact periods of time. The words used may be the same, but the meaning is of another order entirely.

them from Truth Himself. But they would cease to exalt them if they really knew their source and origin, and, while enjoying these fruits, they would whine about the processes which procured them and the mediocrity of the benefits they might expect.

Indeed, the processes of the Hermetic Art cannot unsettle the seat of the *Principle* without unsettling the *Principle* itself, since it is there that it reigns and acts. However, isn't it walking on a path which is absolutely contrary to the nature of material Beings, to wish to control its *Principle* by an action other than that which is similar to its own essence? Doesn't that violate the established Order, both of temporal material Nature and of temporal immaterial Nature?

Moreover, activating this *Principle* by a Law other than *that which is its own*, and through this creating only a weak and fleeting impulse, will only result in a weak and fleeting result.

That is why these results speak only to sight; why we cannot see them except by means of natural or artificial elemental light; why they only exist for a time and why, once that time has passed, they no longer appear; finally, why they have none of the essential conditions to be real, to provide evidence that they have been extracted by means of the right path and to show that they truly have within them the seed of their own *fire* and their own *life*.

This, I know, will not be understood by the Hermetic Philosophers and by men educated in science even more profound and more essential than theirs. However, those who are ignorant of the processes of the Hermetic Art, and who don't know any of the fruits which can come from them, will understand me enough to learn how to discern those fruits, if one day they have the opportunity to see them; and to guard themselves against the abuse of the terminology used by disciples of this science; for they can seem to be clever enough and confident enough to be dangerous. But is it truly possible for them to follow the cult of corruptible substances in good faith, and to hide the fact that what they are actually seeking with so much ardor is a soul made of matter, instead of seeking one which is not?

This abuse of expressions, this confidence – or rather these illusions – reveal themselves in the claims of most of the Hermetic Philosophers who boast of their ability to work on the *prima materia*, or first matter

All physical and material processes, far from happening on the first matter, can only take place upon the second, composite matter, seeing that the first matter cannot be physically experienced by our hands or our eyes or any of our organs, which are themselves secondary and composite.

Moreover, think of the disproportion between the gross and material Fire that they use, and the powerful and free Fire which serves as an Agent of Nature? And what can they expect from their vain efforts, if they compare the object of their desires with what they would receive by *making use* of a *Fire* which is purer and less destructive?

We will not repeat what has already been said in the book concerning the difference between the first and second matter or, put differently, the difference between a body and its Principle. Suffice it to say that this first matter, or this Principle of the body, is constituted by a simple Law and participates in unity, which makes it indestructible; whereas the second matter or body is constituted by a composite Law, which never shows itself in the same proportions and which, because of that, makes all the material processes of man uncertain and variable.

In not making these important distinctions, the Hermetic Philosophers are, at every moment, dupes of their first mistake; and their doctrine, like their path, leads into error all those who allow themselves to be seduced by the wonders of the things they show us.

The use they have made of prayer for the success of their work, and their conviction that it could never have been accomplished without doing that, shouldn't concern us. For it is here that their error can more evidently be seen, since their work, being limited to material substances, cannot rise above secondary causes.

Now, since these secondary causes are, by their nature, beneath man, it wouldn't be deceiving man to tell him that he is made to use them. If the Hermetic Philosophers have sufficient experience and knowledge to prepare the matter fundamental to their work correctly, and that work is possible, they would most surely achieve this without any need to introduce another *Power* than that innate in all matter, and which constitutes his manner of Being.[91]

Moreover, there is an almost inevitable danger to which the Hermetic Philosopher is exposed: that in praying for his work, only too often he prays to the material itself. The more the results he obtains seem perfect and liberated from coarse substances, the more he tries to believe that they

---

[91] Saint-Martin is saying that prayer isn't necessary for Alchemical work, despite the well-known motto of the Alchemists, *Ora et Labora* or 'work and pray', since the work being performed on lower substances is beneath the level of man, and therefore requires no Divine intervention.

are drawing closer to the nature of the Divine, for since his senses see something higher than what he ordinarily perceives, he is seduced by those appearances and believes he has the most valid reasons for justifying his error. In this manner, the Hermetic Philosophers, by sinking into new shadows, perpetuate the sad results of their enthusiasm and presumptions.

I don't agree with the grounds which they claim prevents them from revealing their alleged secrets, for fear that if their knowledge became universal it would destroy civil society and even empires, and thus destroy the harmony which seems to be on Earth. How could their knowledge become universal if, as they teach, it can only be shared among a small number of the Elect of God? And besides, what would civil societies and empires have to regret if, by changing their form, they were composed solely of virtuous men and women, educated enough to know how to cure diseases of the body, the vices in their hearts, and the ignorance of their mind?

Bringing together all these observations about the great Law of inferiority which should have their own symbols, you will recognize that Hermetic Philosophy is unable to be the true goal, or the true subject of the allegories of Fable. It would be against all probability that the nature of enlightened man would had led him to envisage the intervention of the Divinities to veil a knowledge which contradicts itself and which injures itself; a knowledge which nourishes this man of hope of immortality, and which allows him to hold its hand; which promises him, without their aid, the most powerful right over Nature; which, if it is possible in all its breadth, should be found in the simple Laws of elemental substances and therefore beneath the knoweldge truly proper to man; which, if it had a higher source, is no longer at our disposal; and which, finally, contains within itself more illusions and danger than all the other material sciences combined, because although being false in its basis and its object, nevertheless through its processes, doctrine and results, it has more similarities with the Truth.

If in the different Orders of Hermetic Philosophers, there are those who seem to take a higher path, and who claim to accomplish the Work without using any material substance, we cannot deny that their walk is most distinguished. But we cannot find their object worthy of them, nor their goal any more legitimate.

Kaph (כ) – Original Intent of Traditions and Myths

The more I have shown, with evidence, that Agriculture and Hermetic science were not the object of symbols and allegories, the more I am committed to clearly identifying what may have been their true purpose.

Several Observers [92] have already given those Traditions an interpretation which is livelier, nobler, more analogous to us than those we have just considered. I would not fear deceiving myself if I firmly adopted the doctrine of those wise interpreters. The more sublime the doctrine is, the less chance there is of being wrong by agreeing with them.

Man, his beginning, his end, the Law which should lead him to his goal, the things which keep him from it, and finally the *Knowledge of man*, inseparably linked to that of the First Principle: these are the things which the authors of the earliest traditions wished to describe. This alone is what ennobles and justifies their symbols. This is the only use worthy of their emblems: for here the object is clearly superior to the allegory, while the allegory is perfectly suited to the object.

Indeed, there is no man instructed in his true nature, who, if he seeks to penetrate the meaning of the Mythological Traditions, won't have a sense of admiration as he perceives in them symbols of the facts which are most important to the human species, and which are also the most similar to himself.

Alcyoneus, Pandora, Deucalion, Sisyphus, the Danaïdes, Hercules, the Tunic of Nessus, the Caduceus, Argus, the Fates, the Elysian Fields, the River Lethe, the boundary of the River Styx, Semele consumed by the presence of Jupiter in his glory, Pygmalion, Circe, the Companions of Ulysses, Tiresias becoming blind in a instant for having looked at Pallas while she dressed, Centaurs: in a word, almost every detail in Mythology offers man profound instructions, which reassure him in the knowledge his efforts have procured for him.

---

[92] This is the one positive reference to 'the Observers' in either of Saint-Martin's first two books. This is quite surprising, since he usually equates them with Deists, Atheists, and Scientists who discredit Creation and God's hand in earthly matters. It seems he finally decided to show a more even hand towards them.

But do these emblems have a basis in anything other than the imagination or genius of those who transmitted them to us? Did the Mythologists put forward these images of their own volition, or did they receive the designs already drawn up? This is a question which is important to resolve.

Making simple connections between the various concepts in Mythology and man's history does not provide us with knowledge sufficient or sure enough to decide, unless we trace our thinking back to their origin. To do this successfully, let us remember that the epigraph of this book imposes on us the duty to 'explain things through man, and not man through things'.[93]

Considering man in his intellectual nature, we repeat that nowadays he is subject to receiving a multitude of diverse thoughts; thoughts which are both bright and obscure, vast and limited, correct and false, beneficial and harmful. Moreover, by the Law of Supreme Order, we see that chosen men who pass their days delighting in truth should be seen as true symbols of the *virtues*; whereas others through their negligence or laziness become symbols of the *vices*.

Then, remembering the need for the manifestation of visible signs of the superior powers on Earth, and recalling that invariable Law by which all Beings linked to time, whether good or bad, can learn nothing except through the physical senses, we will see whether it isn't natural to accept that there must be a similarity and a proportion between those visible signs of all the types and diverse thoughts of man, and that both must follow the same direction and the same path.

Aren't the reflections of solar rays proportional and analogous to the nature of the substances that receive them: none on black surfaces, weak on colorless liquids, stronger on colored liquids, powerful on colored and compact solids, and immense on pure and integral solids such as glass and diamond? Isn't this clear evidence that intellectual results take on our manner of being, and that they necessarily reflect brightness or obscurity, strength or weakness, ultimately the vices and *virtues*.

There is within us another indication of the existence of those physical signs. We are unable to communicate a single thought if it isn't preceded by an image generated within us by our mind. When our

---

[93] This epigraph, on the front page of this book, was taken from Saint-Martin's first book *Of Errors & Truth*.

thoughts are active, the image which represents them within us is often physical enough to offer us a kind of reality; and in all our forms of expression we are satisfied to a greater or lesser extent depending on how closely their physical signs, through which our thoughts are expressed, are like them and communicate their character.

If we want still more sound proof of the relationship between physical signs and our thoughts, we will draw it from the present state of our Being and the violent Law to which it is subjected. For if it is evident that we cannot receive anything in the mind except through physical channels, yet however we don't doubt that man's intellect has received thoughts as it receives them every day, it follows that those thoughts have taken on a physical modification before arriving in him. It follows, then, that this modification or this physical sign exists invisibly around us, by us, in the same way as the source of thoughts; and that, if instead of the secondary thoughts that we receive from men, we were to raise ourselves up to the level of those *living* and *original thoughts* which are drawn from their own *source*, they would necessarily be preceded by *similar living signs* which belong to them, in the same way that, for us, coarse and conventional signs such as writing and speech precede the thoughts which men communicate to us.

Finally, if man's education weren't so false and improper, those *original* and *natural signs* would be the elements of his instruction, and he would begin the development of his intellectual existence by perceiving and having physical knowledge of those signs, whose meaning would only be communicated to him at a more advanced age.

Though we can only support this Principle with a very small number of examples, it would be wrong to deny its certainty. Consider the feeble child, enclosed in his organs: the watchful tenderness of those to whom Nature has entrusted him uses every physical means necessary to care for him. He accepts their efforts, and although the people who transmit them and the beneficent reason which makes them act this way are unknown to him, this in no way negates their existence; and it is no less certain that without them, the child would never receive any care, or any pleasant sensations. Such is the image of what takes place in the Order of thoughts relative to bodies and the signs which are necessary for them to come from their source to us.

Without going further into the nature of those signs, which should be very similar to those which we ourselves use to communicate our thoughts, since we cannot invent anything new, we can say that, if there is an extreme variety among mens' thoughts, so there can be considerable differences between the visible signs which belong to them, since those signs are only the organs and modifications of those thoughts. Then the relationship that we have established between thoughts and their analogous signs becomes even more necessary and more indispensable to avoid confusion.

According to these principles, just as the child who begins to grow also begins to perceive, though dimly, those objects which surround him, so man who, during the early *progression* of his *intellectual abilities* may be ready to begin to receive thoughts and might therefore perceive the signs which represent them in an uncertain manner. But as those *thoughts* and those *signs* become more perfect as he grows older, just like his physical abilities, it follows that the *natural growth* of his intellectual Being would lead him to the point of being gifted with living, true and expansive *thoughts*, and also to receive their analogous *sign*, that is, a *sign of complete regularity*, with features so perfect and so exquisite that he would take it to be a faultless man, a Superior Agent, a Divine Minister; as a man on leaving childhood, then visibly recognizes those physical Agents who cared for his first needs in his childhood, and those to whom he owes his existence and his life.

He who, on the contrary, has *false*, depraved and wicked *thoughts*, would distinguish them in *signs* which were *malformed* and irregular enough for them to appear to him to come from the very *Agents* of error.

Indeed, since man is the most noble thought of God, it shouldn't be surprising that the *Divine Thoughts* which come to him have similarities with the most beautiful of forms, which is that of man. And it is here that the passage of Sanchoniaton, cited above, in which he represented the God Thoth drawing the portrait of the Gods to make of them the sacred characters of the letters can be applied; because man's body is the most beautiful letter of all alphabets that exist on the Earth, and consequently the most accurate copy of the invisible portrait of God.

One could even extend this inference up to the shape of the stars which, like man, are *living letters of the great alphabet*; and if they appear to us to be spherical, it is because that was the form which all objects took for man in his childhood, when everything seemed to be equal and uniform, for we can't deny that down here we are in our infancy with respect to a *true understanding* of the stars.

Finally, we should apply to the development of our intellectual abilites and to all the wonders which belong to them the same progression as that observed in the development of a child's physical abilities. There is a similar progression of degrees from darkness into light, even a mixing of gentle and vexatious impressions, the same perception of graceful things and contrary or mischievous things.

If we add to this the mixtures those which are within our Being, where vices combine with *virtues*, light with darkness, there we will find as their analogies a new order of signs, that is, mixed signs containing both truth and falsehood, with infinite variations depending on the various measures of *correct* or *false thought* from which those mixtures are formed.

But there is a broader and more convincing truth: which is, according to the principles which have been considered with regard to man's degradation and the links which he still has with the Principle from Whom he has descended, that the Principle must have communicated to those men especially charged with competing the *Great Work* all the thoughts relating to their former, present, and even future estate, in order to show them at the same time what they had lost, what they are suffering, and what they might hope for.

Those chosen men must therefore have physically seen the Universal Table of man's history, in which they must have understood his original privileges, all the *combats* he had to endure, which have been renewed and multiplied to infinity since the demolition of his *First Temple*; the *perpetual and powerful relief* which the Supreme Hand constantly places around us; the harmony and the progress of all the principles of Nature; the form and structure of the Universe; the *Laws* of the *Earth*, the powers of those bright *stars* which illuminate us; and finally the *stars*, even more alive, which have the same nature as man and which, for that reason he will, one day, be permitted to contemplate.

In a word, it was necessary for each of these thoughts, or that knowledge, to be accompanied by the physical sign which is analogous to it, so that the chosen men to whom Wisdom wished to communicate His light, might receive the full instruction they need.

But if man portrays the same truth under varied images and forms all the time, it shouldn't be surprising that the various men chosen to serve as the *Columns* of the *Building* should have received their knowledge concerning the great facts and the great truths through different signs, and through connections which didn't use all the same characters, since we see that the languages were only multiplied and diversified because each Nation considered the same Being under an appearance which was specific and acceptable to them.

We should no longer be surprised that the succession of Centuries has multiplied the images of truth and the signs relating to them, so that men today are able to draw from reservoirs far more abundant than they would have had in the first times, because the wellsprings which were opened at the moment of the fall of man have never ceased, and still continue to flow over his unfortunate posterity.

From what we have just explained, one may easily see all the Traditions of Earth and all the different Mythologies of the Nations coming down to us.

The men favored by great enlightenment only received it for the purpose of utility, and for instructing their fellow man. In order to fulfill that purpose, they were expected to communicate them to the small number of people they felt were properly prepared, and that communication had to be done in two ways: one through discourse and instruction, the other through the *exercise* and *use* of those actions taught to the Sages by those Superior Powers whose existence and connections to us have been sufficiently demonstrated.

The Sages, in performing those *acts* in the presence of those to whom they had given their trust, made them witnesses of all the *physical outcomes* which could occur, and since the knowledge and the signs which the Sages had received from those Superior Powers contained the complete story of man, both in his glory, and in his state of degradation and suffering, the *results* which their disciples received contained the same mixture of light and darkness, good and evil, perfection and disorder, pain and remedy, danger and the means deliverance.[94]

Those same disciples, either through the command of their Masters, or through zeal, would have communicated to the Nations in which they lived, if not the facts, at least the description of those facts and the instructive disourse from their meetings.

That is why, among the Ancient Nations, the Traditions spoke of a Golden Age, of Giants, Titans, of the usurpation of the Celestial Fire from

---

[94] This is clearly a reference to the *Order of Élus Cohen*, whose leaders were charged with performing theurgical operations, for them and the students to observe the results, usually called 'passes', in which signs such as flashes of light, noises, sparks and sigils were sought. The references to 'witnesses' and 'physical outcomes' makes this clear.

the Throne of Divinity, the anger of the Father of the Gods against the prevaricators, the various scourges visited upon the Earth and in the various regions of the Universe, the powers poured upon the pious and faithful mortals on whom those same Divinities granted their favors, and the hope that they would admit them to greater felicities still if they observed the Law of their Principle and knew how to respect their *Being*.

One shouldn't be surprised that these Traditions and Doctrines are universal because in the beginning, they formed the basis of the historical records of all the Nations. It is only as a result of time and political events that civil history has come into existence, so that in Ancient Times we have so few monuments to the political history of Nations and so many to Theogonic Traditions; whereas in modern times we see few Traditions and facts relating to *natural* and religious history, though we have so much civil history, since these two Orders rarely have much affinity between them.

Although the Sages educated by the Superior Powers and the disciples educated by the Sages, basically received the same *knowledge* and the same *results*, nevertheless they each only received a *full understanding* of the *great concepts* of man's universal history through those *signs* and *images* that were specifically pertinent to them. For if it is true that all men have the same Being with regard to their essence, it is also certain that they show a universal variation in talents, abilities, ways of understanding things, and wisdom; and by sending such gifts to men *physically*, those teachings can always take those differences into account. Those Sages and those disciples, receiving the same instructions, could therefore each conform to the notions which their particular talents allowed them to take from them.

From this comes the infinite variety that can be seen in the stories among all the different Nations of the Earth, even though the basis of those truths is usually the same.

The disciples admitted to that *knowledge* and to those *manifestations*, were not only unable to grasp everything with the same level of understanding, but a few even added personal and corrupted interpretations, while others confused emblematic things with the symbols they should be expressing, and then replaced the facts themselves with the allegories, forgetting that the similarity between *natural* and *superior signs* to physical objects only existed in relation to their form, and because of our subjection to inferior and material Laws, whilst that similarity never extended to their essence.

Yet others, giving themselves over to depravity, deliberately altered symbols and emblems, or didn't adhere to all the wonders in which they participated, preferring instead confused and *irregular things*. And each of them then professed that the knowledge was too confining or even corrupted, and created new and absurb Traditions, an infinite multitude of ridiculous tales which were both godless and foolish, and whose new Mythologies were upturned and no longer agreed at all with the fundamental original truths; and because of that, many of those stories have so little connection to the true source that they have no connection at all with us. Finally, it was from that that the various religious sects of men and all the branches of idolatry were principally derived.

For if it we know there is a kind of idolatry in which one sees only ignorance and nothing else, there is one which clearly lends itself to depravity and leads to still greater crimes, even than those which fanaticism and superstition have been able to generate on Earth. Both of them are a corruption of true worship; they both set up a false God in place of the True God. The difference between the source of these two kinds of idolatry is that in one, man has abused his knowledge to form a culpable science, and in the other, he has been poorly educated.

But all these errors also introduce the idea and the knowledge of a Sovereign Being, for if the idea of a God was not analogous to our nature, neither the objects of our physical emotions nor the very instructions of the Superior Agents would ever have come to life, either in the souls of the teachers, or in the souls of other men. Again, if man had never physically known anything superior to him and worthy of his homage, he would not have been able to have the notion of *sovereignly criminal* idolatry since, to be truly *idolatrous*, not only must he begin by recognizing a Divine Principle, but he must also have understood this in such a way as to be unable to ignore that it is due a pure and lawful worship.

So, when we are filled with admiration for natural beauty, veneration for a hero, or tenderness for a friend we are still a long way from idolatry, and we would never attribute to any lesser Being the names or titles which belong to Divinity if the idea of the Supreme Perfection had not previously developed in us, either *by nature*, or through the example and instruction, even if altered, of our educators and those who surround us.

And similarly, when we forget ourselves to the extent of seeing men or purely terrestrial things as Divine, it is not really those things which we are raising up to the quality of a God – for they are too weak and too infirm to lead us into true idolatry – but rather the majesty of our Being that we make descend to the level which example and instruction had brought us, and because we let ourselves focus on lesser things. It is this Being who, knowing that it is meant to pay homage to and contemplate the Supreme Divinity, abases itself before Beings beneath it, and takes them to be the object of its worship.

It is therefore less through seeing physical things as being Divine than making himself more material that man makes himself an idolator. It isn't through physical emotions that man has raised himself up to the thought of Divinity and that of His Agents; it is on the contrary by debasing this sublime and natural thoughts that he has lost sight of the superior things which his essence should approach, to attach himself instead to the coarse and perishable Beings which have neither reality nor power. For I repeat, if man hadn't initially had proof of the existence of those Superior Beings, and if he had not communicated that fact to his fellow man, either through facts or through traditions, none of them would ever have been in error about a Principle which they knew nothing about; and one can see as an absolute truth, that if a man were completely separated from other men from childhood, it would have been much easier for him to accept and practice the worship of the Supreme Being than for him to begin by creating a single idol.

Those people who have worshipped the Sun and those wish to claim that such worship is the most natural, since its subject is nearer to us, don't in any way destroy the principle that I am outlining. Those Nations who have practiced the cult of the Sun only came to that idolatry through the debasing of a worship which had previously been more sublime, and it is sufficient to convince us of this fact by comparing their antiquity with that of those other Nations which have adored the invisible Being. Chinese Tradition tells us of such a pure and enlightened worship in that Nation long before the establishment of the cult of the Sun in any other Nation on Earth.

As for those who claim to justify material idolatry, they close their eyes to man's nature, and they don't see, too, that such worship cannot meet his needs for long; for since man is an active Being he needs to pray, to contribute to the *work* that he wishes to perform, and since the Sun regularly performs its functions toward us without us having to act and without the need for us to address prayers to it; since man is destined by his origin to exercise a sacerdotal function which puts him into correspondence with his Principle; and finally, since man, like all Beings, can only thrive among Beings in whom he recognizes his likeness, then the Sun, majestic as it is, has no point of similarity with man.

We saw previously the need for the Superior Powers, in communicating to man, to present themselves to him in a form similar to his, being the most expressive of all forms, and so that the aid of those Powers would be beneficial to him. It was therefore under similar *forms* that the Sages and their disciples had to receive the principal *signs* and the most essential *outcomes* of those *pure and regular actions* which they used for their own education and to spread the truth.

Their followers, when transmitting to the different Nations those stories and facts whose knowledge which they wished to communicate, would have represented them in their speech by expressions and images familiar to those to whom they transmitted them; and the Nations they taught, wishing to retain the memory of everything they had heard, drew, painted and erected material monuments which their descendants ended up regarding as being the reality of the things those monuments had been intended to represent, though they were only meant to be their copies and emblems.

That is why, among the ancient Divinities of material and ignorant idolators, there were many who were honored as corporeal human figures and represented by statues.

But it is also true that alongside all those *regular signs* which were similar to the human form, the Sages and their disciple received signs and forms connected with all the objects of Nature, for since the *superior aid* had the goal of laying man's former grandeur before his eyes, it showed him in stages every part of his domain.

The disciples of those Sages transmitted that new order of knowledge to their Nations, just as they had done those which had basically taught about man's superior nature, and once again the Nations confused the signs with the earthly objects; so, it isn't surprising that the different Nations on Earth have had so many idols which were both oddly formed and monstrous, and that they took as the object of their worship stars, animals, plants, reptiles and other things in Nature.

Kaph (כ) – Original Intent of Traditions and Myths 147

And really, if we consider the level of degradation to which man's soul can descend through ignorance and the little care he takes to cultivate his intelligence, if one considers the many and varied degrees to which he can descend through the confusion of his thoughts, we will find the evident source of that multitude of idols distinguished from one another by so many different forms and powers, because in the whole extent of the circle of Beings, there are none, whether they are true or false, on which man won't place his reliance and towards which he cannot direct his worship.

And so, it is not surprising to see Empyrean Gods, celestial Gods, earthly Gods, aquatic, fiery, vegetable, reptile and mineral Gods, and ultimately even infernal Gods and Gods of crime and abomination honored physically on Earth, because man has the right to stand before any object he chooses and to give it the honor and respect which he should have for the Supreme Dvinity alone.

But if it is true that man's form is the most expressive of all forms, on which is founded all connections and relations, the more signs and monuments of idolatry are distanced from it, the more they will be inferior and changed. It is therefore by comparing everything physical shown us with the regularity of our form that we can judge not only the different degrees of idolatry of material Nations, but also which of them follow either a more criminal *idolatry*, or a pure, active and legitimate *worship*, because the correspondences connected to our form are universal.

Let us agree for now that Mythology, in its most physical and apparently regular accounts, must be inexplicable to those who have not grasped an understanding of man and Nature. Even those who have made some progress must still find great difficulty in this kind of study, because, to ensure the accuracy of the connections, one must in some way review the *original signs* themselves on which they are based. However, copies alone of such signs are not sufficient for such verification, and they must seek the originals in the very *deposits* from which the first writers drew them, that is to say in their *natural reservoirs*.

Let us not therefore be surprised that so large a number of Observers have consumed their time in vain, using their work to explain the origin and purpose of Mythological Traditions, trying to convince us of the truth of their various theories, since they haven't based their works on a general Principle, nor true understanding. How can they explain the obscurity of the origin of Fables and Allegories if they don't have a true idea of man, and not know nothing about his primitive and fundamental relationships?

But one might ask why, since the same *lights*, the same *signs* and the same *facts* are still present to men, allegorical and emblematic language has almost disappeared today from the Earth? I have already answered part of that question, by explaining how religious Traditions are older than the civil history of Nations, and showing why these two kinds of Traditions have followed a reverse order. It will therefore be sufficient to say here that present day men make use of those *major aids* less often than in earlier times, and that they are without doubt all the more guilty in that, since those signs and emblems are still around them and available for their use. Besides, when they make use of them today, they are so obsessed with *reality* that they no longer think in *symbols*.

Lamed (ל) – Religions, Signs of the One Tradition

Although the origin and purpose of Mythological stories are almost universally unknown; although they have so often been changed, either due to the ignorance of Translators and rivals, or writers and poets, we have mentioned a number which demonstrate clear connections with the truths outlined in this book. We will give a few examples, drawing from the Egyptian and Greek fables.

Who won't recognize in Alcyoneus, that famous giant who aided the Gods against Jupiter, whom Minerva cast out from the globe of the Moon where he had been stationed, and which had the ability to resuscitate him; who will not recognize in him the ancient Prevaricator excluded from the presence of the Supreme Principle, reduced to the horror of confusion and chained in a dark enclosure where higher forces endlessly constrain him and trouble his ever-renascent will?[95]

We see with equal clarity the story of criminal man in Prometheus; and that of the various crimes committed by his descendants in all the unfortunates whose names and torments mythology recounts.

Such was Epimetheus, who opened Pandora's box.[96] We will note here that Prometheus means *seeing before* or *foresight*, and Epimetheus *seeing after* or *hindsight*[97]; an expression which we shall revisit in light of other connections.

---

[95] Saint-Martin appears to be confused over his Mythology. Firstly, he seems to confuse two Myths: one involves Alcyneus who was a giant slain by Heracles, who discovered that he had to move the body from its native land where it could spontaneously revive itself; and the second concerning the Giant Enceladus who battled Athena (the Greek manifestation of Minerva) – which is amusing since in the previous chapter he accused others of doing precisely that! In neither case did the Giant assist the Gods, and indeed in the latter case led the Giants *against* the Gods (as described in the *Gigantomachy*). Neither story mentions the moon. Also, although Saint-Martin says he is drawing from Greek and Egyptian mythology, he uses the Latin – rather than the Greek – versions of most of the Gods' names.

[96] Epithemeus was Prometheus' brother, and strictly speaking he accepted the gift of Pandora, the first woman, from Zeus and married her: it is usually told that Pandora opened the box she was told never to open. In fact, she opened a large jar (*pithos*) and not a box (*pyxis*), but a mistranslation of Hesiod's myth by Erasmus in the 16th Century has left us with Pandora's Box.

[97] Also, *second sight*.

Another was Ixion who planned an incestuous liaison with the wife of Jupiter, his father, and who, in fact only embracing a cloud, produced the Centaurs, the monsters who were half man and half horse; by which our mixed nature is clearly represented.[98] His punishment was a faithful image of that suffered by man, cast to the extremities of the circumference around which he moves, where he encounters only furious and implacable enemies.

Yet another was Sisyphus who revealed the secrets of the king, his master, and was sentenced to forever push an enormous rock to the top of a mountain, from where it constantly rolled back down: that is, to persevere in bold undertakings is to be continually thwarted and to see them continually reversed.

So, as a final example, is the allegory of the Danaïdes who killed their husbands and who, without the virtuous conduct of Hypermnestra, would ave forever degraded the perfect centenary number of which that family was composed.[99] Also, being reduced to forever drawing water in bottomless vessels, they help us understand what Beings who are distanced from their *Guides* and their support – as portrayed by the chiefs or the husbands of these criminal girls – might be capable of.

Perceptive eyes can no doubt identify the direct and clear relationships in all these symbols, such as the picture of the fate of those culpable beings who, each being condemned to perform a single action always behave in the same manner; who betray themselves through that monotonous consistency, thereby protecting the well-intentioned person from their assaults, which we ourselves experience in the different *passions* which obsess us, which always appear in the same manner which each of them had when they first begin to pursue us. But since those notions are not within the grasp of the vulgar man, let us be content to observe in the image of Tantalus, the sufferings to which we are heir: to

---

[98] To clarify this shorthand myth, Jupiter found out that Ixion wished to sleep with Hera, his wife, so substituted her with a cloud in Hera's form. The result of the union between Ixion and the cloud (a nymph called Nephele) was Centaurus, a hideous misshapen man who was banished to Mount Helion, where he mated with the Magnesian mares and thus founded the race of Centaurs, also known as Ixionidae. As punishment for his incestuous designs, Ixion was punished by being pinned to a fiery wheel, which spun through Hades for eternity.

[99] Saint-Martin is alluding to the fact that 100 is considered in his philosophy to be a good number, and the 50 Danaïdes and their 50 spouses would have made 100, and by killing their husbands they would have forever cursed that number. However, in not killing her husband, Hypermnestra preserved the integrity of this number.

see in the three-headed dog, the three rivers of Hell, the three Fates, the three judges, and the three different kinds of trials, the sufferings and challenges which we must endure because of the *Three Superior Actions* from which we are separated, and the three degrees of atonement which every man must show before reaching the end of his rehabilitation.

The Greek and Egyptian Mythological Traditions aren't limited to presenting us with to the effects of the judgement of the Heavens upon man: they also provide an image of the evidence of their love by offering us – albeit beneath a veil – the rays of their own light.

It is true that due to our unfortunate situation this light cannot shine forth in all its splendor, for in spreading its light over the dangers and evils which surround man as well, it would only lead to horror and terror if man were to see all the enemies that surround him and all the obstacles which he must fight and overcome, all at once.

And Wisdom ensures that he is only exposed little by little to the formidable *adversaries* which pursue him. For He only allows him to open his eyes with caution and over time. Wisdom watches over him as if over a child who would tremble with fear and terror if, in his weakness, he were to recognize the strength and violence of the Elements, or active Agents which assail his puny envelope.

And if we find that most men are still children when it comes to such great matters, it is because they see these facts like those of the Elemental Order, where throughout their material life thousands of men who experience the actions and counter-actions of the Agents of Nature are nevertheless neither able to recognize their Laws or their usual Causes, not observe their actions. Finally, because of the weakness of their thinking, they let all those phenomena pass before them without understanding them, and without learning anything from them.

But if the doctrine we previously established above concerning our relationship with our Principle is indisputable, we can no longer ignore the signs of the vigilant love that Wisdom has for man, which we see in the symbol of Minerva, Jupiter's daughter, as she covers her favorites with an impenetrable shield. We see it in the hope left to Epimetheus after he had opened the box; in the counsels which the Gods gave to Pyrrha his daughter and her husband Deucalion, to repopulate the land after the human race had been destroyed.[100]

It was as a consequence of this same love that the piety of King Athamas resulted in his receiving the Golden Fleece from the Gods; that the courage and virtue of Theseus won him Ariadne's thread[101]; that Orpheus stilled the Wheel Of Ixion; that Jupiter made a present of the Horn of Plenty to the Naiads in exchange for that which had been wrested from their father; and finally, that the Gods placed a caduceus upon the Earth to bring about the Rule of Order and Peace; and a tripod to deliver their oracles and the people selected to pronounce them. All these symbols clearly indicate the interest Divinity takes in man, and the indestructible notion which those who gave us these symbols had of them.

We know already what to think of the famous Hercules, whom commentators of all kinds have made an archetype in their systems. His many tasks, all performed for the benefit of the human species, clearly tell us what kind of model he symbolically represents; and without going into all his labors in detail we should get a sense what he teaches us when he killed the vulture by which unfortunate Prometheus believed he should be eternally devoured; when he crushed the giant Antaeus who had taken a vow to build Neptune a temple out of the skulls of men; and when he took on the weight of the Earth to relieve Atlas, which in its true etymological sense means *a Being who bears, an encumbered Being*. Now in that sense, who could it better refer to than man overwhelmed by the weight of his terrestrial and shadowy realm? Finally, we should remember that, after his death, the gods rewarded Hercules for his glorious work by having him marry Hebe, or eternal youth.

Physical truths also pierce the Mythological emblems. Argus is an active example of this living Principle of Nature, who never ceases His action on it, who penetrates and animates it throughout, who maintains harmony and who keeps watch everywhere to prevent disorder from drawing near.

The Divinity, Who presides both over the Heavens, the Earth and the Underworld, demonstrates the triple and quadruple link that unites all the parts of the Universe; a link for which the Moon is for us the true sign

---

[100] Interestingly, by a flood. Prometheus warned Deucalion that Zeus was going to destroy mankind by a flood, and Deucalion built an ark, eventually landing on the top of a mountain – in this case Parnassus. A familiar Myth indeed.
[101] With which he navigated the labyrinth and slayed the minotaur.

because it receives the quaternary action of the Sun; because, not only do we find the powers of all the other stars contained within it, but also because, by inhabiting the heavens like them, it also has a direct action over the Earth and over the Waters, which are the physical symbols of the abysses.

It is without doubt because of that great power that the Néoménies or New Moons were so often celebrated by the Ancients.[102] As the Moon was the vehicle and organ of *actions* superior to it, it wasn't surprising that they honored its return with celebrations. And if the Ancients had considered this return only in terms of elemental light, they wouldn't have instituted festivals to celebrate it.

Moreover, this custom was all the more natural since, in an early language with which we will not concern ourselves here, the words *planet* and *influence* are synonymous.

Finally, the famous caduceus, separating two snakes who fight one another, is an expressive and natural image of the purpose of the Universe's existence, which is repeated in the least of Nature's activities, where *Mercury* maintains the balance between Water and Fire to support the body, and so that the Laws of Beings might be revealed to men's eyes, they can read them in all the things that surround them. The symbol of the caduceus which Mythology has given us is therefore an inexhaustible field of knowledge and instruction; because the most physical truths portray to man the Laws of his intellectual Being and the *goal* towards which he must strive to regain his balance.

This leads us to symbols and hieroglyphs which, like all other emblems, belong to signs of the many diverse thoughts to which man is susceptible, as we have already seen; and which, in physical reality, should show man the true image of the state of his intellectual Being.

If man here below should have physical evidence of the existence of the Supreme Powers; this is all the more reason he should have evidence of those inferior powers which comprise all of Nature and which are to be found in his domain, and then there would be – not just for all the Intellectual Orders but also for every physical Being in both general and individual Nature – similar fixed signs to lead man along the path of

---

[102] The 'Néoménie' or New Moon was a festival celebrated in Ancient Greece, Rome, Egypt and Israel, according to the French Wikipédia. However, in this context it was much more relevant to Saint-Martin as one of the regular rituals created by Martinez de Pasqually for his Order of Élus Cohen, called the *Rite du Néoménie*.

instruction. Otherwise, his knowledge would be devoid of foundation and support.

Therefore, the signs and hieroglyphs relating to physical Nature cannot bre based simply on the arbitrary conventions of man, as claimed by those who don't follow *sound paths*, and who blindly accept the first opinion presented to them.

The evidence that those signs are independent of our conventions is that, by using arbitrary signs, man could only create hieroglyphs which were *dead* and without any power, and they would therefore be meaningless, and powerless to represent Nature where everything is *alive*.

So, it must be that natural objects themselves are accompanied by similar signs which serve to indicate their essence as well as their properties; and we don't doubt that the Sages were guided by this principle when they applied distinctive signs and characters to all substances: to the Planets, to Metals, to Fire, to Water, to all the Elements. No doubt the men who succeeded them wished to imitate their example when they connected various signs and various characters with many natural objects, such as those whose understanding and study are the subject of Chemistry.

But it is evident that, by supposing that the characters which those imitators used were actually real, they blindly followed the use which they made of them; which is obvious when we see that they gave metals the common names and composite signs of the planets.

From that we cannot avoid realizing that everything of this kind which has been passed on to us in the Sciences, in the Arts, and in the alphabets of languages is wrong, not only in its use but because the figures and the forms of the characters have also been changed. Now, because of those disfigured signs and characters, similar errors have resulted in the natural sciences with regard to the symbols representing the Superior Powers, whose abuse, generated by ignorance, has given rise to *supermaterial* idolatry. This truth will serve as a moment of clarity to show us with what level of confidence we should follow the Sciences and theories of men; but here we need to clarify a question concerning hieroglyphs and writing: that is, whether hieroglyphic signs came before the signs of speech and language.

Men of renown have approached this issue by saying that all writing and signs were hieroglyphic, that is, that they had to contain an element of the object which was meant to be submitted to the mind, and indeed, *speech* itself only becomes intelligible to man by *becoming hieroglyphic* within him, and he only understands the words of languages after their meaning has become familiar to him through the assistance of the physical things to which those words correspond.

However, that decision, adopted all too easily, would result in the need to see hieroglyphic signs and languages as the same thing. Now, one cannot doubt that these two things are very different, while being intimately related, and if we may use an analogy: together they form a fruit, one of which is the juice and the other the skin.[103]

Finally, there can be no doubt that if all the signs of languages are hieroglyphic, in that they relate to the essential properties of the Principle they express, then all objects of any kind, regardless of whether they are hieroglyphic in themselves, must still be the custodians of a name which can be used in man's language, to serve as the subject and guide for his intelligence when the object is no longer before his eyes.

This truth is confirmed by the general experience of all the Nations, all of whom have two ways to communicate their thoughts: through the objects or things themselves, and the words which correspond to them in their languages. And if anyone suggests that when intellectual things aren't present, men should not have words to express them, I would refer to what I said above about the need for the physical presence of the Supreme Powers among men: and even the objection would be supportive of the principle that I am defending; since, in man's present state, since words are as it were enveloped in physical objects, if men have words to express intellectucal things in their languages, it is clear proof that those intellectual things were once physical to them, or to those who passed on those ideas.

So, we can resolve the question raised by saying that in the natural and perfect order of things, hieroglyphic signs universally precede languages; that if one correctly recognizes that men, in their state of degradation, had language before writing, then this confirms our principle; for we shouldn't regard the current and common characters of writing as being the original hieroglyphs, nor as the source of man's speech, but rather as secondary hieroglyphic signs intended to provoke

---

[103] It is perhaps tempting to see here the analogy used by Martinists of the composition of the candle, being the wick, the wax and the flame: all different though each being a representation of the candle. Whether this idea was fully developed by Saint-Martin himself or extended by Papus from this comment when he wrote his rituals, is subject to debate.

the mind and speech in those to whom the same hieroglyphs would be communicated; and one cannot doubt that these lesser hieroglyphic signs have this function when one observes that mutes make themselves understood by their signs, and that many men can write languages they neither speak nor understand.

Finally, if we wish to convince ourselves that signs and the original hieroglyphs came before languages, it is enough to note that all our words are mentally preceded within us by the physical image of what we wish to express.[104] Even more strikingly, it is sufficient to observe that man passes the first part of his corporeal life in the shackles of infancy and bound by his material organs, before coming to the enjoyment of speech.

But let us return to the natural signs of the inferior Powers which act in this Universe and recognize once more the necessary existence of those signs for all Orders of Beings, all Kingdoms and all Realms, for everything is governed by this irrevocable Law.

As with every Nation, each individual man is free to make use of such or such an object, each must also be endowed more extensively with the signs relating to the object with which he is concerned: it is even a sure indicator to recognize the knowledge a particular Nation cultivates, and one does not have to study the hieroglyphs of the Egyptians for long to see that they were less devoted to true knowledge than is commonly believed. The multitude of reptiles, birds and aquatic animals which dominate them tells us clearly enough that they were particularly focused on elemental objects, and even on still more inferior things; since the Water from which all those animals came is, by its number, the true symbol of a confused and disorderly origin. For if it were claimed that they had only drawn those hieroglyphs from among the most common objects in their aquatic country, it would suffice to recall what we have already said concerning the origin of idolatry, which is simply a deviation

---

[104] This is a nod to Plato's belief that within us we retain an archetypal memory of perfection, and that when, for example, a person says the word 'chair', our mind's eye doesn't conjure up an image of a wooden stool, or a sofa, or a throne, but rather an abstract and perfect image of 'chairness'. This belief is quite close to Saint-Martin and Pasqually's own theosophies. Consider the following comment from https://plato.stanford.edu/entries/plato/ (May 16, 2018): "We must recognize that the soul is a different sort of object from the body – so much so that it does not depend on the existence of the body for its functioning, and can in fact grasp the nature of the forms far more easily when it isn't encumbered by its attachment to anything corporeal. In a few of Plato's works, we are told that the soul always retains the ability to recollect what it once grasped of the forms, when it was disembodied prior to its possessor's birth (see especially *Meno*), and that the lives we lead are to some extent a punishment or reward for choices we made in a previous existence."

from the true Religion, and which is necessarily preceded by original and hieroglyphic signs.

Similarly, there is convincing evidence of a Nation's ignorance: that is when it has no *natural hieroglyphic writing*, and its monuments are adorned with arbitrary and meaningless figures to which one can only attribute a conventional and ideal sense. One may then be sure that the most renowned scholars of that Nation don't even have the first idea of the title with which they are honored, and that, if they hold a distinguished rank in common opinion, they occupy a very inferior one in the true order of knowledge.

Here it is appropriate to present a few examples of those natural signs which should be connected to temporal objects and denote the properties of Beings.

While all the Nations on Earth have used the triangle in their hieroglyphic monuments, few have known or revealed its true relationships and its true meaning. Those which have used it as a symbol of the Sacred Ternary should have shown us an intermediate symbol between that Supreme Symbol and the corruptible ternary since, without that, the distance between the Invisible and Invariable Being and a dead figure, like a triangle, is too great for us to be able to raise ourselves from one to the other: and, as we will see shortly, the intermediate figure is man.

And so, we should simply contemplate the corruptible triangle in its temporal connections, and through this it becomes the perfect emblem of the Principles of Elemental Nature, which are three in number.[105] It therefore becomes the emblem of all individual bodies, since they are constituted by the same number and the same Laws as Universal Nature. Finally, it is the physical expression of the fundamental basis of things, and if it is the first and simplest figure that man can produce or design – for the *circumference* is less a figure and instead the whole and universal image of all actions and all figures – it is without doubt a vivid image of the specific Law which Wisdom followed to produce His physical creations.

With relationships so vast, it is not surprising that this figure holds such a distinguished rank among the hieroglyphs of the Nations.

---

[105] In his first book, *Of Errors & Truth*, Saint-Martin expressed a belief that there were only three true Elements – Earth, Water and Fire.

Chemists, whose research is to study the separate parts rather than the whole, have employed this sign in their Science: but, instead of considering it under its true relationships, they have only used it as the sign for Fire, or Phlogistics; and even though, under this limited point of view, there would still have been a certain correctness in the application if only the Chemists had known how to show us what is contained within Fire, it is clear that by not understanding this, this sign has become dead in their hands and its meaning has become arbitrary.

Some Chemists have believed they see Fire expressed by the triangular faces of the pyramid; and have based this on the fact that the first syllable *pyr* means *fire* in Greek, and on the fact that there are a number of these pyramids in Egypt where they celebrated the cult of the Sun or of Fire, and from whom the Greeks obtained most of their knowledge. But if the pyramid had connections with Fire, this would not exactly be due to its triangular faces, but rather by its vertical direction, and by its form which ever decreases until it comes to an imperceptible point. It is there that we would find the Laws of Fire; because it always rises vertically when external causes don't impede its natural action; because it decreases, for us, to the extent that it rises, and because it ends, like the pyramid, by becoming imperceptible to our senses.

The Chemists made the same errors regarding the figure of the cross, which they have adopted to represent universal acid. This sign, corresponding to the precise center of the circumference since it is formed by two diameters, is the visible symbol of unity.

We know that *Fire* is *one* everywhere[106], that it occupies the center of all bodies, and ceaselessly works to separate itself from any coarse substance with which it is combined. The figure of the cross would therefore logically be the real symbol of Fire, rather than acid: because although acid is a Fire, as it is never without Water, it is not pure Fire; and so the sign of simplicity and purity isn't appropriate for it.

Also, the Ancients were so convinced that the cross was the symbol of Fire that the Priests of the Sun among the Egyptians wore it on their vestments.

---

[106] As we just saw, the image of the candle and now fire is used effectively by Papus in his Martinist rituals. One of the symbols employed is a triangle composed of three lit candles, used to portray three separate fires which are at the same time one fire, since all fire is homogeneous, and used to explain, among other things the individuality and unity of the Trinity.

Lamed (ל) – Religions, Signs of the One Tradition

Finally Chemists, by combining the triangle with the cross, have taken this union to be the symbol for sulfur because, as sulfur is composed of vitriol and phlogistics, those signs individually claimed to represent acid and fire can be chosen to represent their union.

But without saying anything more about those conventions, other than that they tell us little, we believe we can discover higher and more interesting relationships in those two signs; and it will still be man who will be their symbol.

The triangle, as the universal symbol of those specific Laws which produced the body, must apply to man's body with regard to its constitive Principles, as to all other bodies. The cross being the emblem of Fire, of the Center, of the *Principle*, should symbolize man's intellectual Being, since it is linked directly to the center of the Superior and Universal Principle of all Powers.

In bringing together these two signs in the same order that the Chemists use, that is, by placing the triangle above the cross:

We clearly and physically have the image of the two opposing substances which compose us, and at the same time an image of the imperfection of our current state, where the thinking Being is overcome and as if buried under the weight of the corporeal form; whereas, being intended by its nature to rule and to dominate it, that form should be subordinate: and that is how all the Laws of Beings might come to instruct us. There, we can even find fresh evidence of the need for Superior Manifestations to help man reestablish himself in his Natural Order, and so that our intellectual essence may be restored to its primitive rank, superior to matter, so that the edifice which had been overthrown according to this figure:

is seen raised up, thus:

Finally, it may be noted that when bodies decompose, their Fire principle, their phlogistics, escapes from all the corporeal means used to contain it. This is to indicate visibly to us the distance existing between matter and its Principle, and by analogy how man's Intellectual Principle is foreign to his envelope.

If we turn from natural signs to symbolic signs, we will find the same instruction.

The Mythologists show us Love armed with arrows, and Minerva coming out of Jupiter's head. This is to remind us on the one hand, that all physical emotions which come to us by means of external objects are destructive; and on the other hand, that Wisdom, Prudence and all the *Virtues*, having their seat in the seed within man can be born of him, in imitation of the Being of which he is the image and Who produces everything: that is to say, that had intellectual man fulfilled his original purpose and had not let any part of his intangible substance change, he *would have lived* less by what he allowed to enter into himself, than what he would have allowed to emanate from him through the efforts of his desire and will. A just Principle, true, fruitful and informative, in which are contained all the secrets of knowledge and of happiness. But what makes the use of this Principle so difficult for man now, is that the application that he should make of it has become dual and divided, in that it must relate not only to objects of intelligence and reasoning, in which all the transactions occur in the head, but also to all *virtuous* emotions of desire and love for the truth, which have their seat in the heart of man. Thus, being linked to two *centers* distanced from one another, his action is infinitely more painful and uncertain than when they were united; so that, seeing the huge distance which separates them, their communication can often be intercepted: and in any case, if they don't act in concert, they produce only imperfect works.

The Mythologists show us a sphinx at the door of the Egyptian temples, to remind us how much wisdom is enveloped nowadays in enigmas and obscurities. But they teach us that this light isn't inaccessible, by transmitting to us the emblem that the Sphinx represented when it was sent to Thebes through the jealousy of Juno; for we know that Oedipus, by solving the mystery that the Goddess had created by sending it, reduced it to the need to take its own life. However, we should agree that it is quite wrong to assume that in the symbol of the Sphinx we should see it come to such an end, since Oedipus only gave an explanation of a man who was animal and physical, and that there is within us a Being who is infinitely superior, which is the only answer by which one might truly explain all the *enigmas*.

Those same Mythologists show us at what price we can hope to attain that light when they tell us about that piece of gold that the Shades gave to Charon in order to pass the river.[107] Man can never gain access into the domains of peace until, during his stay here below, he has acquired enough intellectual wealth to win over and subdue those who defend the enclosures of light; and even then, during his physical and material existence, he cannot take a single step towards the truth which he doesn't pay for in advance, through desire and dedication, to the faithful guide who must lead him along that path.

Finally, the Mythologists remind us visibly, and in nature, of the presence of that guide to man, by showing us the palladium or statue of Minerva which came down from heaven with the aid of Abaris, when the Temple to that Goddess had been build in Troy. At the same time, they show us the confidence we must have in that supreme Gift, since, in the example of Troy and according to the oracle which had announced on what the preservation of that city depended, we would be forever safe, so long as we don't allow *enemies* to penetrate the *Temple* by *subterranean* paths, come to our Altar and remove our *palladium*.

All the allegories we have just seen are sufficient to convince us that by beginning with the first origins of temporal things, the Mythological Traditions present man with a host of images faithful to all the facts of the past, present and future which should be of interest to them: that there they can see the history of the material and immaterial Universe, indeed their own, that is, the image of his original splendor, his degradation, and the means that have been used to rehabilitate him in his rights.

As to those who wish to confine the traditions of Mythology to historical facts, and who only see heroes or famous characters in the ancient deities, we believe that they may be right on a few points; but they must also admit that most of those specific changes were made later on,

---

[107] In passing, it is interesting to note that Saint-Martin uses the phrase 'passer le fleuve'. Although this is a valid construction for the phrase 'to cross the river', there are many other words he could have used. *Passage du Fleuve*, or 'Crossing the River' is also a reference to an esoteric alphabet mentioned in Agrippa's *Third Book of Occult Philosophy*, in common use at the time when secret codes were all the rage. Saint-Martin never disappoints in his Masonic and esoteric references. An example of this alphabet may also be found at: www.omniglot.com/conscripts/ptr.htm (as of June, 2018).

and after the Mythological Traditions had already come into existence: so that we cannot avoid recognizing that the original Mythologies were hieroglyphic and symbolic; that is, that they contained most important truths for man, and so necessary that there is no way they would not have existed, either in Fable or in some of Tradition which would have outlined them to us.

We will end our review of those Traditions here, so as not to slow down our journey, and so as not to go into interpretations which, being too profound to be generally understood, would not all appear to have the same level of truth, in that they would not all present the same evidence, and which, because of that, could spread doubts and concerns about those which are much clearer.

But the observations we have just studied are limited to the Mythological traditions of the Greeks and Egyptians: the Theogony, Cosmogony and Religious Doctrines of all the Ancient Nations, having had but one Principle and one common goal across the entire human species, should show us the same images and the same truths. Indeed, open the Shastah of Gentoos, the Zend Avesta of the Parsis, the Edda of the Icelanders, Chongqing and the I-Ching of the Chinese: in a word, consult the Sacred Traditions of all the Nations of Earth, and we are not afraid to assert that you will easily recognize man in olden times, the present and the future, as well as a natural expression of his needs and his thoughts; for since man is a Being of all times and all places, everywhere he must have the same needs and the same ideas.

From among all those Traditions, let us take those of the Chinese as an example; for regardless of what their antiquity predisposes in their favor, they present the most striking connections with the fundamental truths which concern the Order of all visible and invisible things.

They talk of the fall of the first criminals, the formation of the Universe through the *Powers* of the Great Principle, of *a Life which had never had life given to It*. We see the origin of humankind, the state of man in innocence, enjoying the comforts of a delightful home, which was *watered by a fountain of immortality divided into four marvelous springs which was called the way of the Heavens, and from which life came.* Everything for him was in *perfect harmony: all the seasons were regulated, nothing could be disastrous nor give death; and this estate was called the Great Unity.*

They teach that an *immoderate desire for knowledge condemned the human kind; that after man's degradation of man, the animals, birds, insects and snakes began to want to make war with him, and that all creatures were his enemy*. We find there that, *once innocence had been lost, Mercy appeared.*

We even recognize the physical images of the paths of this wisdom in the famous Fou-xi or Fu-xi[108] whose fabulous birth is depicted in an extraordinary manner, and which is claimed as having established the cult, whose traces still exist in China. It is also claimed that he invented the *koua*[109], which are the hieroglyphic signs and the characters of the first writing of the Chinese, and which by their sense show connections with the Hebrew language, where the word *koua* also means: *he has said, he has indicated*, and these connections are all the more justified since the Hebrew language can, on more grounds than one, pass as the symbol of other languages.

Note that those Chinese *koua* were established on the arrangements and divisions of three basic lines, whose different dispositions indicated everything that the Master wished to teach to his disciples, that is to say, without exception, all that it is allowed for man to know, as the three constituent Elements of the Universe were sufficient for the Creator to multiply to infinity the images of His thoughts in the eyes of those that know how to read them.

Fu-xi made known also to this people the *Qi*, a word that is physically rendered as the *breath* of the *Almighty*, but of which are still found more expressive traces in Hebrew, by *ki* or *kai*, meaning the *living*, or the power and the virtual action of the Universal Principle which gives existence to all Beings.

According to the knowledge that *Fu-xi* is supposed to have transmitted to the Chinese, one should not be surprised to see him hold an elevated position in their Traditions, and that they wouldn't fear attributing to him the Creation of the Heaven and the Earth.

---

[108] It is easier to understand this passage if we remember Saint-Martin's original spelling, which is *Pho-hi*. As with many Chinese names, the orthography has changed over time (just as the 'Peking' of older readers' youth is now spelled 'Beijing').

[109] Saint-Martin may be referring to *Zhou*, the generic term for I Ching, or even the individual lines of the I Ching called *yao*. Either way, the terminology has changed since 1782, and we will preserve his term 'koua' here.

If you ask why I cite the Hebrew language as the symbol of other languages; I would say it is because the original language from which it is derived is no longer spoken generally in this common world[110]; that we cannot regard as primitive a physical language which was originally founded on the form, Laws, and the *sounds* and *actions* of all natural objects, whereas the language of thought was foreign to them: I would say it is because, in some dialects considered to be from the Hebrew language, Syriac or Arabic, be they Samaritan or Chaldean, it offered indications of all the Principles we have discussed; because its roots were almost always composed of three letters, reminding us of the three universal roots of all things; because all its roots were words, and don't appear to have been names other that those observed during the order and progression of the language under its most enlightened days; because it expressed all its roots by the third person to let us know at once those of the three Supreme Abilities which are closest to us; because it only used the past and future tenses, only being affected by temporal and apparent things and not by the present and real things: and finally because the *language* only began to become conventional and corrupted when it used the present tense, which isn't appropriate to uncertain and fleeting things, and which only belongs to the True and Fixed Being, whose action is always present, always what it has been, and always what it will be.

In bringing together the name *Fu-xi* to the Hebrew language, with which all the languages of the Earth have primitive connections, we could extend our ideas with respect to this famous Legislator, on which the Chinese scholars themselves are so focused, and whether he existed in reality or only in allegory.

The word *fu* isn't very different from the Hebrew word *phe*, which means *mouth*; the word *xi* is even closer to the Hebrew affix *i*, which, linked to its nominative, means *mine*. The word *Fu-xi*, interpreted in Hebrew, could therefore have connections with the expression the *mouth belonging to me*, or *my mouth*. I am simply stating a few connections, because those we are making are not direct and complete, and because Hebrew itself does not render the words *my mouth*, by *phe* which would seem to be the natural expression, but by the abbreviation *phi*.

---

[110] We must remember that in the 18th Century Hebrew was indeed considered a 'dead' language, spoken in corrupted forms by the Ashkenazic and Sefardic Jews, and in the Yiddish of the Germanic descendents. It wasn't until the middle of the 20th Century with the establishment of the new State of Israel, that a version of the original language was restored.

Lamed (ל) – Religions, Signs of the One Tradition   165

So whether *Fu-xi* was one of the Agents, or one of those subdivided *powers* which necessarily had to show themselves during man's dominion, or whether he was just an ordinary man, it is certain that, given the Traditions which attribute to him the creation of the Heaven and the Earth, given the sublime knowledge of which his Nation has recognized him to be the dispenser, given the very meaning which etymology leads us to discover in his name, it is certain, I am sure, that China received the most vibrant glimmers of light.

There can be no doubt regarding the natural Arts and Sciences, that the Chinese had very profound insight, when one sees the traces which remain, either in their astronomical monuments or in their musical system. The Art of Music is the simplest and the most powerful of all the temporal Arts, the only one that embraces in an active and physical way all the Laws of Beings, the only one among composite things which is subject to an equal and constant measure; since even the stars themselves, though having regular periods, still have a path whose progressions vary continuously by the common Law which has them each depend on one another.

Not only were the Chinese profound in their knowledge of Music, they also paid tribute to its sublimity by applying it specifically to religious worship, and the ceremonies by which they honored the Shades of their Ancestors. They even claimed that it was necessary for their musicians to be of pure morals and imbued with a love of wisdom in order to obtain regular sounds from their instruments.

Of their ancient and sublime knowledge, the Chinese no longer possess anything other than the monuments left to them. And what has taken place in all Nations has also happened to them, in that some have worshipped those monuments without understanding them, while others have despised them; or to state it more clearly, the Chinese Nation has directed all its thoughts towards morality and perhaps a wise administration, but their fruits don't rise above the politics of prosperity. Even its educated Orders, who believe they fulfill the function of protective Gods, have forgotten their original purpose and are buried in laborious research on the veracity of their known history, on their civil laws, on the Government, and principally on the literal and typographic understanding of their books.

Those famous *koua*, which they were told contained all knowledge, receive no more than a sterile respect from them; and no longer understanding their use, they replaced them with a frightening multitude of characters, which no doubt provide a physical expression of the signs and intellectual factors working on Earth; but today they are limited to representing visible things, as they no longer know how to apply them to Nature and the Laws of Beings; and from this point of view, these are just so many prisons which they build for their souls. So, it is man who in turning his eyes for an instant away from his Principle, ends up by corrupting everything, and comes to see as fictitious what he no longer has the intelligence and strength to see as reality.

For that reason we cannot by too prudent and discerning when we consider those allegorical Traditions, both Mythological and Theological, of the Chinese and of all the Nations of Earth, seeing that through ignorance and haste, they all have confused and confounded most of their original Traditions, either with their civil and political history, or with their laws and conventional customs, or even with the monstrous ideas of coarse and unbridled imagination which have completely perverted many of these Traditions.

It is therefore through a profound observation of oneself, and all the Laws of Beings, that a clear confirmation of what we have said above may be found in the greatest number of these stories; and that it was necessary for the Divine Powers to manifest themselves so that degenerate man could regenerate in their image, and that he might manifest in his turn the greatness of the Pattern Who had tasked him to be His sign, and to bear His character in the Universe. With this active and vigilant precaution, we will easily recognize that the Supreme Power could initially only show Himself to man as a sort of subdivision of Himself; yet since they were made for Unity, that subdivision would keep them in inevitable suffering, and should make them feel the rigor of the Divine decrees by the severity of the Law that accompanies them, which is indicated in the Traditions and allegories of all Nations in stories of violence, fury, and the most rigorous justice.

But I can offer the reader one more thread to lead him through this labyrinth; and that is to warn him that since the same allegory contains the truths of several Orders, he should follow those truths according to their natural progression. He should first seek in the allegory that sense which is closest to the letter as being the most understandable and the closest within reach, then raise himself up to the meaning which immediately succeeds this; and by this careful and prudent path he will come to the most sublime knowledge which a Tradition can contain. If he ignores this order; if he omits any part of this progression and wishes to seek an explanation of the extremes too soon, he will only find confusion, darkness and contradiction there, for in neglecting the intermediate steps, he will have deprived himself of the only means that would make these subjects intelligible.

Let us now turn to the traditions of the Hebrews.

Mem (מ) - From Genesis to the Flood

Whatever profit there may be in the discoveries one can make in the Books of the Hebrews, they shouldn't be used as demonstrative proofs of truths concerning the nature of man and his correspondence with his Creator, for these truths subsist by themselves, and the witness of Books can never serve except as a confirmation of this.

Besides, the Books of the Hebrews, given their length and the abundance of language in which they were written, claim such a large number of interpretations that they are like a battlefield on which each side, each sect, finds something to be attacked and something to be defended.

This is why those who, with no assistance but common knowledge, pleading for or against the sanctity of those Books, cannot convince one side or the other because they don't base their opinions on a natural foundation common to them all, so that all their objections appear insoluble to both sides.

If the principles put forward up to now are not based upon a solid foundation, they do little for the advancement of knowledge, since quoting those Books – whose sanctity has not generally been established – as their foundation, still leaves doubts about the authenticity required to guarantee the truth of their arguments. But having established those principles on unshakable foundations, I believe I have the authority to use all that can be drawn out of them or to confirm their certainty; and the Hebrew Books appear to be useful to accomplish this purpose.

The Hebrew Traditions, as much histories as allegories, offer us the same truths as those of other Nations. They also tell us about man's degradation, the efforts he must undertake to erase his ignominy, and the assistance which the Supreme Order unceasingly offers him to accelerate his return to the light.

There we find the same indications of the correspondences between man and Divinity, and between the Earth and all the Superior Powers. In them we also find the same subdivisions of these Powers in relation to man. Everything in them is equally vengeance and strictness; everything shows only the severity of a Justice which never relinquishes its rights.

And so, although those Traditions only offer us physical and corporeal things, although they only show terrestrial powers to some degree, and only appear to offer as hope fleeting blessings and temporary recompense, we should believe that they have the same purpose, and contain the same doctrine as Mythological Traditions.[111]

Nowadays, we may think with some basis that we have discovered striking correspondences between many characters in Egyptian Mythology and the Hebrew Traditions, where the former consequently appear to be the original source of those stories. And if we have perceived the story of man in those original Mythological Traditions, this is all the more reason for us to recognize it in those events which appear to have been the pattern and source of the most famous of those Traditions.

Besides, in the Hebrew texts we can see facts joined to dogma and *action* to doctrine, whereas in all other Traditions, these two things are almost always separate. Egyptian and Greek Mythological Traditions only contain events, and precious little doctrine. The Theological Books of the Parsees, the Chinese and all Nations who, on the other hand, are all distanced from their original source, contain more doctrines than facts, since all those Nations have neglected the true knowledge of man, which must make them stray from their *history*, when it does not rule them through morals, and only leads them to moralize when they don't know how to *act*.

Mohammed, who was born and lived among the descendants of the Hebrews, imitated their Books in the same manner. In the *Koran*, doctrine and historical facts appear alternately, and though that Book, which does contain a few flashes of illumination, is nothing but a shapeless collection

---

[111] It is interesting to note that, while many had taken the biblical stories literally throughout history, it was predominantly the Protestant branches which rejected the 'modernist' biblical studies being undertaken in the 19th Century, though it was not until the end of the 19th Century that a specific movement coined the term 'fundamentalism' and insisted upon an adherence to certain statements as essential to belief, including a literal interpretation of the Bible. This was a movement specifically confined to the United States at the time. Gallup undertook a survey in the United States in 2017 and found that 38% of adults believed that "God created humans in their present form at one time within the last 10,000 years", which was apparently down from the prior survey. As an example of just how different belief in the United States is from Europe on such subjects, a Gallup poll in 2012 discovered that around 80% of British, Swedish, German, French and Italian adults agreed with the statement: "Human beings, as we know them, developed from earlier species of animals"; while only 40% of American adults agreed with the statement. This absence of a formal sense of Fundamentalism in the 18th Century would perhaps explain Saint-Martin's interesting claim that the Hebrew Scriptures don't provide "demonstrative proofs of truths concerning the nature of man and his correspondence with his Creator."

of stories, and though it does not lead men to their true nature and debases the means by which the Supreme Wisdom prepares their regeneration, there remains enough to recognize it as a natural child of the natural child of Judaism.[112]

Indeed, it is through its emanation from Judaism that it shows us more clearly its illegitimacy, because things which are true and which lead towards a real goal are perfected over time, rather than deteriorating; and the more they advance in years, the more they must show forth their beauty, their grandeur and their simplicity: in other words, the correspondence with the pure and living Laws of the original type, which all Beings are charged with manifesting in their Order.

Although Mohammedanism presents itself in this manner and claims that it is more perfect than Ismailism and Judaism, it is infinitely beneath both of them. It possesses neither the *divine knowledge* of the Hebrews nor the *natural knowledge* of Ismail[113]; and being distanced from *power* and intelligence, it is unable to offer anything other than the Law of the sword and the reign of the senses.

If the Books of the Hebrews, despite their obscure expressions and the singularity or even atrocity of the majority of their narratives, tell us of other rights and powers; if they unite events to those dogmas closest to our Being and most appropriate to remind us of the *Powers* of our Principle; if they present us with the most expressive images of what man seeks and what he may obtain; and lastly, if those Books don't contain a single material *talking idol,* and only contain living animals, men or superior Beings, we should give them a distinguished rank among all the Traditional Books which are known to us.

---

[112] When this book was published in 1782, the prevailing Western view was that Christian and Jews were People of the Book, while Moslems were part of the same family but somehow lesser. This was a view created by centuries of Catholic propaganda, and indeed extended to all other religions, seen as being outside of the perfection of Christian salvation. Therefore, this section should be read in that historical context.

[113] Wikipedia says of Ismailism: "After the death of Muhammad ibn Isma'il in the 8th century CE, the teachings of Ismailism further transformed into the belief system as it is known today, with an explicit concentration on the deeper, esoteric meaning of the Islamic religion." (https://en.wikipedia.org/wiki/Isma%27ilism). This would certainly explain why Saint-Martin found this path of Islam of greater interest to him.

The name *Hebrew (Ghibri)*[114] does not indicate the true type of present day man; it signifies *passing* or *passenger*, to indicate to man that he is a sojourner on Earth.

In these Books one finds clear correspondences with the most profound truths, both intellectual and physical.

Universal creations are represented as being the fruit of those invisible abilities which precede any action. The word *Resh*[115], which signifies Creator, head, or the duration of thought, can also signify thought itself; *Be<u>r</u>eshit*,[116] which is the first word of the Hebrew text, can therefore be denoted equally well by these words: 'In thought', as by the words: 'In the beginning', which makes it an action in time. Thus, without rejecting this version: 'In the beginning God created, etc', one may read it intelligently as: 'In thought God created, etc.', and through that we discover another truth.

Universal creations are represented as being the fruit of many Agents, through the singular expression *Bara Elohim*, 'the Gods created': a vivid image of the truth of the original events, in which one sees both a single thing, and six Agents cooperating to produce it, from the fact that the word *Elohim* contains six distinct letters in its pronunciation, which is also the number of its characters in the Greek version by Sanchoniaton, although it has five letters in Hebrew.[117]

So, it is a weak and false notion to fear setting limits to the omnipotence of the Universal Source of life, since we can recognize in Him those Secondary Agents which operate perishable actions for Him and who perform those actions for the duration prescribed to them; for that power sheds light on so much more, by directing results which are

---

[114] The Hebrew word עברי ('Ibri) comes from אבר (Abar) which means to pass by, or nomad. The page in Abarim Publications on this word is fascinating. It tells us that the root עבר ('Ibar) also refers to the idea of passing over water or a river (remember the *Passing the River* alphabet, which was discussed earlier). It can also mean passing over a river to dry land, as in the use of river symbolism to denote the passage from one state of consciousness to another. Indeed, it does not take much of a leap to see the connection with the name Abram/Abraham. For a more in-depth discussion of this fascinating word, see: http://www.abarim-publications.com/Meaning/Hebrew.html#.Wy0c2_ZFyfM.

[115] Also, the Hebrew letter 'Resh' (ר).

[116] Underlining is the Translator's, to show the root 'Resh' in the middle of the word.

[117] In Hebrew the word Elohim is spelled לּהים. Incidentally, the direct transliteration of these letters can result in a word sounding like 'Al-Cheem' (the 'ch' guttural as in the Scottish word 'loch'), which is rather like *alchemy*: another theory for the origin of that word!

executed punctually, and those concern those works which His Grandeur and Sublime Simplicity did not allow to be executed by Himself.[118]

Those who would ridicule the extraordinary expression: 'the Gods created', only show that they have little understanding of natural truths.

They have affected to translate the word *Bara*, by 'He made', which can also mean: 'He produced', 'He created'. Let us not fall into the same error. That expression: 'He made', suggests a coeternity of matter with God, Who would have had no other task than that of modifying it; whereas that coeternity was only referring to the non-material Principle of matter.[119]

In those Books, immaterial creations are referred to as serving as the basis and seat for the Spirit of God which, according to common translations, *was carried upon the Waters*, or upon the primitive and invisible seed[120] of the Universe, just as we now know that in the order of the corporeal Universe water is the primitive seed of material forms.

Instead of the *Spirit of God*, those translations should have said the *fructifying action of those Agents*, the *Elohim*, charged with the production of the Great Work; for in Hebrew proper nouns are real and essentially constitutive. Now the word *Ruach*, which is translated as 'Spirit', is absolutely not of that elevated Order: it merely signifies 'breath', or 'expiration'; so when it is applied to superior emanations and actions, it can perhaps only be by analogy to the breath of the wind, or to the expiration of animals which, in their respective Orders, are a kind of emanation; but in neither example would this sort of emanation bear the name of the individual Being who is its Initiator, and there would be nothing to be gained in confusing the action with its Agent if one wished to proceed correctly.

Now let us bring together the three images contained in those three words *Bereshit*, *Elohim*, and *Ruach*. The first gives us the Supreme Thought conceiving the creation of the Universe; the second, the number

---

[118] This suggests that Saint-Martin believed that God, being omnipresent and eternal, could not create something limited and temporal by His own act, and therefore had recourse to six lower Agents to create the Earth and Universe for Him. This idea is straight out of Pasqually's *Treatise*.

[119] The French word *faire* can be translated as 'to make' and 'to do', which perhaps gives a sense of the broadness of this verb in French. For example, *faire le menage* means 'to do the housework'; while *faire la cuisine* means 'to cook'. The point, as Saint-Martin says, is that the word *faire* is not used for a purely creative act, but rather an action which modifies something which exists. This reinforces the point made in Footnote 118 above.

[120] Or 'origin'.

of Agents, or the active plan for its execution; the third gives us the means that this action is realized. We recognize in those three Agents a natural correspondence to the three intellectual abilities whose existence in man I have previously demonstrated.[121]

As for the perceptible development of these Universal creations, we see in those Books that it is operated through a means similar to that which man uses to execute his will, since if he does not *speak* – in whatever manner that might be achieved – to those whom he wants to act, his desire will remain null and without effect.

Finally, those Universal creations are represented as separating the inferior *Waters* from the superior *Waters*, darkness from light: and consequently, this is the purpose of their existence, for this is their Law. Even today the least vegetation can neither acquire nor maintain life unless it occupies a place between the shadowy abode of its creation and the region from which elemental lights shines down. This is the physical image of a more important separation which was operated at the beginning of the Universe, which is repeated in prevaricating man and in all of his posterity and which, in order to come to an end, expects nothing less than the coming together and joining together of all that has received existence.

This important fact is also indicated in the word *Aretz*, 'Earth', which signifies both Realm and Universe, for it derives from the word *Ratzatz*, or 'he has broken'[122], 'he has compressed', 'he has crushed'. And if one mistrusts this idea, note that the word *Aretz* has preserved in the majority of our modern languages a similarity which is evident in its root, as much in for the meaning. The Germans call the Earth *Erd*, the English *Earth*[123], the Latin by inversion *Terra*, from whence the French *Terre*, *arrêter*, *hart*.[124] All are expressions in which the original sense is easy to recognize, and this is why Earth is called the theater of expiation.

---

[121] That is, Thought, Will and Action.
[122] This first word hardly seems similar to the other two, but the phrase in French, '*il a brisé*' means precisely that, a word used in the Bible to suggest an act like crushing skulls: and soil is after all a crushed composite of the three Kingdoms, containing organic (animal and vegetable) and mineral (rock) matter.
[123] Oddly, Saint-Martin actually says: "l'Anglais, *heartz*." The Translator can find no origin for the word 'heartz' in Old or Middle English and has no idea from where he obtained the word.
[124] *Arrêter* means to stop (as in 'arrest' in English); *hart* could be seen as a further reduction of the word '*arrêter*' and means rope or halter. This is an interesting etymology, further supporting the idea that we're all 'bound' or 'arrested' in mud or earth.

The Laws of Physics are expounded in those Books with complete accuracy, and the senary [125] division, which the Author symbolically presents as *Days* in the work of Creation of temporal things, conforms with Nature. That Law is manifested in the relationship between the radius with the circumference, by which the Author wished to teach us that it was a number of six united actions which resulted in the material corporization of the Universe; that this number of six actions must consequently direct all material things as it directed their Creation; that this should be understood not only with regard to Universal and individual bodies, but even to the length of time they were given for the duration of their existence. [126]

Independent of the metaphysical relationship between the radius and the circumference, these truths are represented at the celestial level, where six planetary bodies act and move beneath the eye of a seventh star which is their chief and ruler.

They are found materially in the six simple mechanical Forces, which provide the mobility fundamental to all movements of the body.

They are found temporally and intellectually in Music, which cannot have regular movement unless its movement is senary since, although we can only auditorily perceive the fifth between the dominant and the tonic, it is no less true that this fifth contains two distinct thirds. [127]

Finally, they are found corporeally in the six white lymphatic corpuscles which, according to Physiologists, constitute each red corpuscle in our body. [128]

The people of the Orient, from whom all knowledge of the Universe has been communicated, offer us facts which apply the principle which we are advancing: in all their measures of time, in all their periods, they count by the number six, or by its multiple, and the famous period of six hundred years, known to all these early Nations in antiquity, is a most important period which Astronomers have subsequently discovered has been used in various places across the Earth.

---

[125] That is, into six.

[126] Those familiar with the Martinist Pantacle will find much to think about in this paragraph, which clearly affected Papus as he (re)constituted the Order in the 1890s (and see Appendix I).

[127] A slighty suspect argument in that the median note is counted twice. If one considers the notes C, D, E, F and G. If C and E are played one hears a third. If E and G are played one hears a third. If C and G are played one hears a fifth., However, Saint-Martin argues that, since the interval from C to G contains two thirds, then $2 \times 3 = 6$.

[128] A curious insight from 18th Century Physiology.

Finally, the people of America believed that the Universe had been created by six men who, before there was an Earth, were carried in the air at the whim of the winds. From this we may infer that those precise correspondences, known to Nations which were so far apart and so different from one another, would not have been discovered if in following the senary division of the circumference by the radius, they had not found the true and natural measure of created things. We can similarly conclude that the Hebrew Author[129] has not communicated anything fictitious to us in representing the Creation of the Universe by the Laws of this same number.

This number of six days, which is perhaps only symbolic, since God acting *at the summit of the angle* is unaffected by time; since our temporal days are only formed by the revolutions of the Sun; and since, according to the same Author, the Sun was only created on the fourth day; that number, I suggest, shows by its division into two ternaries the Law of Action and Reaction necessary for the existence and production of corporeal Being, and it is that number which is observed by the Hebrew Author.[130]

For it represents the Earth and all that belongs to it as the first ternary, since it was on the third day that all things were formed, and it represents the stars and everything which isn't essential to the Earth, as the second ternary dominates and acts upon the first.

It is only in the second ternary that all Beings having life have birth, and it isn't unimportant to note that the Sun and the Earth fulfilled functions similar to those which we see them perform today, since it was through the heat of this Sun acting on the fourth day on the Earth (itself

---

[129] As an aside, until the 1600s it was still generally believed that the Pentateuch was written by Moses. From then, the belief moved to the idea that the Old Testament had been written down much later, during the Babylonian Captivity, by one or a small group of Scribes preserving an oral tradition in danger of being lost. However, by the late 19th Century most biblical scholars have believed the Books to be an amalgam of writings by four authors of various Rabbinical schools, usually referred to as the Jahwist, the Elohist, the Deuteronomist and the Priestly sources, identifying four separate styles within the Books. However, it is not easy to tell whether Saint-Martin was referring to Moses or to Ezra when he wrote of the 'Hebrew Author'.

[130] Here we have another piece of the puzzle which comprises the Martinist Pantacle. The circle contains the hexagram denoting the six days of creation, and now the six-pointed star reflects the evolutionary and involutionary forces (see Appendix I).

formed on the third day) that all animals received life; a Law repeated in the reproduction of all species, through the joining of male and female.[131]

Here we part company with Physics.[132] We present the Creation of the Universe as being performed without time, yet the terrestrial globe offers apparent indications of a slow and successive formation. We present the birth of the Universe as a single event, yet the surface of the Earth is covered with a number of substances which seem to have been created and consolidated only after many Centuries. Finally, the chronology of the Hebrew Books gives the world a middling antiquity, compared to that which observations of Nature appears to attribute to it. We need to examine these difficulties.

The Observers of Nature teach that a very extreme heat accompanied the origin of things, and that the Universe was uninhabitable for a long time following the moment of its birth.

We would ask them firstly if their minds were not repulsed by such retarded progress, by this hiatus in the acts of an Almighty Hand Which, by His nature, would not wait for an instant without acting; we would also ask them what purpose, what object was being met by this interval which they would like to claim between the origin of things and their creation; what function they supposed for a world without inhabitants – for the picture these people paint is one in which the work of such a Creator is without purpose and reason, a Being devoid of wisdom: and it would abuse reason itself to use such an image to introduce such a Being.

They only put forward these theories after relying on secondary facts which they saw before them, such as the present-day reproduction of various Beings which can only occur in the intervals of time proportional to their species, and in the various sediments and mineral deposits which have only accumulated after a long period of time.

---

[131] Since an increasing number of people are unfamiliar with the Old Testament, in summary: Day 1 – Light separated from Darkness; Day 2 – Creation of the Sky/Heavens; Day 3 – Creation of Earth; Day 4 – Creation of Sun, Moon, stars and planets; Day 5 – Creation of life in the sea and the air; Day 6 – Creation of life on earth, and finally Man. Day 7 is the day of rest, the still Point in the center of the Circle.

[132] The following section is a very pre-Darwinian justification for reconciling biblical narrative with proto-evolutionary theory and provides a fascinating insight into the mind of a well-read European at that time. Anyone who has read Immanuel Velikovksy (*Worlds In Collision*; *Earth In Upheaval*; *Ages In Chaos*) will especially appreciate Saint-Martin's theories as an early pointer to some of Velikovsky's writings: if he had never read Saint-Martin, he should have!

These comparisons have led them astray: they have not distinguished between primary and secondary facts, the inferior and passive outputs of primordial productions given off by the act of living.

It is a certain Law that the more Beings approach the Original Principle, the more powerful their generative force becomes, and this Power manifests itself not only in the quality of their creation but also in the speed with which it is generated, because the Original Principle is independent of time, and Beings cannot rise up towards Him without rejoicing, according to their measure and number, in His *rights* and *Powers*. And if we wish to find proof of this in man himself, we can compare the slowness of his physical, corporeal movements to the promptness of his intellectual Being, which knows neither time nor space, and which can transport itself instantly in thought to the most distant places.

Now, without leaving the Physical Order, we note that the slower the growth of a Being is, the larger the seed which produces it. This is why the seeds of all specific Beings in Nature are corporeal and visible, seeing that their creations only form over a period of time. But general Creation is the fruit of a Principle and a seed which is not corporeal but invisible, like the interior motivation which directs us in all our actions, and this general Creation must be born outside of time.

Therefore, we won't deny that those Principles which are the product of the material Earth and Universe are superior to those terrestrial Principles which have engendered the animals and plants. Moreover, animals and plants must originally have had a power, a life superior to that which they now enjoy, since nature changes like all corruptible things. As a result, present day animals and vegetables could be regarded as secondary fruits relative to the originals and those which the *original* Earth had created by means of the immense heat of its Central Fire, just as these latter are secondary in relation to the invisible and superior sources which constituted universal Nature.

In the present day Material Order, we can only find proofs of this truth with difficulty. Everything being secondary, the difference between the reproductions and their Principle, though certain, are too imperceptible to find a place in rigorous demonstration, and besides, when these reproductions come to their final term, they revert to the opposite condition of their original creation, because the circle must be closed. It is for this reason that the caterpillar[133], after falling into the state of a chrysalis, bursts forth in the glory of the butterfly, which gives rise to a new caterpillar; and it is for that reason that all mortals, engulfed in the somber horrors of Earth, come closest to the pure rays of light when they wander over its surface.

But if we don't currently have any clear and visible evidence of the difference between the first and second Principles, at least we have them in analogy. A first example is the many experiments undertaken by those who, knowing how to release to a greater or lesser extent the *Principle of Fire*, work on material vegetation in a shorter time than that employed by Nature to produce them. Another is the precocious nubility of animals which inhabit climates nearer to the Equator; and finally, the changes which Nature shows as it becomes more distanced from the time of its Creation, since by the enormous bones and petrified vegetation which remain from those ancient times, it is clear that the first creations must have been much stronger and vigorous than those of our times; and that similarly through the diminution of Nature, more species, both aquatic or terrestrial, have been lost.[134]

If it is clear that the secondary Principles are inferior to the primary Principles in all species, why compare them? Why would we want to make such unequal Agents appear to be the same: and are those who make statements based on such theories not exposing themselves to false conclusions?

The slowness of the daily creations of Nature would accordingly have done nothing contrary to the action of the Agents which directed the origin of things and all the primordial creations.

When the Observers want to consider the origin of those calcareous sediments they see over the whole surface of the Earth, they realize that they offer two problems: one concerning their enormous number, and the other to the time necessary to make them permanent and convert them into stone.

So, is the same doctrine of that Great Central Fire sufficient to answer these questions without having recourse to explanations which run

---

[133] Saint-Martin used the French word for worm (*ver*), and it is hard to tell whether he is making a metaphorical point, or more likely, that he is ignorant of Biology. After all, in his first book published in 1775 we saw him citing examples of *spontaneous generation*.
[134] The next few paragraphs give a fascinating insight into the views of the 18th Century on such subjects as the Earth's creation, geological formations and the existence of fossils.

contrary to the natural idea which we have of the activity of the Great Being, and which cannot be recognized as right, because they only offer activity devoid of reason or purpose?

Without doubt the Central Fire was greater in the past than it is today, but it is not necessary to believe that it was so to the point of rendering the Earth uninhabitable, which would contradict the wisdom of Nature and the object of its existence. It only requires the Earth to have been hot enough to give sudden birth to the original creations which, in their turn, could give birth to numerous secondary creations in a shorter time than is required today for the same things.

It is that Fire which enabled the rapid concentration of minerals, the vitrification of granites, sandstone, jasper, porphyry, living rock[135] and quartz; that is, gave rise to all the vitrification which compose the tops of the mountains and the majority of rocks. It is that Fire which also calcinated that multitude of shells with equal rapidity, from which marbles, fluorspars, chalks, stalactites and all creations which can be transformed into limestone resulted. It is that same Fire which would have been able to layer together those clay soils and calcareous earths, and those enormous banks of complete and perfectly preserved shells which are to be found in many places of the Earth.

Moreover, one must also accept the action of Water in those great events. Everything tells us that it acted with just as much potency as the Fire, for even nowadays it makes basalt and lava solid, as well as dissolving both metallic and calcareous vitrifiable matter: like Fire it divides as much as it consolidates and vitrifies. Finally, if the action of Fire still shows us that it can take things apart before our eyes by showing us volcanoes in the middle of the oceans, the action of Water is no less powerful.

If we are certain that Fire acted in those First Times – when there was an explosion of creations – with infinitely more action than it does nowadays, and that the diminution in Fire is the cause of the present-day sterility of the poles and the loss of many species of animals, we must hold the same belief for Water, since we see it noticeably diminished on

---

[135] *'roc vif'*: this has a specific meaning, but other than the fact that it is sometimes listed along with granite and sandstone as an example of metamorphic rock, the Translator was unable to find a precise translation. It is also worth pointing out that Saint-Martin wants the Central Fire to be lukewarm enough to accelerate the development of animals and plants, while being hot enough to create precious stones, volcanic and metamorphic rock!

the earth, and we also have evidence that many species of aquatic animals were destroyed.

Finally, the Earth itself had its own work to fulfill in those First Times, and that work also had far more intensity than it has today: for if Fire is the beginning and the end of the Elements, and if Water is the beginning and the end of corporealization, then Earth is the beginning and the end of form.

The *powers* of those Elements are thus balanced, the one by the other, and it is when they cease to be in equilibrium that the Universe will cease to exist.

Let us say in passing, that Fire being the beginning and end of the Elements, everything suggests that Fire will end the existence of the Universe, just as it began it; and here we see the passage of this Agent, both creator and destroyer. Since its origin the Earth has been sinking towards its Central Fire in order to reunite with it; the heavens with their planets follows it to reunite with it. We see little of it in the physical, since the atmosphere is carried along with everything else, but the more those masses approach the Central Fire the more the Water disappears; and finally, there will remain nothing but a mass of salt. Then the igneous Principles enclosed in this mass of salt, working on themselves, will cause it to catch fire, and will go through it in order to rejoin their fiery origin.

If the power of Water and that of Earth was greater in earlier times than it is today, we have in them another means of explaining ancient and prodigious terrestrial phenomena, as well as famous catastrophes of Nature, without needing a fourth Agent which is even more active than Fire, Water and Earth, and about which we will have cause to talk in a moment when we take a look at the origin of those catastrophes.

Finally, if we wish to reflect on those sudden consolidations which earthly substances undergo each day by means of the power of the Waters of some springs, or even through the manipulations of Engineers who know how to direct the forces of Nature, we will no longer be surprised that the original Elements could bring about the same results; and it would be pointless to lengthen the age and time of the Earth's origin – as many have done – in order to clarify the difficulties presented to us, .

The Hebrew Books tell us of a seventh day, or the Sabbath, which ended the work of Creation. This word *Sabbath*, which has been translated as *Rest*, is simply saying that the number of the Universe was completed; and it doesn't really indicate a cessation or an absence of activity by the

Divinity, for it is written that He *blessed* this same day; and this signifies that, when the Universe came into existence, He joined *Superior Powers* with those which had formed it, since the latter were not *holy*.

If it doesn't abuse the privileges of etymological science, one might find in the Hebrew word *Shebet*, or *Sabath*, a sense of great sublimity. For in its root this word also signifies: 'He is seated', 'He is placed'. And that is to say that *on the seventh day, God placed Himself, came to inhabit, came to establish His seat in all His works*. These are sacred and worthy correspondences of the Universal action of the Great Being, but which cannot be presented in an open manner since they would be disputed according to the letter of the text, though they may be justified by the purest rays of wisdom.

It is no less true that on that seventh day, Supreme Wisdom presented man things nearer to His Being than from all the *senary powers*, for it is important to note that man received temporal birth after all the Beings in Creation, and that he was thus closest to those Holy *Septenary Powers* which consolidated existence within them.[136]

One also sees in the Hebrew Books the dignity of man, who alone among the Beings has the sublime dignity of being the creation of Divinity Himself and, according to the texts, *in God's image*, that is to say as being His expression and sign: living and active correspondences which the Translators have weakly expressed with these words: *in the image and likeness of God*, but which I explained at the beginning of this book, and which finds a happy confirmation here.

Here one sees this man set in a place of delights, near to *Life*[137] itself, from whence flowed *four rivers*, and receiving no interdiction other than that of approaching *knowledge of good and evil*, which existed with him in this enclosure, as it still lives with us today. One sees him established by the Author of All Things over all the works of His Hands, as overseer to command them and submit them to his control; and one can no longer doubt that man, even in his degradation, manifests that glorious Law,

---

[136] Remember that God, according to this theogony, did not create the Universe personally, but emanated six (i.e. senary) Agents or Powers to accomplish this. Man was placed last on Earth, although he was the greatest of all Beings, as Martinist ritual reminds us. Saint-Martin therefore suggests he was closest to the source, and nearest to the perfect septenary number (or seven). For him, the Seventh Day was not a day of rest, but rather an active day of completion, when God blessed His creation, bound it together and made it holy.

[137] A reference to the Tree of Life.

created exclusively for him alone since, despite his ignominy and weakness, he continues the work of subjugating all of Nature.[138]

But there one also sees man ignominiously stripped of that empire, today preserving only the most imperfect image of it, having made an alliance with illusion and error; for the Hebrew word נחש, *Nahash*, from which is taken the word for serpent, signifies *spell, enchantment*.

And that very serpent, that disproportionate animal, that Being without corporeal armor, without scales[139], without feathers, without hair, without feet, without hands, without fins, having all its power in its mouth, a power which is but venom, death and corruption; that serpent, I say, carries with it the physical signs analogous to seduction to which man's thoughts are susceptible, since that animal alone, among all others, has the ability to form a perfect circle with its body, and through that to show us, under a regular appearance, the shape and the basis of all sensual and created objects – that is, to focus our eyes on matter and illusion. Finally, by forming an empty circle in which we can see no central point, it has the ability to make us lose sight of the Simple Principle from which all things come, and without which nothing would exist. So it is not surprising that we find such an antipathy between man and the serpent, since man, on the contrary, retains the center *through the proportion of his form, whereas with its form the serpent only shows the circumference or nothingness. Please don't take this to be merely a play with the imagination: important truths are contained within those correspondences. It is there that we may find the means to instruct ourselves in the* metaphysical relationships *which formerly existed between man, woman and the serpent; and which materially manifest themselves between them today, in all the regularity of the numbers.*

In these Books we see the grievous punishments attached to the criminal error of mankind. In seeking the light in another Principle than that which alone possessed him, he lost sight of the least of His rays, like all those who, since then, have sought their education and knowledge elsewhere than in the immaterial Principles of all Orders, and have become strangers to understanding. It is that *nudity* which made man

---

[138] At the time the book was written, controlling and subjugating Nature was seen to be a *good* thing.

[139] This is an odd description to use for a serpent, but the phrase used here, *sans écailles*, means exactly that.

blush after his crime, and which keeps all his posterity in the same shame, until he shall have recovered his original *clothing.*

For the nudity which the Hebrew Books attribute to him before his crime and which it is said caused him no embarrassment, presents us with another truth. The word gharoum *(naked) comes from the Arabic root* ghoram, *which indicates a bone stripped of its flesh. Now,* bone *is the physical symbol of the word* strength *or* power, *since bone is the strength and support of the body. On another side, that word* bone *comes from the Latin word* ossum, *originally from the Hebrew root* ghatzam, *which means a* strength, *a* power. *And so, we find original man in a state of nudity, which tells us that he was an immaterial Being, a power, a force, a* strength *devoid of flesh, without a material body.*

In the same manner, it seems even more true that in the next passage man is described as not blushing at all because of that nudity, and indeed, since the embarrassment which inspires shame is only concerned with carnality, if man, being pure and enlightened, was not concerned by his nudity and felt neither shame nor any sense of modesty, it clearly proves that this was not meant in the carnal sense.

Nun (נ) – From the Flood to Moses

If the Hebrew Books teach about the horrible degradation of man, as confirmed by our present state, they explain even more clearly the various assistances offered to him for his regeneration and the need for which we have seen, founded upon the indissoluble link between the Divine Master and His image, and upon the love towards man which burns within Him, and which is the distillation of His essence and His *Powers*.

It is for that reason that in the midst of all the scourges[140] which followed the various prevarications[141] of man's posterity, and which Nature has experienced in its fundamental Principles, those Hebrew Books which have preserved such stories tell us of great *powers* successively set in motion to repair the disorders. There we read about the different periods, about virtuous Beings, some of whom could act on Water, others on Fire, and still others on Earth, and which repeated in those specific regenerations what had occurred at the time of the original regeneration, when before man's rehabilitation he had to reestablish his domain.

The first example which Hebrew Tradition offers us about those truths is the story of that ancient prevarication, in which entire Nations of the first times were depicted as having given themselves over to the empire of the material senses, to the extent of having perverted all *the ways of Nature*, and thus merited punishment by the element of Water. At the same time, it is a portrait of the means which the Supreme Wisdom then used to preserve a sanctuary on the Earth for the *powers* of just men, and those of all Beings of His Creation.

The more the general influence of man's crimes upon the Element of Water appears astonishing, the more one is compelled to admit that it is only the greatness of his Being which could resolve this problem. His sublime origin is a true witness of the extent of those rights: for just as one cannot put an end to his powers, nor in consequence the fruits which

---

[140] This can also be translated as 'plagues'. For consistency, the word 'scourge' has been used throughout, even when referring to the 'plagues of Egypt'.
[141] Or 'betrayal of trust'.

are their reward; so one cannot put an end to his prevarications, nor to the results which must naturally accompany them.

Just as man can exercise the sum of his legitimate rights and receive from all Nature the homage due to a sovereign, so he can show the signs of a traitor, a rebel and attract upon himself the severity of all the Powers which he had wished to usurp.

But one shouldn't dwell exclusively on the carnal crimes of the first posterity of man if one wishes to discover the true reason for the Flood. There is too great a discrepancy between the influence of that kind of excess on the dissolution of the body, and that destructive phenomenon which the Author describes being produced by the concurrence of all of Nature. The corporeal decay of the individual who abandons himself to those excesses, being his natural punishment, is found by Superior Justice to be adequate without needing to extend the activities of the original Universal Elements.[142]

One must therefore accept that those early descendants must have given themselves up to considerable aberration and powerful criminal acts in order to attract upon themselves such boundless and measureless scourges. If man's first crime subjected him to the Elements and plunged him into an immense realm of physical and confused activity[143], what error could he have committed, other than a similar crime, to expose himself once again to the fury of those Elements?

The only difference we should note is that original man, not yet being material at the time of his first crime, experienced the action of the same Elemental Principle, whereas in the prevarications of his descendants the Elements only acted on man through coarse action, since he himself was coarsely corporealized. Now, after all the physical ideas which have been presented in this writing, we should understand that the first appearance of the corporealization of coarse and physical things is Water.

This extraordinary scourge should not be seen as impossible, since it isn't impossible for man to expose himself to it; and if men have within them the right to be able to provoke justice in different ways, that justice

---

[142] Saint-Martin is claiming that carnal excess draws its own debilitating punishment, which no doubt refers to syphilis and other venereal diseases which were incurable in his time and points out that we must look to other reasons for the Flood. This would suggest that, although we know him as something of a ladies' man, it is highly unlikely that he took advantage of any of his enthusiastic female disciples!
[143] This is another reference which Papus used to good effect in his rituals.

must always be ready to bring the kind of punishment appropriate to their type of crime down upon them, for the possibility of crime must be not above the possibility of punishment, without which truth would be in peril.

We note, still taking the physical body as a guide, that in human individuals the greatest excitement of the senses is felt during the first third of life, and it follows that the same period would hold for man in general; and that the intellectual crimes which must have accompanied those errors and attracted the great catastrophes, must by analogy have the same date; from which we can, with care, obtain some clarity on the age of the World and the period of the Flood.

The Observers have attacked the reality of this Flood in vain, arguing – according to their calculations – of the impossibility of a volume of water sufficient to cover the whole surface of the Earth and high enough to cover the highest mountains. These objections are based only upon the lack of understanding of the Translators, and upon errors which Philosophical systems have spread concerning the nature of Matter, by recognizing no other Principles than Matter itself.

In fact, although the Hebrew word ארבת *aroubboth* signifies *cataracts* according to the letter, is it not, according to the same interpreters, a derivative of the word רבב *rabab*, or רבר *rabar*, which means *it has been multiplied*? So the text gives us a clear image of a more extensive action by the Agent which produces Water, and not Water which had previously existed simply flowing around, because then there would only be a union or coming together, and we would not see the action of a living Being who creates and multiplies.

According to this principle, we cannot contest the possibility of great revolutions in Nature, the excess of one Element over another, and in consequence Universal scourges which can fall upon Regions, Nations, and the entire Earth.

For then we would have to deny the existence of the world itself, since it is the visible result of the living and combined action of the Elements which strive against each other, and in succession overwhelm each another within Earth's boundaries, each manifesting to the other the life and Laws which they have received from the Supreme Powers.

Those Observers have also contested the existence of the famous Ark, built by order of the Supreme One to preserve an offshoot of the human race. Whatever this Ark was, since it represented the Universe, like the

Universe, it had to enclose – either in nature or in *Principles* – all the Agents and all the powers which comprise it; and if these things appear inexplicable to the man who walks without his Law, they are not at all inexplicable to him who knows them, and who accepts the idea that he must have the greatness and the rights of his Being.

We would add that, like the *first vivifying seed* of all things, the Ark was carried upon the Waters; that similarly the Ark floated upon the chaos and terrestrial abyss to restore to him, at the prescribed time, the life of which he had been deprived; and like the *vivifying seed*, it contained a pure Agent, a living source of justice and sanctity, in which men coming into the world should still find traces of their original splendor.

Regarding the Ark, I cannot spare myself from telling the Observers to look at Chinese Traditions. They would see there that "the character used for *boat* or *vessel* is composed of the figure for *vessel*, the one for *mouth* and the number *eight*, which could make an allusion to the number of people who were in the Ark. One also finds the two characters *eight* and *mouth* with the one for *water* to express *successful voyage*." If this is by chance, it accords well with the facts.

Let us turn our gaze for a moment to those confused and diverse remains of the general inundation and universal destruction, whose signs are written on this terrestrial surface attesting to the certainty of that event. Regarding Physics, which I have already discussed with regard to the origin of the Universe, at that time I only covered the normal consequences which appear to have accompanied its birth. Here I will consider Physics in the context of those disorders.

In that general inundation which the Observers cannot deny, they only wish to see a physical event, isolated and independent of any connection it should have with the *Great Work* on which all the *powers* of Beings are employed. But if the immense plan which has been exposed in these Writings could broaden their ideas on man's nature and on his connection with all things visible and invisible, they will find fresh explanations in those very Hebrew Traditions where the Laws of things are faithfully drawn, because they set to work all resources and all Beings. There they will see that to end the Flood, independently of the activity and all the convulsing Elements, a *Superior Power* had to end the action of the Principle of Water, and that at the same time He sent a *wind* or an *active exhalation* which, stirring in every sense the Waters spread over the Earth, could control those enormous movements of terrestrial matter from one region to another and, in a very short time, make upheavals which would require an endless amount of time if they had only been the result of simple Elemental actions.

So, we should not be surprised that a combination of actions which were so opposed and so violent would result in physical effects which were so bizarre and inexplicable, when one of the Agents which should have contributed to their creation is suppressed. Let us accustom our eyes to understanding all the Principles, if we want to understand all the facts.

The famous epoch of the Flood was followed by another event when the posterity of man strayed, when the criminals strived to usurp the *Powers* of Heaven by terrestrial means which were both material and impure, concealed in the expression of that audacious edifice which, only being constructed with brick and having bitumen for cement, indicated both the impious folly of those who erected it and the lack of consistency of their work.[144]

The consequence of this crime was the famous confusion of tongues which divided the one People into many Nations. This is an image which again clearly explains as much obscurity and confusion in the knowledge of those Nations, as the variety in their physical and habitual languages: though it is true nevertheless that, having afterwards formed many scattered and separated groups, they would have then seen their common and original language altered by time to produce an innumerable multitude of other languages, almost completely different from one another.

That division of languages, perpetuated over all the surface of the Earth, repeats in a typical manner the present situation of man for whom, from the time of his Fall, the language of all the real *Beings* which surround him is intelligible; and who no longer knows the means to use in order to revive his communication with them and recover his original empire.

As a result, these two punishments being similar tells us that they are the fruit of the same crime, and that man finds himself today a stranger to the language of truth, because at the beginning he dared to speak another language than that of this truth; as his original posterity have never stopped realizing when they ceased to have the exclusive dominance of

---

[144] This is referring to the Tower of Babel.

the *First of All Beings* as their goal, and when they formed the idea to substitute Him with another *Principle*.

Here I am explaining a truth which will one day shed light on our origin and on the degradation of knowledge. Some have claimed that early men were in the most profound ignorance and reduced to reliance on the sole resources of their instincts: they have been painted in the colors which we give to savages, having nothing to fight but Nature, nothing to satisfy but their physical needs, and nothing to communicate among themselves than their physical thoughts; and they would have us believe that such was the foundation on which the different levels of the edifice of human knowledge were successively raised.

They are mistaken in using this argument to explain the expansion of man's knowledge. When, after his degradation, he was placed on the Earth, he came there with more light than perhaps was possessed by the whole of his posterity, although this light was inferior to that which he had enjoyed before his descent. He was like an offshoot of those General Elect used by the Divine Goodness for the reparation of his crime; he communicated to his descendants the illumination he still enjoyed; and it is here that we find the true heredity for which the first men were so eager, and of which men in the following Centuries only preserved an appearance through their material inheritance.

So, those early descendants allowed this heritage to change, as man himself had lost that which he enjoyed during his glory; and ignorance joining with iniquity could only grow until both being filled to overflowing, the scourges of justice reduced men to deeper shadows and to a total *dispersion*.

It is to this last epoch that one must transport oneself in order to find man languishing in uncertainty and misery and reduced to the sole resource of his instincts; it is in this epoch that one must seek the origin of regular languages, since all true knowledge had been lost to men and they had to use physical descriptions to signify their ideas. Finally, this was the origin of all the effort they were obliged to use, having abandoned the infallible motives which could still have led them over the Earth.

Their efforts, stimulated by need, soon led them by various means to discoveries and ideas, though imperfect, about those Universal motives which were so necessary to them, without which no Nation, no tribe, perhaps no individual can walk through life taking the same steps, or along the same paths.

This was how knowledge continued to grow among men, and one can follow the uninterrupted chain from this secondary epoch up to the present day. We can similarly be reassured that this body of knowledge will continue to develop more and more if we reflect on the innumerable means discovered to propagate it.

It has been so for the general species of man as well as for its individuals. There is nothing purer than the first rays of light which illuminate our Being, when it begins to become capable of receiving them. Soon those precious rays find themselves stopped, and often even obscured by stormy emotions which lead man to lose his memory of those first favors of wisdom, which he had tasted at the beginning of his infancy; but soon we also see him deliver himself from these shackles and rise up towards the *regions* of knowledge and reason, to walk in the immense *paths* of light and truth, which extend each day before his eyes, losing themselves in *infinity*.

It is as a result of that progressive growth that, in the middle of the prevarications and the dispersal of the ancient Nations, a Just One[145] was chosen from among the Chaldees to be the recipient of knowledge for the various natural Laws of our Being. This Just One was drawn from the town of אור Ur[146], which in Hebrew signifies light, to remind us of the emanation of original man and all his species, who was born in the bosom of Truth itself and which belongs and corresponds, by his nature, to the Universal center of *Life*.

This Just One was physically favored by three higher signs, or by the presence of three immaterial Agents who were corporealized in human form, even receiving hospitality from him. These signs, having allusion to the three *Supreme Virtues*, declared the sublime rank to which this man had been called; and this rank was to be the *father* of a posterity as numerous as the stars of Heaven and the dust of the Earth. That is, by penetrating the sense of this figurative expression, to receive all the *Superior Powers* of which man had been stripped, and to bring back the

---

[145] This was Abram, who later took the name Abraham.
[146] The English Bible translations tell us that Abram (Abraham) came from Ur, which is spelled in Hebrew as '*Aur*' or '*Our*', translated as 'light'. This should strike a chord with students of Kabbalah who will recognize '*Ain Soph Aur*' as the Source of the Sephirotic emanations. However, it, should be noted that the Papus edition of the book spells the word וי, (in fact יי to be completely accurate) or simply 'Ur'. However, most references give the city as 'Ur Kasidim', meaning Ur of the Chaldeans, where 'Ur' is always spelled אור ('Aur').

inferior Beings who had strayed. And finally, he was to be the the head and father of a People chosen from among all the Peoples of the Earth, destined to be the object of the Divinity's favors, and to serve as a beacon for all Nations. This idea shows us this choice of a People as being necessary, so that man might have before him, and in his own species, the living representative of that which he had been himself.

To fulfill this glorious task, that was the order which he received before taking possession of the Earth which had been promised to him. He was advised to traverse both *latitude and longitude* [147]; a new indication of the quaternary superiority of man, and of those two diameters of which we have already spoken.

If one sees that privileged man commit adultery which not only goes unpunished but is even authorized, seeing that it did not stand in the way of his appointment, and also noting that adultery was later considered so great a crime among the Hebrews, it is because the Law had still not yet been published; it is because the *Great Work* had not yet, so to speak, been started and because men still did not understand their *powers* other than through carnal generation, not yet being brought into regular order by a *superior and luminous Law*; and such is the power of the physical Laws to which man is subject, that the more they approach him the more his true nature returns to silence, so that only these physical Laws hold sway.

That is why, at the beginning, he was allowed to marry his own sister, though later on men weren't permitted to marry except at the *fourth* degree of consanguinity, because that number, being that of universal action, gives the same blood time to renew itself, and to demonstrate to man that his intellectual or *quaternary* Being should be in control of all his abilities.

After the glorious promises which were made to the first leader of the Chosen People, one may easily recognize in this Just man, in his son Isaac and in his grandson Jacob, the successive and subdivided expression of the three Supreme Abilities from whom he had received the signs all at once, and who served as an example to those who manifest the human soul. He himself visibly exhibited *Thought*, through the rank of his appointment which made him the first depository of the designs of the Great Being for the posterity of men; his son is the symbol of *Will*, through

---

[147] Genesis 12:14 – 15 "…look from the place where thou art northward and southward, and eastward and westward; for all the land which thou seest, to thee will I give it, and to thy seed forever." (KJV).

the free sacrifice which he made of this individual, and the son of his son represents *Action* through the combat which he entered into against the Angel, and through the numerous offspring which came forth from him. Here cannot the freedom of understanding be extended, for we see in Rebecca the image of the physical world, and through the two children who fought in her womb, we can recognize the image of man and his *elder brother, his enemy*, with whom he is imprisoned in the Universe?[148]

Later, the descendants of that Hebrew Just One became slaves to the Egyptian Nation, from whom they had sought help. The sense of the word *Egypt* expresses sorrow and tribulation, and the union of the Jewish descendants with that Nation recounts what the original criminal did in his abomination, and shows that no Being can throw himself into such a abyss without being condemned to suffer and to sojourn there for a length of time proportionate to his iniquity.

The Hebrew Books paint for us the consequences of that criminal alliance. Those people, reduced to living out their days and labors in the dust, exposed to the unjust impositions of their tyrants, repeat the humiliating situation of man here below, where despite his action being horribly restricted, he had however to support fights which were far greater and more numerous than in his first estate; where he now had *to live*, being, as it were, separated *from life*.[149]

Now one sees a famous Agent appear, who, as the Child of the Hebrews, escaped from the cruelty of the king of Egypt, or from those *impure Virtues* which had set themselves against the first efforts of our sentient Being, and which work solely to prevent him from regaining his liberty. That famous Agent floated, like man, upon the *waters of the abyss*, preserved from their whirlpool by a *cradle*, as man, by the powers of his body, is raised and directed by a faithful teacher, and as man would

---

[148] This is in reference to Pasqually's *Treatise*, recognizing that man was initially placed on Earth to watch over God's first creations, who could be regarded as man's older siblings, who had turned against the First Principle, and who tempted man to operate an act of creation.

[149] In this passage Saint-Martin equates the story of the Hebrews – firstly being in command in Egypt in the person of Joseph, then being subjugated by those very people and turned into their slaves – with the story of man, created to rule over the original prevaricating spirits, being tempted to perform an act of creation, and as a consequence being made flesh, and now being subject to their torments. Incidentally, the reed boat in which Moses, the liberator of the Hebrews, floated on the waters of the Nile is also referred to as an 'ark': for nothing symbolic in the Scriptures is redundant.

forever be if he were active and docile; and finally, charged like him to watch over the reestablishment of order and the destruction of iniquity.[150]

Through his works, and his victories over the Egyptians, this Just One paints us an image of the powers of man over the *Powers* of the Universe and over the Principle of Evil. Those who have claimed that this Lawgiver had gained all the knowledge of the Egyptians have not observed that, before his battles with the Sages of that Nation, this Just One spent many years at the house of his father-in-law Jethro, who was a *Priest*, and that he sat near a בור *Beour*, a word translated as 'a well', but which can be analyzed as ב *beth*, 'in' and אור *aur*, 'light', signifying nothing less than the seat of knowledge and truth.[151]

Man's superiority over physical things, and his powers over corruption, is outlined for us in the portrait of the flight from Egypt, and in the passage of the Red Sea. The first Table paints for us the Egyptians annihilated, so to speak, by all the scourges which they had brought upon themselves but hadn't ceded until the *tenth*. It describes them stripped of their wealth, in which we surely understand the criminal instruments of their Religion; it paints them as pursuing the Hebrew People by uncertain roads, who alone rejoice visibly in the light, while the shadows have spread over her enemies and over the whole of Egypt. The second image represents the Elements obedient to the voice which commands them to open a free passage to those who were led by *wisdom*, and to resume their natural course at the approach of the impious who, having none of the *powers* necessary to defend themselves, became their victims.[152]

This second Table[153] teaches us again that the corruptible substances of blood are the true shackles which keep man in his suffering, and that it is only by breaking those links, or by the separation of his intellectual

---

[150] Biblical commentators had long since made the connection between certain acts of Moses with the Redeemer in the New Testament, for example with the raising up of the brazen serpent on the Tau Cross to heal the people of Israel as a harbinger for the time that Jesus would be raised up on a cross to redeem his people. However, Saint-Martin appears to be explicitly using Moses himself as a harbinger of the Repairer, or Héli (Elias) of Pasqually, whom Saint-Martin equates with the Christ.

[151] *Beth* also signifies 'house', so a simpler translation might be 'House of Light' or 'House of Ilumination', an equally powerful concept.

[152] Once again, we see the theme of 'Passing the River'; in this case crossing the Sea of Reeds.

[153] Again, one can imagine with profit these images, portraits, tableaux as Tracing Boards presenting these symbols as pictures for contemplation. Willermoz was to make much of this approach in the many Tracing Boards he designed and used, many adapted from the 'Rite of Strict Observance' of Baron von Hund, in his 'Scottish Rectified Rite'.

Being from blood, that he recovers some measure of liberty. This has already been indicated by the spirit of the precept of circumcision, which was followed by the prohibition given to the People against ingesting blood, because the life of the flesh is in the blood, and the spirit of the flesh had been given to the Hebrews, or to men, for the expiation of their soul. This a sufficiently clear expression to justify the reproach made by the Lawgiver of the Hebrews that many of the People had not distinguished in man a Being separate to the physical Being.

Finally, in the many encampments and the different works which followed the flight from Egypt, that Lawgiver paints the various interruptions which man must endure after his corporeal passage, to realize what he can only know here below in appearance, just as Moses alone showed in himself a complete example of the Universal course of man, from his terrestrial origin until the end to which his original nature never ceased to be called.

We come to that period when the Divine Voice made itself heard to the Hebrews, where the Lawgiver himself, like all the people, heard the Sacred Word which was communicated to men, to teach them not to act except in accordance with it, not to put their confidence in *strange Gods* and *idols* which could not *speak*. In the events which followed, we see the First Law of man presented in his state of splendor, and the Second Law of that same man in his state of reprobation. Indeed, his First Law was taken away from him when he distanced himself from the center of truth, just as the first Stone Tablets were broken at the time of the idolatry of the Hebrew People.

The Second Law, though containing the same precepts as the first – that is to say the indispensable obligation to manifest the properties of our Principle, and to be in some way the living organ of *His Virtues* – that Second Law, I say, is inferior to the first and infinitely more rigorous one. Outside the daily experience which our present situation compels us to have, we have a sign in those very Tablets which Hebrew Tradition gives us.

The first Tablets of the Law are described as having been not just written, but even carved by the hand of God. An instructive Table, whose true meaning is the emanation of man outside the realm of light, on whom the same Hand which gave him being, engraved at the same time the

Nun (נ) – From the Flood to Moses   195

Number, or the Covenant on which all his power and all his glory should be based.[154]

On the other hand, the second Tablets were explained to us by the Writer as having been written by the hand of God, like the first ones, but the difference between them was that the second ones had been carved by the hand of man, and that it is on that work of man that the Necessary Being, filled with love for His creations, again deigned to engrave His Seal and His Covenant, as He had done on the pure substance of which the first Tablets were the image; such that the Law of man, not being engraved upon his natural material, operates in him that violent and painful state which all men experience when they seek that Law with sincerity and draw near to it; because such suffering and vexation is inevitable between heterogeneous Beings.

The majestic and terrible refulgence which accompanied the promulgation of those Laws reminds us of the Table of the origin of things, where disorder gave way to harmony; when each Being received its Order and its Law; where the light, mixed and confounded with the shadows, strained violently to separate from them; where the criminals who must inhabit these shadows were dragged along with the debris of that frightening explosion; and where those who had been faithful to their Principle rallied to His Divine Light, there to read the irrevocable Decrees of His Eternal Wisdom and to exercise them throughout the Universe.

It is always in elevated places that those great facts are presented to us; in those places where the Air, being purer, seems to communicate the most salutary influences to our whole Being, and a life which conforms best to our nature and to our original destiny.

For later on, when this same Law condemned the Hebrew people and those of its leaders who sacrificed in *high places*, it did not exactly claim to be speaking about the mountains, but about specific objects of Nature to which men had often given a blind confidence, and which, having begun by serving as instruments of Sabianism[155], ended by giving rise to the abuses of judiciary Astrology.

---

[154] That number, of course, was ten, the number of the Commandments, and that of perfection and completion for Pasqually and Saint-Martin.

[155] The Sabians were known for worshipping the sun, moon and stars. Saint-Martin appears to have a distrust of Astrology and those who put their faith in the motions of the planets for purely short term divinatory purposes, and yet as we see, he had less issue with reading the course of man over longer periods in them.

Some particularly large changes were introduced into the body of knowledge of the Hebrews. One finds the proof of this in the waters of jealousy[156], by which the Priest determined the guilt or innocence of a woman accused of adultery. These proofs, stripped of the superior *power* of man, where the Priest was supposed to be specifically dressed, appear suspect and give us an impression of sorcery and illusion. But when one ascends to the nature of man and when one reflects on the extent of his rights, nothing should surprise us in similar stories, because the *secondary Causes* are subordinate to him and he has the *power* to direct these *actions* to the glory of his intellect and to the maintenance of the Law of Him whom he is charged to represent on Earth.

As a result, although this *Superior Power* was weakened among men, they nevertheless preserved the formulas. From this came proofs by Water, by Fire, by red Fire[157] and by the arms of the cross, which have for a long time been the only criminal jurisprudence in many Nations. These same Nations, held in thrall by superstition or blinded by ignorance, only judged after the facts and did not check to see if those who appeared to have these facts were sufficiently trustworthy to merit their confidence, and they did not doubt the innocence of the accused when his courage or his cleverness allowed him to endure the proof.

Finally, men's eyes were opened, both to the lying pretensions of the judges and to the abuses of that extravagant form of justice. But men, while saving themselves from those atrocious crimes, were no further advanced towards their Principle: they had suppressed those abuses without making their footsteps any the more assured, guaranteeing that they would make the same errors as their ancestors, and they became no wiser. They even fell into yet another excess for, not understanding those proofs at a time when they had already been deprived of their underlying basis, they believed that they had never had any at all.

It is the same with the leper: this illness was regarded by the Hebrews as a punishment for erring against the *Law*; it could therefore not be cured except by the possessor or the depository of the Law, and in reality, that privilege or gift belonged to the Priest.

Later on, when the art of healing no longer belonged to the Priesthood, when the Doctor believed he could stop being a Priest, the

---

[156] See Numbers 5:11-15, 27-28.
[157] Most likely branding. Nowadays *fer rouge* ('red fire') means a red traffic light!

sources of leprosy remained unknown, as they still are, and the sources of remedies were therefore closed to him. So, in the darkness in which man finds himself, he has sooner thought leprosy incurable than see what he lacked for its cure; just as the evils of man have more than doubled, for he has always had the *means* to prevail over leprosy and yet he cannot find the means to deliver himself.[158]

---

[158] It was not until 1832 that the first scientific study of leprosy was undertaken, and the root causes began to be identified. Before then, and in Saint-Martin's time, lepers were still seen as unclean – both physically and morally – and separated from the general public in sanatoria. It is interesting to note that Saint-Martin suggests that Doctors should be Priests: one might either see this as a case for witch-doctors, or on the contrary, for the power of holistic medicine!

Samekh (ס) – From the Tabernacle to the Temple

The Sabbath, so recommended by the Laws of the Hebrews, corresponds to the original Sabbath, both in its number and by its reason; and it is assuredly in the spirit of this original Sabbath that it was ordained for them not to sow, not to till the earth, not to tend the vine during the seventh year, or sabbatical year; during this year not to sow anything at all, nor harvest anything; and not to expect any kind of subsistence other than the natural products of the earth to meet their immediate needs, without any anxiety about the needs to come.

Doesn't this in fact make us remember the difference between the material Laws and those of the intellect? Doesn't it show that matter only exists, produces, sustains itself through violent means and by means of laborious cultivation; while intellectual life, being self-supporting, promises the man who can attain it easy delights and an assured nourishment?

Doesn't it show us in advance what man's destiny will be, when the Great Sabbath comes, and he will be reunited with the true Divine *Virtues* themselves, and come into possession of that *Uncreated Earth*, which will endlessly yield fruit without cultivation; when being an *adherent* to the springs of life, he can continually quench his thirst there, with the confidence that they will always be more abundant than his needs, and that they will never run dry?

One shouldn't forget that the true temporal Sabbath should be on the fourteenth day of the Mars moon, that it was at this time that the deliverance of the Hebrew People took place, and that this is the time in Nature when we find the first signs of creation, for it is around this time that the vegetative Principles receive the first influences of Spring, which for us should be counted by the course of the Moon and not that of the Sun, when both of those stars are found together at the same equinoctial point.

I would add that the Hebrews have moved the time of their Sabbath by beginning it at the appearance of the first star, instead of beginning it at midnight, which is the time of its original institution, considering that

Samekh (ס) – From the Tabernacle to the Temple

this is a central hour; but this isn't the only carelessness for which they can be reproached, for at its institution their Law was pure and supported by invariable foundations.

There one may see that, so far as the regulations relating to aliments, everything was founded on the healthiest of Principles. The prohibition against eating animals known to be impure by the Law[159] considered the nature of these animals whose impurity for us is written in their very shape.

Those whose head and body are stripped of offensive or defensive members; and those whose neck is so large, that in other words, the neck and body form a single mass, those I tell you are the least pure, the least regular Beings, and at the same time the most harmful to man; for it is them whose blood is prone to be carried more abundantly in the upper part of the body; and to preserve the language of the Hebrew Law, their blood is physically on their head[160]; and frequent use of similar meats would not fail to produce the same disturbance in the equilibrium of our own humors[161]; it is then that the gross sulfurs, which our nature seeks to purge, flow back into our Being and block up all the organs.

Certainly, no Being is more interested in avoiding that terrible effect than man, for when the seat of his Principle is disturbed, the Principle itself can suffer because of that disturbance.

Man is destined by his nature to be superior to all those that are bloody *and impure, since his own head, being separated from his body by a thin neck, appears to be vertically set, so that the* blood *not being able to rise up, reigns and dominates over all things which hold to* blood. *And since we have the example of the brutishness of the Negroes, which is due in part not only to their* blood, *but that their* fat *is also on their head; for this fact is visible in the dark and reddish color of the marrowy substance of their brains, and by the wool which they have in place of hair.*[162]

---

[159] The list may be found in Leviticis 11:1-30. It is most useful to know that one is not permitted to eat vultures, camels, tortoises, mice and moles!

[160] The unusual rendition of 'on their heads' rather than 'in their heads' is the terminology used in Leviticus, and also refers to the passage in Matthew (27:25) when the Children of Israel respond to Pontius Pilate with the words: "His blood be upon us and on our children", when calling for the crucifixion of the Repairer.

[161] The French word is 'liqueurs' which directly translates as 'liquors' or 'liquids': here the older interpretation has been substituted.

[162] This paragraph is of course, a classic example of the ignorance of Europeans with regard to other cultures at that time. All the Translator can say is, firstly this paragraph appears in all French

What I said about the deformities in animals which are described as unclean also applies to fish, whose body forms a single mass with the head, and appears to carry all the marks of impurity, so that one might ask why the Hebrew Law only banned those which had neither fins nor scales.

In general, the impurity of unclean fish must be less than that of terrestrial animals, because the blood of the former is so moderated by the aqueous fluid that it is neither abundant nor of a temperature capable of producing great havoc. It is for that reason that the Law tolerated those which did not have all the signs of impurity at the same time.

However, as the Element which they inhabit bears within itself the character of the confused origin of material things; and as it is in Water that all material Beings take their corporealization; the Law regarded fish as participating to some extent in the confusion *of their Element, and for his reason too, they did not use them in their sacrifices.*

One cannot ignore the fact that salt, so useful for our food, was strongly recommended in sacrifices, and that almost everywhere on Earth it has been the symbol of wisdom. Salts in general are very instructive substances for man. They only come into being through the reuniting of their different parts contained in Water which holds them in solution, and through the action of Fire – be it general or specific – become active and powerful combinations, custodians of all the qualities manifested in the body. In a word, salt is Fire set free from Water, and Water has a number so impure that the Hebrews only express this word by the dual number מים *mayim.*

Let us add that, if preference was given to marine salt over other types, that was because it is square on all faces and has seven centers; this is because it directly receives the higher influences through the action of the Moon on the oceans, and because its acid has less affinity with metals than other salts.

Unleavened bread, so recommended for festivals, no doubt has a very great significance, for it represents at the same time the affliction of deprivation, the preparation for purification, and the memory of the origin.

---

editions, and that he consulted a prominent African American scholar on the propriety of retaining this passage in the book, prior to publication. He agreed it should appear, but with this *caveat*.

Samekh (ס) – From the Tabernacle to the Temple

The word *manna* comes from a Hebrew noun which means *to number*, and to understand that daily distribution which the Hebrew Books tells us were made to the people, this is what it is necessary to know.

Just as the Sun traverses all the points of our horizon each day to revivify the whole circumference, in the same way all men receive a ray of the *Great Sun* every day, which is enough to restore them intellectually, if they have not allowed it to be intercepted by a thousand foreign obstacles. Finally, each day in the Physical Order there is a Universal movement by which all the spheres act upon one another, and mutually draw near to the foundations on which, while passing, they imprint actions and numbers analogous to the traits they find there; and it cannot be denied that it is the same in the Intellectual Order, since the one is the model of the other.

But in neither Order can man pass beyond the limits and measures of his abilities without destroying them, and despite the fact that he received those abilities by his nature, he must wait for the *powers* and the higher numbers to come and complete them and nourish them; just as he should not cease relying on that superior aid and believing that they can renew themselves like his needs. This is what is symbolized by the vases[163] of the Hebrews, the manna with which they filled them every day, and the interdiction against collecting double portions.

If one doubted that this manna existed in material form, one need only recall what one has just read; and if we recognize that intellectual manna is given to us every day in life, we will have taken a large stride towards believing in the possibility of the material type, for the latter could well have come from a common branch of the same tree, but which had grown lower down, having the body as its object.[164]

Regarding the Criminal Laws listed in the Hebrew Books, though they are founded on the most precise justice, I do not propose to justify their origin with as much care as those Laws of Precept and Instruction which we have discussed up to now. They present too many difficulties to dare to be certain that man's hand, in drawing them up, never took the place of the Supreme Hand; and the main objection is that, if the Head of

---

[163] Or 'omer': Exodus 16:18-22.
[164] This appears to be a reference to the Kabbalistic Tree of Life, specifically to the Four Worlds, and suggests perhaps that physical manna comes from a lower branch of the Tree than intellectual or spiritual manna, as physical manna is in Assiah and spiritual manna is in Yetzirah.

the Law was obliged to *consult* the Higher Light in all doubtful circumstances, it would have been pointless to have written out a Criminal Code.

Indeed, if he knew by *consulting* the Code what the punishments set forth by the Law against such and such crime were, he knew it on the *deposition* of *two truthful witnesses*, of which I can give no clearer idea than comparing them to the signature on a letter and its contents, for we know that in Ancient times man wisely began their letters with their name, and this custom still exists among many Nations and in the ordinances of sovereigns.[165]

But the Head of the Law, having amassed many of these *judicial sentences*, must have used them to serve as guides when he found himself presented with similar cases, when he was limited to *consulting* them on the guilt or innocence of the accused.

Following this, the form of that jurisprudence must have been further debased; and the successors to the true Heads, finding the Laws for the punishment of crimes written down, took those Laws to be the only rule which they needed to consult, together with the testimonies of human witnesses, to be those the Lawgiver had in mind; from which we can see the abuses which must have been the result of this misunderstanding.

I willingly explain this problem so that my train of thought does not appear suspect, and in order to have the right to defend the treasury of teachings which, despite this adulteration, can be found contained in the Hebrew Books.

Let us now consider the Ark of the Covenant, the repository of all the *ordinances* which the People should observe in order to retain their power over their *enemies*. Let us compare that Tabernacle, and the Ceremonies ordained to be practiced there, with the *original occupations* of man: we will see that they offer a description of those ancient symbols which Wisdom should show to man once more, so that He might never be

---

[165] This passage appears to refer to Deuteronomy 19:15-21, which lays down the Law requiring two truthful witnesses, which also includes the famous "eye for an eye, tooth for a tooth" passage, and links this to the tradition of edicts being prefaced with the name of the sovereign, as is still practiced in a way in Last Wills and Testaments, as in: "I, John Smith, being of sound mind...". The underlying point seems to be that, even if the original Law was given by the Supreme Being, the practice of Common Law, where decisions are taken with reference to previous and similar cases, has moved us away from God's original Law and closer to a man-made Law which is both imperfect and which has lost its connection with the original Law. This is borne out by the next two paragraphs.

accused of breaking the Covenant which He had made with him in forming it.[166]

Also, it was commended to the Agent chosen for that work to conform to the plan which had been shown to him on the mountain, so that through the visible copy, being similar to the model which man could no longer see, man might be able to draw closer to his former glory and original knowledge.

And so, it is important to study this copy with care if we wish to recover some ideas of the original. We should think about the various areas of the Tabernacle and the different veils which separated one from another, in order to retrace the various progressions and suspensions of the light for us: the *Oracle* enveloped and covered by the wings of the Cherubim; the crown, or circle or gold which surmounted it and seemed to be placed there like Saturn's ring[167], to serve as the organ of the higher *Powers* which must descend to that place; the *tables* erected in various

---

[166] It is important to later sections and arguments to understand that the French word '*arc*' or '*arche*' can mean 'arch' or 'ark', and also note that the French for rainbow is '*arc-en-ciel*', literally 'arch/ark in the heavens'. This allows them to draw some conclusions not immediately apparent to English speakers. The first Ark carried the remnanats of humanity over the waters for forty days, and the first Covenant of God with man was symbolized in the Arch or Ark in the heavens, in a way a celestial correspondence with the Ark upon the waters, and which also symbolized the moment that the terrestrial Ark was reestablished upon firm ground at Mount Ararat. Moses was carried in a second Ark upon the waters of the Nile; and later in life (was he symbolically forty years old, perhaps?) he has an Ark built to house the Covenant with God – received on another Mount, that of Sinai: again, a celestial Ark or Arch to mirror the terrestrial Ark which began his life. Note also that the French word used for Covenant is '*alliance*', a word more normally associated with marriage. So, by adhering to the Law man was in a way 'married' to God, suggesting a much more personal and intimate relationship than the English translation of 'Covenant', with its connotations of a political arrangement. This will also help us to understand God's fury when Israel was 'unfaithful' to its 'marriage vows'. Four 'arks', four 'arches', forty days, forty years. Moreover, the Keystone completes the Arch or 'Ark' which binds the two pillars together, and Christ – or the *Repairer* in Saint-Martin's terminology – was described as the Keystone, thus uniting God and man. In Freemasonry, the two pillars carry orbs depicting the terrestrial and celestial worlds, now united by an Arch which ties both together and is itself made stable and enduring by the Keystone, that "stone which the builders rejected." The symbolism is both rich and compelling. This is one of the reasons why the Holy Royal Arch Degree in Freemasonry is considered the completion and perfection of regular Masonry. One may only imagine how the scales fell from the eyes of those who went through the Degree one hundred or more years ago, when their familiarity with the Bible would have allowed them to recognize the allegory as an old friend, and to take them on a journey of discovery and deep symbolism. Nowadays, sadly, most Candidates for this Degree have never read the Bible, and see the ritual as little more than a quaint story…

[167] A reference to the fact that, at that time, Saturn was seen to have as single ring around it, rather than several.

locations; the twelve loaves of shewbread arranged six by six, to give us a picture of the two *senary Laws*, sources of all things intellectual and temporal; and finally the seven-branched candlestick repeating the number of that *Superior Light* which invisibly illuminates and vivifies that Mysterious Sanctuary, the seat of His glory.

Not only must the Tabernacle have correspondences with the destination of the Universe; it must also have correspondences with man, since man is its primary object, which is clearly shown by that square Altar[168], in which it was ordained should be placed there together with the vases and instruments relating to the worship which should be practiced there. That square form is a symbol identical to the number of intellectual man, a symbol which one can easily penetrate, and which will be further considered later. *Now, man's own body also appears to have correspondences, since it forms a square shape itself by its dimensions. Moreover, this Altar was supported and transported by means of four hollow batons which could never be detached; and this type is found in physical nature in the material form of man.*[169]

One cannot contemplate the physical end of the Lawgiver of the Hebrews, whose sepulcher remains unknown, as well as the story of those Elect Ones who we are told were raised up in chariots of fire, without taking away a vast and instructive idea of our true destiny.

Man is a fire concentrated in a gross envelope; his Law, like that of all fires, is to dissolve that envelope and reunite with the source from which he is separated.

If, by neglecting those activities proper to his Being, he allows himself to be dominated by that physical and shadowy envelope, it gains a more or less strong influence over him, depending on the rights that man has ceded to it through his weakness, his penchants or his pleasures. Then his fire is stifled or buried, so to speak, beneath that obscure veil, and at his death, man finds himself mingled with the ruins of his corporeal form. That debris must remain heaped upon him so long as he feels nothing *vital* enough in the center of his existence to break and destroy the bonds which attach him to the inferior realm of the body.

If, on the contrary, by following the Law of his nature, he knows not only how to conserve the power and rights of his own fire, but also how

---

[168] That is, the Ark of the Covenant.

[169] To state the obvious, man's square shape is 'supported and transported by means of four hollow batons which could never be detached', meaning his arms and legs.

to augment them further through the action of the higher Fire, it should come as no surprise that, at his death, their ardor more quickly consumes the impure form which till then had constrained his movements, and that the disappearance of that form is quicker.

So, what happens if the whole man is burned up by this higher Fire? He is obliterated down to the least vestiges of his matter. One will find nothing of his body, for he will have left nothing impure, like those Elect who, at the end of their career, appeared to rise up to the Celestial Realms in luminous chariots, which were in fact the explosion of that pure form which is more natural to our Being than our material envelope, and which we have never ceased to have, despite being joined to matter.

What should we make of the translations which have Job say: *In my flesh I shall see God*? One might think that this text is contrary to our thesis. In fact, the word נקפו *niqfou* comes from the verb נקף *naqaf*, which signifies: *he has broken, he has cut, he has corroded*, and not *he has been encompassed*. And Job, having recognized that his Redeemer lives and that He must raise him from the dust, naturally adds: *When my evils will corrode or destroy my corporeal envelope, I shall see God*, not *in my flesh*, as the translators say, but *out of my flesh*. For in מבשרי *mibbesari*, as in a thousand other cases, the particle מ *mem* is an extractive ablative which represents existence, outside of a place, outside of a thing, and not existence in that place or in that thing: so here the text carries exactly the opposite meaning to the translations.

I will leave aside the multitude of facts and scenes contained in the Hebrew books from the time when Moses was replaced by his worthy successor, up to the time when the form of government changed. With the principles which we have established we can easily discover what Joshua represents when he introduces the people to the Land promised to their fathers; when he has his meeting with the Prince of Armies of the Lord[170] and when he took on the enemies of his people, the towns of *Kirjath-sepher* and *Kirjath-arba*[171] or the *City of Letters* and the *City of Four*; then I say one will understand what the Hebrew people themselves bring to mind, by allowing many of the criminal Nations which they had been ordered to exterminate to endure, and forgetting so far as to make Alliances with them.

---

[170] Joshua 5:13-15.
[171] Joshua 15:15 and Joshua 15:54.

As for the other scenes we find in the Books, we can uncover natural and instructive interpretations easily enough, in the same way that in our times it has been shown that the majority of those facts which appeared inconceivable were in fact far less dramatic than the translations led us to believe. In Samson's foxes[172], for example, one can see that it was nothing more than bundles of combustible matter, which nevertheless could have been combined with a more *active fire* than normal fire.

I will also leave aside all those facts which could appear to be revolting, such as the bloody executions, the cruelties undertaken or ordered by the chiefs and the Agents of Justice, as I intend to talk about these in a later book.

As for the rest, perhaps it is best only to pour out a little knowledge and wisdom rather than undertake a universal explanation of all that is contained in the Hebrew Books; since not only is the life of one man insufficient, but it would perhaps even require a labor of many Centuries to develop all the points contained in them.

Let us observe that, when we discover many more inexplicable things in them, for whatever reason, that does not diminish the merit of the facts, whose correspondences with our Being and with the nature of things provides the most perfect evidence, in the eyes of intelligent men.

Of this number is the fact of the sudden change in the kind of Hebrew Government. Most importantly, when did this change occur? It was when the sanctity of their Law was profaned; it was when the avarice of their Priests led them to appropriate the objects of sacrifice and when they only exercised their sacred profession as an expedient to their cupidity; and finally, it was when those same Priests, being incapable of defending the incorruptible Ark of that Covenant among man, had let it fall into the hands of the enemy, and when the people thus found themselves stripped of all that was their strength and their support. It was then that the Hebrew People, despite the wise advice of the last of their Judges, wished to be governed by a King like the other Nations.

But just as original man, separating himself from the center of light, was reduced to having no more than a feeble spark of that light as his guide; in like manner the Hebrew People, abandoning their natural guides and submitting themselves to a King, now only had the *powers* of a single man – even if he be weak or wicked – as their recourse. And in this manner

---

[172] Judges 15:4-5.

Samekh (ס) – From the Tabernacle to the Temple

the history of the Kings is the most instructive Table that Hebrew Tradition could communicate to us. For of all the Kings of Israel, we are not shown a single one who did not commit a *crime*, and among the Kings of Judah, we are shown only a very small number who were exempt, such as Asa, Jehosaphat and Josiah, even though one might reproach the first one for making alliances with foreign Kings, and for having had less confidence in God than in Doctors when he was sick.

Let us hasten to get to the famous period of the Temple which was built under the *third* King; a monument which Hebrew Traditions represent as the first wonder of the world, and to which even today the bastards of Ishmael still offer a form of homage.[173]

The construction of that Temple, made a short time after the Hebrew people had abandoned their natural guides, is a perfect repetition of the fate experienced by man after he was separated from the source of his glory, when he was reduced to no longer seeing the harmony of the *Divine Virtues* except in a coarse and complicated reflection.

These images, completely material though they must be, still provide guilty men with traces of their original model: the Author of Beings, forever jealous for their happiness, offers them the image of His Strength, His Glory and His Wisdom, to fix their sight on the greatness and beauty of the light, when that light will be fixed in their senses through His Own Symbols.

The edifice of the Temple also united everything that had been foretold through the physical signs of previous manifestations.[174]

It had, in its true – rather than literal – proportions and measurements, correspondences with the Ark of which Hebrew Tradition makes mention at the time of the scourge of Divine Justice upon the prevaricators by means of the element of Water; and thus the Temple, like the Ark, was a new representation of the Universe.

It offered the same attributes as the Tabernacle whose model was given to the Jewish people at the time of the promulgation of the Law, for in the Temple there was a place for sacrifices, just as they had been performed in the Tabernacle. In both there was a *place* set aside for *prayer*, which was like a conduit for the light and the gifts which the

---

[173] Once again, one must remember the times this was written and the ignorance of the author who was repeating calumnies then perpetuated by the Catholic Church: this refers to Al Aqsa Mosque.
[174] Here Saint-Martin sees not only the Tabernacle, but also the Ark as earlier manifestations of the Temple, as a sacred space set aside for prayer, sacrifice and contemplation.

beneficent hand of the Eternal One spread over the Elect People and on their leaders.

But everything in that Temple was more numerous, more abundant, more vast, more extensive than in the previous Temples, to teach us that the *powers* are always going to increase over time; and that as time advances, man will see assistance and support multiply in his favor.

It is in order to instruct us in these truths that each of the three *Temples* was marked by a particular distinction. The Ark of the Flood wandered and floated upon the Waters, to paint us an image of the uncertainty and darkness of those early times. The Tabernacle was alternately on the move and at rest, and moreover, it was man himself who transported it and set it down in the chosen places, to recount the rights given to man in this second period – rights to which he could aspire now and then, when he possessed the light. Finally, the third Temple was stable, and adhered to the Earth, to teach us physically about the privileges to which man may one day lay claim – privileges which extend to establishing forever his abode in the place of truth.

And so, the Temple at Jerusalem not only represented what had taken place in the previous ages but was also one of the most instructive physical signs that man could have before him, in order to recover knowledge of his original destination, and the paths which wisdom had taken to lead him there.

There, in the sacrifices and the effusion of the blood of animals, he found the image of that Universal Sacrifice which pure Beings never cease to offer the Sovereign Author of all existence, promptly using their own life or actions to support His Glory and Justice.

We would add beforehand that all this being concerned with man here below, it is by *man himself* that this sacrifice should be performed, and that sacrificing animals was only a secondary means to manifest the Glory of the Great Being. Man alone in Nature has the right to offer Him tribute worthy of Him; but being nowadays at the far end of the chain of Beings, he raises himself up successively through their means: by exposing the *power* of the most inferior Beings he can ascend to the *powers* which govern them, and through this progression reach a *living* power which brings him to the level where he can fulfill His Law, that is to say to worthily honor His Principle by presenting Him with offerings on which are imprinted the characters of His grandeur.

If the Jewish people had been the depositary of such instructions; if they possessed a Temple which appeared to be the Universal hieroglyph; if those who fulfilled the functions in the Temple acted as we have described as Agents of the Laws of Religion; and if they also did everything I have described to show that the source was in man: it is likely that the Jewish People would indeed have been the People Chosen by Supreme Wisdom to serve as a sign to man's posterity.

If this is true, would we not then believe that this Nation was sent forth – preferably to all the other Nations in possession of the means of regeneration we have already discussed – so that this Religion would necessarily be carried across the Earth by means of the Agents who had been made the depositaries of the *powers* subdivided from the *Great Principle*, in order to provide man with the knowledge of that *Principle*?

In the same way, we believe we can recognize in the Religion of those People a correspondence with the true nature of man and his true purpose, as we have already remarked between the Temple at Jerusalem and the harmony of the Universe.

We will see that the frequent ablutions, the careful preparations, the holocausts of all species – whether animal or the produce of the Earth – and the Sacred Fire which forever burned the sacrifices and offerings, are most instructive symbols of all the functions of Beings towards the First Principle, and of the superiority of that Principle over all Beings. The single order for the times fixed for the different sacrifices, the disposition of all the *instruments* which were employed, the quality of the *substances* involved, the number and arrangement of the *lamps*, and finally all the parties to this ceremony, are no doubt so many signs of a few of the higher powers which Wisdom has subdivided for man after his corruption.

However, all these things which are, so to speak, common to all Religions, being exterior and foreign to man, do not give him a sense of his true character. It is necessary for those great signs to be experienced by him, that they be represented and carried out by members of his own species, so that he will have personal and intimate evidence that it was for such work that he had been created.

If, from his origin, he could have had three great objects for his contemplation: the *Source* of all *Powers*, the *Virtues* which descend from Him to accomplish His *Laws*, and the *Beings* which never cease offering Him *homage*, then there must remain with him in his degraded state some indications and traces of that sublime spectacle. Then all those great objects must be presented to him, as well as those men who must represent them to him.

Now, in the practice and totality of the Hebrew Religion, we can see those three Orders with the greatest precision.

The people arranged about the Temple or on the parvis, recalls to man that multitude of pure creations of the Infinite One who remain faithful to that Principle, as much due to love for His Glory as interest in their own happiness.

The Levites busy about the Altar represent through their actions the functions of those privileged Agents chosen to send forth the gifts and *powers* of the Great Principle to the least of His creations.

Finally, the High Priest entering the *Holy of Holies* alone and only once a year, to bring the prayers of all the People and to have flow down to him the benefit of *life*, becomes a telling image of the invisible God, for whom a single act of power is enough to animate the whole circle of Beings, such that, of all those Beings who perpetually receive from Him the very seed of their existence, none have ever penetrated into the inaccessible Sanctuary of His essence.

And that is how man can recover the idea of his original abode, since he has before his eyes a reduced – but exact – image of it, and because he has finally seen recounted in his own species the God of Beings, his Ministers and Worshipers.

There he also sees *physical signs*, both of his former delights, and of the *fruits* which served as recompense for his *prayer*, since Hebrew Tradition gives us to understand how these sacrifices were rewarded, by teaching us that the Temple was filled with the Glory of the Eternal One, that is, with those positive indicators of *pure thoughts* with which we have seen man surrounded.[175]

As for the extraordinary multitude of animals which it is said were immolated at the time of the Dedication of the Temple[176], and in general in the sacrifices of the Hebrews, we have no intention of justifying those descriptions nor of refuting everything that has been said about the impossibility of the small country of the Jews containing enough livestock

---

[175] This is also a thinly-veiled reference to the work of the Elus Cohen, or Elect Priests who, following their Operations, were expected to sit in the darkness and seek signs that their Operation had been a success, by means of a communication from *La Chose*, or 'The Thing', discussed in an earlier footnote, and which would be manifested by physical signs.

[176] See I Kings 8:62-64.

to provide so many victims, and there being enough Sacrificers to slay them all. Those who occupy their time and exercise their minds in critiquing these Scriptural texts could find more useful employment for both.

It would be more useful to seek the means of penetrating these symbols than to stop at their outer envelope. One should note that the more the Hebrew Traditions offer justice and profundity in their passages when they are clearly expressed, the more one should admit that, when the passages appear to be obscure or invariable, that this is deliberate in order to conceal from us those truths which only belong to knowledgeable men, and which would be meaningless or harmful to those others who were not prepared for them.

It would be more valuable to remember that the Hebrew language is in harmony with intellectual things, since it has no words to express matter or the Elements[177]; there is more value, I say, in showing us how the *original meanings* of its most common words are sharp, correct and sublime, and to teach us that, instead of limiting the Hebrew language to a specific and literal sense, it is so vast that to understand its true spirit one should focus on drawing out its full meaning: for in the true order of things, it is for the subject matter and intelligence to direct language, and not for language to direct intelligence and the subject matter.

Finally, it has been more useful to teach us that every corporeal Being is a symbol of an *invisible ability* which is its analog. Then one can take the idea of *strength* from the bull, that of *gentleness* and *innocence* from the lamb, that of *putrefaction* and *iniquity* from the he-goat, and similarly for all species of animal and even for all the substances which were offered in kind in the sacrifices.

Perhaps with this in mind, we would have already succeeded in piercing the veil. For it could be that the species of animal sacrificed was the physical sign of the *ability* which corresponded to it, and that the quantity or number of victims was the allegorical expression of that very *ability* which the Sacrificer sought to combat if it was *evil*; or which, on the contrary, he strove to obtain from the Sovereign Being if it was *pure*; and finally, to Whom he offered homage when he had obtained it.

---

[177] This reference is odd, since it is clear that Saint-Martin is familiar enough with Hebrew that he should know it has words for the elements – indeed he uses at least two in the text: *mayim* for 'Water' and *aretz* for 'Earth'.

Ayin (ע) – From the Prophets to the Wanderings

Among the important things that Tradition presents to us, there is nothing which should interest us more than the appointment of the Just Ones, raised up by Divine Wisdom, Who being unable to abandon men – since they should be *signs* of His Glory – from time to time presented them with Patterns.[178]

None of those Patterns more resembled the ideal than the Just One Elijah, whose name embraces all Orders of Beings which are higher than matter, and who was made known through most extraordinary acts. But it is because he participated in the strength of the Principle of All Things that we should cease being amazed by such things. If he remained close to the *Being* Who had produced all things, to the Source from whence flow all perceptible *signs*, both material and immaterial, which operate in the Universe, what problem is there with the idea that, under the emblem of a crow[179] he received his nourishment from a Superior Hand? What problem is there with the idea that he unveiled the deception of the Priests of Baal by manifesting the powers of the True God? What problem is there with the idea that gave life to a cadaver, since he was acting by the same God who had given it life in the first place?

So let us not be surprised by the rights which he was accorded to multiply the aliments of the widow in Zarephath, to hold back the rain or dew or to let it fall according to his will, to consume the Captains of Ahaziah with Fire from Heaven: for if we do not lose sight of the designs

---

[178] The word *modèle* means 'model' or 'pattern'. The Translator selected 'pattern' in remembrance of the first two lines of the fourth verse of the popular Christmas carol "Once in Royal David's City": 'For he is our childhood's pattern, day by day like us he grew'. Thus, Saint-Martin states that the Prophets were sent to the Hebrews to provide an ideal 'pattern' for them to follow in their lives. This is an interesting variation as the Prophets are usually seen as people who warned the Hebrews and their leaders against errant behavior, and not a role models whose example was to be followed, especially given their general hygiene and unusual eating habits…

[179] From I Kings 17:4. More often translated as 'raven' in English translations. Curiously, in French the word *corbeau* means both 'crow' and 'raven', although 'crow' can be translated as *corneille*, which is helpful seeing that they are completely different species. Incidentally, *corvus* is Latin for 'crow', while *corvida* is a corruption of *corvidæ* meaning from the crow family – a meanginless observation to most Readers, unless they belong to a certain Order…

which the Divine One has for us, if we read the Book of Man[180], there we find the elements of all these marvels.

One can surely see here how advantageous it is for us to be ever strongly joined in Thought, Will and Action to the *Powers* of those privileged Beings, since the faithful disciple and successor of Elijah repeated almost all the miracles of his Master.

But one of the most beautiful teachings which Elijah has left to us is when, while on the mountain he recognized that the God of man was not in a *violet wind*, nor in the *trembling air*, nor in a *great and devastating fire*, but in a *soft and gentle wind* which proclaimed the calm and peace with which *Wisdom* filled all the places it approached, and indeed, this is a sure symbol of separating *truth* from *lies*.[181]

The various Just Ones who followed the same career were charged with telling the Kings and their People the fate they must expect if they proceeded to deviate from their Law. And just as there are numberless roads along which to stray, and just as the hardships which correspond to those deviations are equally innumerable, these Elect, by presenting pictures of them fulfilled their duty by means of signs which were the most appropriate for what they had to tell.

It was for that reason that the Supreme Justice, desiring to make the Hebrew People feel the horror of their idolatrous alliances, presented them with the symbol of union between one of His Delegates and a female prostitute; a union which also represented original man when he had covenanted with impure substances so contrary to his Being.

It was for that reason that Justice, wishing to give notice to His people of the dispersion with which they were threatened and the shameful state to which their enemies were going to reduce them, commanded another of His Agents to appear, stripped of his clothes, exiting through a breach made by him in his own house, and secretly taking flight.

---

[180] This is explained in detail in Chapter 4 of Saint-Martin's book *Of Errors & Truth*, and later in this book.

[181] A note on the name 'Elijah'. The original Hebrew is אליהו (Eliyahu) meaning 'Yahweh is my God'. The Greek version is Ἠλιας or 'Elias' in English. In French the name is rendered as *Élie*. This list explains the variants we hear, for example, when Jesus on the cross calls out to 'Eli' (Matthew, 27:46), and according to the New Testament the people there understood as him calling out to 'Elias', or 'Elijah'. Also, Pasqually termed what Saint-Martin called 'The Repairer' or *le Reparateur*, *Héli* – another variant on 'Elias'. Finally, the muse of the Rose-Croix, often mentioned by Papus and Paul Sédir was known as *Élie* or *Elias Artiste* or in English 'Elias Artista'.

Finally, it was for that reason that, wishing to show the Hebrew People the undignified treatment to which they were going to submit in their servitude, Justice did not hesitate to have them see a Just One plunged into the most terrible suffering and taking for nourishment the most disgusting things.

Man can recognize himself in those various Tables, which he can compare to his deplorable situation.

That was the source of the multitude of allegories and emblematic events which the stories of the Prophets offer us in such extraordinary passages, and which one could not conceive if they were separated from the secret events which are their purpose and reason.

From this we see the errors of those who dared to judge those passages, without knowing either their meaning or their correspondences, multiplied. Those Observers created chimeras in order to argue against them with more success; and for that they can only claim imaginary victories.

When, in defiance of the teachings of the several Elect Ones, the People and their Masters abandoned themselves to crimes of *putrefaction*, the Hebrew Books tell us the story of a new servitude even more humiliating and harsh than the first, since, at least in their Egyptian bondage the Hebrews had come willingly from a foreign land, whereas, in this second servitude, the enemy came to attack them in the heart of their city, shed their blood, drag them from their hearthsides, ravish and profane the most precious articles of their Religion.

We can even see it written that those cruel enemies blinded the king of the Hebrews, and since that Leader represented the Light of the People, it was to show that the manner in which Justice dealt severely with those prevaricators was to extinguish the flame of their knowledge.

That symbol was repeated during their servitude by the flight of many Tribes who, having escaped the yoke of the tyrants in Babylon, went far away and by hidden paths to dwell in an unknown land on the Earth. There they still practiced the Religion of the Eternal One in its pure state, according to the Law of the Hebrews; there they made expiation through mourning and sadness for the prevarications of their ancestors, and represented that *pure living organ* of our thoughts, which withdraws when we are *craven*, and which laments our voluntary errors, so that all their tears might be offered as tribute to Supreme Wisdom and Justice, Who

Ayin (ע) – From the Prophets to the Wanderings

forgets the crimes of the guilty in order to attend to the sorrows of the innocent.[182]

The same symbol is seen in the Ark of the Covenant which Maccabees tells us was deposited by Jeremiah, during the captivity, in an unknown place where it must remain until the end of time.[183]

But in all these symbols we always see mercy accompanying justice, ever giving hope to unhappy mortals condemned to privation. It is for this reason we are told that at the end of time the Tribes who were exiled will reunite with their people, and that the Ark will come out of the hidden place which concealed it, with the same refulgence and majesty which surrounded the famous mountain where the Law of the Covenant was given to man.

A conquering King of Assyria, wise and participating in a knowledge of the Hebrews, knew that the end of their slavery had come. He charged a Just One, indicated by Divine Wisdom, to lead them to the Land of their Father to rebuild the Temple which had been abandoned for the entire period of this horrible servitude, where they had been deprived of their Religion and their true sacrifices; where also, plunged into sorrow, they had hung their *musical instruments* on the branches of the willows rather than mix their *songs* with the *impure harmony* of their *Masters*.[184] These images are so plain and so strikingly similar, there is no need for us to explain these correspondences.

It is the same with the differences found between that Second Temple and the First. The First had been so impressive that those who had known the old Temple, and who saw the new one built, could not stop themselves from shedding bitter tears, so much did they sense the value of what they

---

[182] One can only conjecture which of the many theories about the final location of the 'Lost Ten Tribes of Israel' Saint-Martin subscribed to. There was not much traction to the Ethiopian theory at the time, probably due to racial prejudice. The Afghanistan theory was in the process of being rejected, as was an extraordinary one about the Lost Tribes founding the Incan Empire. However, one with some currency at the time was that descendents of the Lost Tribes made it to North America, being absorbed into or founding the Native American Tribes; and this was probably the most accepted theory of the day, following a popular book published by James Adair the Explorer, in England in 1775, with a long title beginning "*The History of the American Indians…*", and a legend which would be claimed by Joseph Smith when he founded the Mormons in the 1830s.
[183] II Maccabees 2:4.
[184] This tells the story of Zerubbabel obtaining permission from Darius to rebuild the Temple at Jerusalem. This story would be well-known to Saint-Martin since the biblical story of the rebuilding of the Temple is a major theme in Freemasonry, and well-suited to Pasqually's imagery. Indeed, it formed part of the story of the 9th, or Elect of Zerubbabel Grade of the Elus Cohen.

had lost. This remind us that the corporeal Temple which man inhabits today is nothing more than a sewer, a shadowy dungeon compared to the Temple in which he had his first abode.[185]

The Priest in charge of the rebuilding of that Temple rediscovered one of the copies of the Law. Those who have thought themselves able to reject the Prophecies in the Hebrew Books by alleging that Esdras had forged those Books himself, might have been able to give weight to that objection with regard to the Prophecies whose events has preceded him, but not for those whose completion could only have taken place after him, and they cannot deny that those are not very numerous.[186]

In re-establishing the Religion, Esdras re-established the offerings of corn, wine and oil, which had been the custom during the great days of the Hebrew people. I will not conceal the fact that these three substances combined form the fundamental materials on which rest the intellectual edifice of the *Great Work* of the restoration of all things; because the first is the *recipient*, the second the *active and generating Agent*, and the third is the *intermediary link*.[187]

To give an idea of the properties of oil, I will make the observation that it is composed of four elementary substances which give it active correspondences with the four cardinal points of the Universal circumference. Among various oils, that of the olive holds the first rank, since the flesh of its fruit being on the outside, because of that it receives the *original effects of the influences, without forgetting that, due to its*

---

[185] This is an intriguing comment, since during the same year this book was published, 1782, Jean-Baptiste Willermoz was helping to organize the Convent of Wilhelmsbad, which was to see the establishment of the Scottish Rectified Rite (the R.E.R.), in which the story of the Second Temple is used for far nobler instruction, concerning the building of the Spiritual Temple rather than the 'sewer, a shadowy dungeon' of Saint-Martin. Pasqually didn't cover the Second Temple in his *Treatise*, and the only mention he makes of Zerubbabel is as "a man who had been established by God to represent those Beings who were to manifest God's justice." It is interesting to note how Willermoz and Saint-Martin went in completely different directions in their interpretation of the Second Temple, given that their original Master had left no instructions concerning this particular story.

[186] As mentioned earlier in the footnotes, by Saint-Martin's time the educated classes were less inclined to take the Pentateuch to be literally written by Moses himself, and accepted that an oral tradition had finally been written down by Ezra or Esdras during the Babylonian captivity. This would naturally have given rise to claims that the Scribe had used the opportunity to literally rewrite history, a claim supported to some extent by later Exegists who believed the writing of the Pentateuch gave an opportunity to insert further stories – or confirmations – into the existing verbal records.

[187] Corn, wine and oil is also a significant image in the rites of Freemasonry.

natural quality, it fixes and retains those very influences. It is for that reason that, when describing the prevarications of the Chaldees, Baruch depicted the women as burning olive stones before their false gods.

A short time after the deliverance from this second captivity, the *strong* ceased to *fight* and became *like unto women*; one sees all their *powers* consumed and corrupted; one sees that *chosen tree* become so weak and so sterile that, in the allegorical expression of the Prophets, it could not produce even a single *branch* strong enough to make a *prince's scepter*; one can clearly see these People fell into such blindness that they didn't fear to go for money, and solicit from among the idolaters the High Priest for their own Temple.

One then sees another *powerful enemy* surrounding their walls, making them experience all the horrors of war and want, and one recognizes in these numberless evils and terrible scourges the fulfillment of the menaces which had often been reiterated to the Hebrew People if they did not keep the Law of His Covenant; when unfortunate spouses who fed on delicacies found themselves so harried by hunger that they would tear out their own child, and having devoured it, would quarrel over that unformed and disgusting mass by which man is attached in his mother's womb. A horrible image which teaches both us about corporeal man and his abominable origin, and the strong necessity for him to daily devour the bitterness and impurity with which the first crime had commingled him.

Soon, the perpetual sacrifice was interrupted for want of victims; a pile of dead bodies had accumulated around the altar; soldiers armed and covered with the blood of their brothers set themselves up in that redoubtable place, where the High Priest alone could enter but once each year. It is then that, subjugated by numbers and by wretchedness, the people strayed, without a Temple, without Sacrificers and without an Altar, as man after his fall groveled shamefully in the privation of his original rights and the sublime functions which he fulfilled in the Universe.

The Hebrew Records, considered in this context and point of view, present us with a faithful mirror in which we can contemplate the history of man. One should also not refrain from recognizing in them traces of a light and a superior power, of which man left to himself was completely incapable. I speak of those *powers* which must have brought visible assistance into his tenebrous abode, or of those Agents, many of whom were proclaimed in the Scriptures as having neither genealogy nor Ancestors.

Finally, the number of those Agents and the different periods in which they manifested, represent that subdivision of Divine Powers which control the torment of man here below, but to which he must submit before recovering his domain, and whose portraits cannot be painted for him in colors severe enough, seeing that for him whose last thought was a contempt for truth, the first must be the terror of that same truth.

We must now focus our attention on the appearances of cruelty and injustice presented to us by the Hebrew Traditions, and on the choice which Wisdom made in selecting a People who responded to His kindnesses so poorly.

Let us first consider those cruel executions, to that enormous effusion of blood at the hand of the Hebrews despite the formal Law which forbade them to shed it: let us talk about the scourges launched against innocent people in expiation of the faults of their leaders; let us talk, I say, about all the sufferings of the many who were its victims, not only for the prevarications of their ancestors, but also those of other criminals apparently unconnected to them.

The first of these problems is resolved by a contradiction. The greater the prohibition made to the Hebrew People against shedding blood, the more Wisdom made it known that the right of Justice was reserved to Him alone, and having alone been capable of giving *life* to men, He alone had had legitimate power to take it away.

But while reserving the exclusive right to act on man, Wisdom does not lose the right to act *through* him. And so, in whatever manner He manifests His action, He changes none of the Laws which compose man, for it is always He who operates, and since He uses the hand of man, He can only do that in a manner which is closer to the coarse state of us guilty ones, and which He continually exercises over all the posterity of man, as He does over all Beings.

Since Man is therefore merely the Agent or organ of Justice, in this instance there is neither prevarication nor crime, and as man does not shed blood by his own authority and for his own reasons, he isn't accountable in the eyes of Justice. This is a truth which men have often applied poorly to their conventional justice and to the province of social order, whereas it only properly applies to the true Law of man; a truth nevertheless of which human justice still preserves a trace and imprint, for it regards all those who judge and kill in the name of the Prince as innocent, and only deals severely with those who judge and kill in their own name.[188]

The Hebrew Author shows us in effect how the hand of man was passive in those great events, and how it was directed by a Superior Power, since in an instant and despite an insufficient number of men, it so often shows us prodigious numbers immolated to Justice.

As for the bloody and cruel executions for crimes in which the People had not participated, without recalling here what has been said about man's crime, one must distinguish between specific crimes and those which are common to an entire Nation. The constitution of the body is such that evil, like good, is reversible in all its members. We see examples of this in the simple order of human things.

Besides, what should stop all concerns is the uncertainty we have if the Supreme Wisdom does not pay for the services which He requires of us; if having exercised His powers on the recipients of His Justice in order to terrify the guilty, He does not recompense them for the works which they have performed; if being more noble and fruitful than all the sovereigns of the Earth, He cannot pour some rays of His Glory into the soul of men, who look for recompense out of all proportion to the pains and service they have suffered? And when the work of Wisdom is considered from this point of view, what can we answer when people use these arguments? Injustice is not setting a workman to work; but rather making him work and then withholding his wages.

If one then wishes to bring to mind the ills which afflict the posterity of man all over the Earth and compare them to the scourges of all kinds which, according to the Hebrew traditions, were visited upon the Jewish People so many times, one will see that those afflictions were more focused and more frequent upon the People who were intended to manifest all the effects of the Divine Virtues.

For, despite the problem with accepting scourges so widespread and ills so numerous being inflicted upon a single Country and a single People, as I have already said, widespread prevarications must attract widespread attacks; and from what we have glimpsed of the rights of man's will, be it for or against him, there are no means or facts which should surprise him, or appear supernatural to his true essence.

---

[188] Saint-Martin was no doubt referring to Kings and Princes who commanded their armies, when killing the enemy was not considered a capital offense, as murdering a person outside of war was.

It is true that in general, natural ills which afflict Nations, occuring without the hand of man, are not comparable to the facts reported in the Hebrew Books, in which Divine Justice is almost always exercised against the guilty by men. But if the Supreme Wisdom had to choose a People from among all the other Nations to accomplish His designs, if He truly made this choice to remind man about the privileged rank He had given to him in earlier times above all other Powers, whatever the People chosen, we should be able to see united in them all the various actions which would constitute an Order of Beings if they were in their state of perfection.

But man's posterity, being in degradation cannot represent that Order of Beings except with great irregularity, and that irregularity consists of showing in the same people all the action of the people in opposition, too. It consists of so shrinking the image that in the same Order of Beings, we can see both active *powers* and passive *powers*; such that in the same Race, in the same People, we may find both Judge, Executioner and Criminal, while those names should belong to different groups of Beings.

As for the prohibition against the shedding of blood, let us seek why it is said in the Hebrew Books that God once more asked for the soul of man from the hand *of man, and even that of animals.*

On the subject of the word hand, *let's first correct an error of the Translators.* יד *iad, 'hand', comes from* ירה *iadah, 'he has thrown', because in fact the hand is the instrument which throws. But the word* יד *iad also means 'power, force'. Now, if the Translators had been led by intelligence, they would have said in Proverbs that death and life were in* the power of the tongue, *which would have been very expressive; instead of telling us, as they have in fact done, that they were in* the hand of the tongue, *which offers us only an unintelligible and bizarre image.*[189]

Then let us transform the word hand *into the word* power *and let us recall what dangers menace the impure man who leaves his body before his time.*

Since the Law of Beings is irrevocable, they are forced to fulfill it. Now, if intelligent man must live for a time in blood, and if he is deprived

---

[189] Proverbs 18:21 says: "Death and life are in the power of the tongue", in both the King James Version and the French Jeruslaem Bible, so it is difficult to be sure what Saint-Martin is referring to, unless the wording in the French or Latin Bible was different in his day. Yet even the David Martin version of 1707 says: "La mort et la vie *sont* au pouvoir de la langue", so it still uses the word 'tongue'.

of his, then he must attach himself to other blood, usually that of his murderer, be it a man or beast, because then that blood is the closest and the most open to him.[190]

In both those cases, only the greatest disorder can result for him, since a Being can only inhabit the body which is proper and natural to him. By attaching himself to the blood of another man, he constrains him without being able to rest there, since another Being resides over him. By uniting with the blood of a beast, he links himself to even grosser and more alien shackles, and all those ills are so many obstacles which hold him back and trouble him in his progress. Thus, we can see why God once again asked for man's soul in the hand *or the power of all that is blood, since man is his tithe through the original correspondences of his quaternary with the ten. We can see the basis for the horror which men have generally had towards murderers; and finally, why all the Nations on Earth have regarded those whose cadavers are exposed as food for the birds and other animals as clothed with the ultimate mark of disapproval.*[191]

Let us move on to the second question, which concerns the ingratitude of the Chosen People.

Most Observers are shocked that the Hebrew Books, presenting a People elected by the Supreme Wisdom to be a mirror of His *Virtues* and His Laws, depict a People who become the most gross, the most barbarous and the most ignorant on Earth[192]; so that, far from fighting on behalf of the Hand which had chosen them, they arm themselves against Him at every turn; so that, by only observing the letter of the precepts of His Wisdom, they became useless to His designs.[193]

---

[190] This is a strange passage, in which Saint-Martin has a person killed before his time entering the body of the man or animal which killed him! The references to 'blood' hark back to the earlier passage in which Saint-Martin said the spirit of man is contained within the blood.

[191] It is not surprising that Saint-Martin clearly hadn't come across the funeral habits of the Zoroastrians, who make a point of returning their corporeal bodies to nature by exposing them on funeral towers as a feast for the birds of prey. However, here it is more likely he is referring to one of the Masonic penalties, which references this form of reprobation.

[192] Again, an example of an age without political correctness, and this is translated to remind us of the ignorance of the time deliberately fostered by interested parties to present the average man with a distorted image of the great cultures of other Religions.

[193] This reflects the words of the Repairer, who accused the Scribes and Pharisees of following the letter, rather than the spirit, of the Law, and likened them to 'whited sepulchers': "which indeed appear beautiful outward, but are within full of dead men's bones, and of all uncleanness." (Matthew, 23:27).

If those Observers had opened their eyes to man's true destiny, to the inextinguishable love of his Principle, Who burns with zeal and ardor for him, and to the belief found in all Nations that this Principle works ceaselessly to deliver them from their darkness and privation, then they would have realized that the Hebrew Books, like all other Traditions, were only the story of man.

They would have realized that this First Principle, Whose image man was charged with manifesting on Earth, continued to furnish him – even here below – with the means of accomplishing his destiny; that He knew the most sensible way of all was to show him, in his own posterity, what he would have been if he had retained the rights of his origin; that in order to do this the First Principle both could and had to select from among this criminal posterity some Being who was less guilty and closer to Him and make him the Agent of the *powers* which Justice grants to the Earth to lead it to His center; to give that Being, as a result of the original Covenant, the promise that if he used them in a legitimate manner, not only would He conserve them in him and his posterity, but he would also augment those *powers* endlessly and exponentially [194]; but if, on the contrary, he and his descendants scorned them, all those gifts would be taken away, and instead of enlightening the Nations and leading them to their center, they would become the object of His justice and the disgrace of the Earth.

Those Observers would finally have seen that the Books repeated in a physical and temporal picture that First Covenant on which the emanation of man was founded, and through which he should enjoy all the advantages inherent in the splendor of his source if he had remained in compliance with it, as he might expect every torment and degradation if he separated himself from it.

But although the Supreme Wisdom could and had to make the temporal choice we have spoken about; although He selected a just Being in whom to confide the treasure of his kindnesses, since no impious person could participate; if the later posterity of that Just One came to deviate from His Law, and if in consequence became a receptacle for ignorance and the object of contempt of all Nations, would we say from this that the choice of that Supreme Wisdom had been unworthy of Him? And would the first choice He had made had become any the less pure if man's

---

[194] *Jusqu'à l'immensité des nombres*: literally 'up to the immensity of numbers'.

posterity had become uncleanness itself? If that were true, then one would have to say that man, emanated from the Supreme Wisdom, was without glory and corrupt at his origin, since today we see him groveling in crime and opprobrium.

So, we must say that this People, despite the fact that they gave so little support to the Hand which had chosen them were, at the time of their election, no less the living flame which should have shone in our darkness and recalled the temporal image, of which invisible man is the model. Finally, let us recognize that he should have been the living proof of the Principle which has been described, concerning the necessity for the Supreme Wisdom to communicate these subdivided *powers* among men.

We cannot deny that, given the complete dispersion across the world in which they now find themselves, they no longer exhibit the signs of that truth. The People, chosen by Wisdom to be His sign upon Earth, represented the glorious estate of man in the purity of his origin and the sublime functions to which this Wisdom had called him to manifest in the Universe. The People also represented the order and harmony of that Supreme Unity which all Beings should ceaselessly contemplate, so as to conform to the regularity of their pattern. In other words, they were to be the beacon of Nations and the flame which should have progressively enlightened them.

When the Hebrew people fell into the camp of the guilty, when their crimes led them to forget their rights, into a false and impious Religion, and into the harsh *diasposa* which was necessarily its result, their original nature didn't change at all. Though the exercise of their rights and abilities had been withdrawn, the voluntary Covenant had not been destroyed; though the members of that body were completely dispersed and subdivided, they still retained their fundamental connections.

Therefore, these People still show the original imprint which constitutes them. They have always born upon them the *seal* of the Ministry to which they were called and carried their indelible essence everywhere they went; just as man has retained his, despite his crime and his degradation. So, when Justice let these People wander among all the Nations, they still showed them signs, though modified, of a worthy origin which attested to the existence of *powers* and Divine perfections. Finally, this People still represents the columns of the Temple to those Nations, though it only offers the image of them thrown down.[195]

In this manner He gave the Nations – in distorted pictures – secret signs of those *powers* which love and wisdom had carried into the dwellings of men, to show them for all time the living image of the True Being on which their existence was modeled. And that People, being dispersed among all the Nations of the Earth, had before them both the Agents which must be the organs of truth, and the scourges which followed them for having dared to reject it.

We cannot end this discussion about the Hebrew Traditions in a better way, than by showing on what the sublime privileges, of which those People were the Agents, reposed. This is the fact that in his language he had the first positive and collective *Name* of all the abilities and attributes of the Great Being, a *Name* which clearly encloses the *Principle*, *life* and *primordial* and *radical action* of all that can exist; a *Name* by which the stars shine, the Earth brings forth its harvest, and men can think; a *Name* by which, dear Reader, I have written these truths for you, and through which you can understand them.

It is true that this great *Name* passed into all the other languages of the Earth, but in no case was it carried across in the complete sense which it had in the language of the Hebrews. Some only have an indicative name for the existence of a Superior Being, without expressing anything of His *Powers*. Others preserved some of His principle traits but made an abstraction of all the others, and those do not paint a true picture of our God to our senses. Still others, whose languages are close to Hebrew through their antiquity, preserved the letters which compose the *Name* of the Universal God to a large extent, but altered their form and pronunciation, and soon stopped associating it with the vast and profound idea which is the source of the word. Hebrew alone possessed intact that Supreme *Name*, a stock on which are and shall be grafted all the other *Names* intended to support the posterity of humanity. We are not therefore surprised that this Nation is shown as being the beacon to Nations and the

---

[195] Once more, this is a reference to the Tracing Board which depicts the ruins of the First Temple, on whose ruins Zerubbabel erected the Second. Particularly in the *Rite of Strict Observance* and in the *Scottish Rectified Rite*, being developed by Jean-Baptiste Willermoz at the time, this was presented in the Entered Apprentice Grade as the black and white floor of the first Temple and the two broken columns at the entrance. The Latin motto on the Tracing Board was *Adhuc stat*, or 'it still stands', which contains a number of meanings in the respective rituals.

visible hearthstone on which, since the Fall of man, the first rays of the Great Being were reflected.

We believe we have presented a collection of principles which are sufficiently linked, coherent and true to overthrow all doctrines of error and emptiness, and we believe we have replaced them with a most solid, luminous and consoling explanation. If, up till now, man had neglected seeking to manifest the properties of the Source from which he had descended, at least he can no longer accuse Him or complain that this Source hasn't provided him with the means to do so.

For though man, as a natural consequence of his faults, has been reduced to being unable to contemplate the images of his divine abilities except in a dismal and painful subdivision, they are so multiplied in him that they no longer leave any reason for complaint.

Not only does every substance and every action of Nature exhibit a sign of the creative abilities which produced them, not only do all the facts about man tell us that he is emanated from a sentient source, that he has been separated from it because of a crime and that, because of an indestructible need and because of the Law of which he is composed, both Wisdom and man must ceaselessly strive to reunite: yet still all the Traditions of the Earth show that this Source has never stopped drawing near to man, despite his defilement, and circling about him by means of innumerable channels in all the parts of his corrupt habitation, and shows Himself visibly in every step he takes.

So, all that man can perceive with his corporeal eyes, all the actions he can perform and produce according to the Laws of the physical realm, all that he can receive by thought, all that he can learn through Traditions, through the various doctrines of his fellow men, through the spectacle of a sublime Religion given to the Earth, through the shameful and contemptible state of those who lost it by having profaned it: and finally, in the past and present Table of the entire Universe, we can find so many irrevocable witnesses which speak to him in the language of his Principle and his Law.

If Wisdom formed man under the express condition that he manifest Him in the Universe, we don't believe it poointless nor ineffectual, to contemplate the ways which He has never ceased to use to reestablish the union which should always have reigned between Him and us. Let us recognize, in short, that although we endlessly fail our side of the *Covenant*, Wisdom occupies Himself solely in fulfilling His.

Peh (פ) – Knowledge and Teaching

Let us now seek to be on our guard against the abuses that men have made of truth, and consider the different branches of *knowledge* which, in their hands, have so often been separated from their *true source*.

I will fulfill this task so much more willingly, for the time appears to be coming when it will become necessary to remind men in some way of these important things. The traces of barbarism have been effaced; we grow weary of the vague and pointless studies which have replaced them; the absurd systems, which had been too precipitously built on their ruins, are buried in darkness and appear to be drawing to an end; and although those poisonous plants have grown deep roots in many places, since they have shed all their seeds at once, there is nothing left in them to grow, so that they are destroyed by their own impotence.

Among the shapeless debris of these colossi of imagination and corruption, we see a class of Observers appear who are both prudent and judicious, and who, learning from the aberrations of those who preceded them, endeavor to make their course more certain.

A hidden desire focuses their attention on the vestiges of truth scattered throughout the Universe. Their rivalry, directed to some extent by Nature, has them discover traces of light every day whose existence they hadn't suspected even a few moments earlier. In other words, the spirits ferment and physically purge themselves of foreign substances with which they have been mixed up for so long.

So, it is probable that the Observers, after studying for some time the Laws of Beings, celestial and terrestrial phenomena, the physical correspondences between man and all that exists, the parallels in languages, and the true meaning of Traditions, will finally perceive the immense realm that is the knowledge of man, and that they will then enjoy a system of knowledge which is true, logical and universal.

Let us note here that the most important and the principle of all these discoveries is the recognition of the *physicality*[196] of the *Earth*, for it is

---

[196] *Sensibilité* can mean physicality, sensibility and sensitivity. Here it's translated as 'physicality' to emphasize the materal nature, but one should remember that, to a French reader, it also carries aspects of the other two words at the same time.

easy to assure ourselves that our planet enjoys this facility, since we enjoy it ourselves corporeally, and because our bodies come from the Earth.

Just as the least parts of our bodies communicate their physicality to the immaterial corporeal Principle which animates us, so do all terrestrial Beings invisibly communicate theirs to the *physical Principle* of the Earth. And one can determine the ultimate degree of its physicality, since it combines both ours and that of all the other physical Beings of our realm, not including the fact that it has correspondences of another kind with other Orders of Beings[197] which appear more distant, and which can only correspond with it by means of their *number* and their *secondary actions*.

But to better understand the importance of this doctrine on the physicality of our Globe, let us understand that it is the *basis* of all physical phenomena, just as man is the basis of all intellectual phenomena, and thus Earth and man are the two places in which are reflected all the *actions* and all the *powers* intended to be manifested in time.

Here, then, is one of the sources of that sublime knowledge towards which men seem to walk without knowing it, and which must one day teach them what their true occupation and the true destination of their Being is.

But we cannot reflect on man without realizing that this epoch could be as much something to fear as something to desire.

For at what time has the *Tree of Knowledge* not been weighed down beneath the weight of *strange branches* which are grafted onto it? We have seen that idolatry is the result of man's descent from the pure idea and simple Religion of worshiping his *Principle* to worshiping *inferior objects*.

Now, if material time only began for man after his crime, we can see how for him, being in material time, it was difficult not to fall into idolatry.

In fact, what has become of that *simple Religion* to which man was called by his nature, and of which he has perceived so little trace about him since his degradation; that *Religion* which pure Beings who are free

---

[197] It is worth mentioning here that Saint-Martin envisages five Classes of Being. He explains this later in this Chapter, but to make the text easier to read, they are listed here: 1st Divine; 2nd Spiritual; 3rd Natural; 4th Material; 5th Impure. This is reflected in the five ways man can act: 1. in God; 2. with God; 3. through God; 4. without God; 5. against God.

of the shackles which bind us offer to the Eternal according to their *powers* and their *number*? Too sublime for Earth, He hides from our eyes and no longer allows us to gaze upon Him.

The forgetting of that Religion having been the first step which man made in distancing himself from his Principle, his only resource was in those pure *Agents* who were formerly his *Ministers* and are now his *Masters*; those Agents who are attached to time like him, but who are not contained like him in the shackles of a gross and corruptible body; finally, those Agents on whom God *writes* without cease today as he formerly wrote on man, and who in their turn *write* on all the parts of the Universe, so that man may everywhere be within reach of instruction.

We could say that, in a way, we normally live under the Laws of that *Second Order*, since we receive daily thoughts which can only come from those who comprise and inhabit it. However, as we are almost always *passive* in those communications and as some Religion heralds their *activity*, we must presume that this Second Order presents for our study *objects* which are more *physical*, *insistent* and *positive*; and that from then on more vigilant and better *directed attention* is required than that which the majority of men employ.

That Order, without being as perfect as the *First Order*, is the highest level to which man may wisely raise his eyes during the rapid instant that it passes over the Earth. It does not require any matter, instrument, or organ foreign to those which man possesses as a consequence of his nature. From his birth, man carries with him all the *materials* and all the *foundations*; without which this edifice would never be built.

Nevertheless, this Order knows the *time* and the *suspension* of the actions permitted to it, since such is the Law of all Agents enclosed in time; and if there are Masters who teach otherwise, they are either ignorant or imposters.

But the more this Order is sublime, the more it is difficult for man to remain there. To do this everything that is prideful in him must disappear and be wiped out, so than nothing but his pure and real essence may be allowed to shine forth. While preserving this indestructible integrity of his Being, those illusions which fill him must make room for solid and true substance, just like tender vegetation which, in the soil, loses its softness and takes on a more durable matter in its channels which, without changing its form, gives it a resistance to all trials. Finally, man, joining the *life* of *another Being* to himself, must perpetually renew himself without ceasing to be himself, and the *life* of that other Being is that of the Infinite One.

Let us therefore not be surprised if this Order appeared so elevated to those who knew them that, from the Fall of man, many of them limited their worship to focus on them, and this was the first source of temporal idolatry.

There is an *Inferior Order* to this. Although it is only at the *Third Level*, it is the most in accordance with the infirm and degraded estate of man; It is composite like him, composed like him of two significant *foundations*.

The first of these *foundations* has as its subject knowledge concerning the true nature of man, and the second embraces physical Nature. Both are pure, respectable and full of marvels for him who knows how to follow their correspondences, and to bring to his meditations a simple, peaceful, humble intention, disposed above all to contemplate and admire those beautiful spectacles, rather than to reign over them and to glorify himself for existing there.

Both embrace those hieroglyphic emblems which have served as the seed of the symbols of Fable; both have been known by many Sages in olden and present times; both are the source of many Religions openly practiced on Earth, since there isn't one which doesn't exhibit at least a vestige of them. And when those traces are further distorted, the pure and constant desires of the man who follows them in the simplicity of his heart can help them to recover their original effectiveness.

If the first of those foundations should serve as the model for the second. The second must support the first, to satisfy all the Laws of our Being, and to bring all the abilities which compose us into perfect equilibrium. For if man, aspiring to *intelligent knowledge*, neglects the *resources* which Nature sets before us, he runs the risk of achieving nothing but ignorance and folly.

In fact, if Elemental Nature is harmful to us, it is when we allow ourselves to enslaved by her, and not when we penetrate her *powers*. In other words, to ignore Nature is to crawl before her, to subordinate oneself to her and to remain in the thrall of her shadowy path. But to know her is to conquer her and raise ourselves above her; and those who are focused on real *objects* recognize her usefulness so well that, when they are exhausted from too great an abundance of the *fruits of their studies*, it is enough for them to fix their attention on a physical object to obtain relief.

Besides, if we find ourselves put in the midst of those physical objects, this proves that the Supreme Being wants us to begin to understand Him in this way; if He has given this Book[198] to us, it is so that we may read it before those *Books* which we are still unable to see. This is one of the greatest secrets that man can know: to not go to God immediately, but rather to spend a long time on the road which leads to Him.

Nevertheless, let us take care never to separate that inferior foundation from the *intellectual stimulus* which should vivify it and which is its true purpose. That is to say, let us strive never to contemplate those physical objects without taking the *flame of intelligence* as our guide, for it is the God of Nature. Without that light, we only see a confused appearance, and we will never penetrate the wisdom of the order and harmony which constitute them, just as we will never approach that God who is beyond intelligence if we don't begin by *deifying* our heart, seeing that nothing operates except by analogy.

Let us take care not to lose sight of this higher goal and limiting ourselves exclusively to physical and elemental knowledge. This is the danger into which men of almost all ages have fallen. It is this danger which befell Ishmael, and then Esau, who lost his birthright. And this is why the Arabs who descend from Ishmael, and who have been such fertile sources of the natural Sciences that they are acknowledged to be its founders in all the Nations, still live beneath the true destiny of man.

It is in distancing themselves still further from that Order that the Mohammedans have reduced the Religion of the Arabs to simple bodily observances without intelligence or light; that, for them, the freedom of the senses is so to speak without restraint, and is that not perhaps for reasons relating to the fact that Mohammed claimed to have been inspired by the Angel of the Moon?[199]

So, in order to obtain a complete understanding of knowledge and *powers*, it is clear that the *two foundations*, intellectual and Elemental, should lend one another mutual assistance.

From the division of those two foundations, as was done by the Arabs as well as by early men, came an immense source of abuse and error which

---

[198] Here we find an overt reference by Saint-Martin to the "Book of Nature", described in his book '*Of Errors & Truth*', and in the following paragraph he even makes mention of 'Order' and 'Harmony', two of its pages.

[199] Another reference no doubt inspired by Catholic prejudice.

forms a *Fourth Order*. The men of this Order, attracted to natural substances, narrowed their view by focusing on them individually.

They focused on the Inferior Being of man; and if they occasionally concerned themselves with his Superior Being it was only to present Him with objects which are not worthy of Him.

From this, through the Ages, those Sciences based upon formulae and secrets cme into being. That knowledge whose success, according to those who teach it, depends exclusively on dead matter, amulets, pentacles, talismans, or the observation of physical objects, the flight of birds, the alignment of certain stars, the features and structure of the human body, what is understood under the names of Geomancy, Chiromancy, Magic, Astrology, and all the Sciences in which the Principle, being subordinate to the *secondary Causes*, leaves man in ignorance of the *true Cause*. Now, it only takes one step to go from ignorance to error and iniquity, just as an uncultivated terrain covered with brambles soon becomes a serpents' lair. It is because of this that blind and false Masters, abusing the faith of people whose passions and vices they deceive, daily turn men aside from their original destination and the true goal of their trust.

I am not talking about those who, while enjoying the most celebrated reputation among men, are even lower than those whom I have just described. Not only have they estranged themselves, like those described, from the invisible cause which presides over all the Laws of Beings; not only have they become blind to the destiny and the Principles of natural things; but they have also lost any understanding of the properties of the least substances. They only observe the external effects of the body, without being concerned with the true relationships of these Beings with man.[200]

However, man's intellect cannot always be asleep, and he has at least sought the Laws and relationships which these Being can have between them. But having separated these Beings from their Principle, they are forced to explain them without reference to God, and it is from that which material and incoherent doctrines about the production of stars from the division of a single body of incandescent matter have arisen.[201] These are

---

[200] It is interesting to compare this comment with Papus in his books a Century later. While Saint-Martin normally refers to the Observers in a dispassionate tone, this paragraph sounds somewhat more emotional, and suggests a personal irritation with certain people who may have been known to him.

[201] Of course, this is now generally accepted to be the manner in which new stars are born!

those sadly diminished comparisons of the birth of those great and living impetuses with the dead, passive fusions of our earthly substances, theories which have cost their authors considerably more effort than would have been necessary if they simply accepted an active and controlling Principle of all Beings, Who infuses each with a measure of *power*, *virtue* and *life* analogous to His plans; for only falsehood and error causes man to labor, and it is a peaceful and natural deed when he is working in truth. But as I have already said, I must not speak of that group of experts, for they are worthless relative to knowledge and the objects of our study.

Finally, there is a *Fifth Order* of knowledge, and it is abomination itself. It possesses *means* and *intelligent physical emblems* like the preceding Orders; it knows the number and properties of phantoms; it has a Religion, and a certain purity is required to operate it. Finally, there is a Nation on Earth which sells other Nations a part of the *ingredients* necessary for this Religion, but the *results* are horrible; their *signs* are usually traced on those who profess and practice it, so that men have eloquent examples of justice before their eyes. For as the *object* of that knowledge is *false* and corrupted, it leads men by paths contrary to those which lead to truth. But since this truth is found everywhere, the monsters of whom we speak cannot take a single step without encountering it, and not coming to it by means of *natural roads*, they approach truth only to be driven back; they only know truth through being tested by its severity, and don't enjoy the peace which it offers.[202]

To these different Orders of knowledge, one must add intermediate gradations. We shouldn't forget that each of these classes can lead to unlimited expressions, either in the number of branches which it encompasses, or in the extent of these branches, which allow it to combine completely or in part with other classes, be they the closest or the most distant, to form amalgams which man's conception has difficulty in recognizing.

---

[202] Being described both as 'impure' and 'working against God' one may safely assume that the Fifth Class refers to black magicians, witches, fortune-tellers and their kind. However, the reference to the "Nation on Earth which sells other Nations a part of the *ingredients* necessary for this Religion" is intriguing. We are clearly prior to the rediscovery of ancient Egypt, which later provided many talismans, mummia, mummy bandages and other accoutrements for magical spells. One might hazard the opinion that Saint-Martin is referring to the *gitanes* or gypsies – but that is only an educated guess.

Peh (פ) – Knowledge and Teaching

For from the sands of the sea up to the highest realms of Beings, man can establish many and varied *signs* of his *original titles*; he can, as he proves each day in his arts, his tastes and his passions, put his soul into his eyes, his ears, his hands, his feet, his taste, his head, his heart, in his impure organs. And all these things, corporeally linked to him, are but the image of objects distinct from him with which he can identify.

From this we should not be surprised at the jumble of doctrines on the Earth, and see in them different combinations of the Divine, the spiritual, the natural, the material and the impure, because all the Orders are open to man, and because when he does not regulate his steps by an *infallible guide*, he allows traces of his corruption and ignorance to enter into his *works*. So, it is invariable that man, through his nature, can act in God, with God, through God, without God and against God.

It is not difficult to see why it would be in our interest to distinguish between all these types of knowledge. But seeing the confusion to which they are subjected in passing through man's hands, it would be possible that they could still lead us into error beneath a plausible exterior. Then let us protect ourselves from the Masters who only build their knowledge on a material foundation, on formulae and on scientific recipes always focusing on secondary causes since, I repeat, there is almost no gap between secondary causes and corrupt causes. And those who cling exclusively to similar subjects and those who teach them should only merit our compassion.

Those who claim a more elevated knowledge and *superior means* require our vigilance and reflection even more, for since their path is less well known, it would be easier for them to lead us astray. There are two ways to assess them: by their teachings and by their *facts*. I would say facts are less important for those who only witness them, even though they are most useful to those who have the good fortune to be their instruments. But as this path is also one of illusion, guile and bad faith, and it is important to exercise prudence in carefully observing all which is manifested and all that takes place, so that one does not mistake natural and subordinate Causes for the activity of Superior Causes. Another means of protecting oneself in these types of observations is not to be blind to the point of wanting to explain everything through the sole mechanism of secondary Causes, as have some Commentators on the Hebrew Books who, speaking about the Law given on Mount Sinai, have represented the imposing sounds which accompanied this episode as being simple meteors, and claps of thunder and lightning.[203]

Teaching is therefore the surest touchstone to judge the knowledge claimed by a Master, in order to know the purpose which drives him and the direction he has given to his abilities.

True teaching, we are bold to say, is that which has been presented in this Book, a teaching founded on man's nature, on his relationship with his Principle and with the Beings which surround him.

It is this teaching which shows him how he is superior to Elemental Nature, since this is but a *composite unity*, or a fraction of the great unity, necessarily following the Law of *numerical fractions* which is to diminish in their exaltation, or to be ever more numerous in their roots than in their powers; so that the more the material Universe advances in years, the more it approaches annihilation, since it augments its powers.

It is this teaching which shows the intellectual Being of man as *complete*[204], since he is connected to the intellectual and divine origin in which all powers are complete; which states in consequence that according to the Law of Completeness, he must grow and spread in proportion to how much he raises himself up to embrace his Powers, since the privilege of the *complete ones* is to manifest more and more their grandeur and the indestructibility of their Being.

It is this teaching which, by showing the *number* of man as being greater in proportion with how high he raises himself to embrace his powers, leads us to understand that there must come a time where the temporal action of that *number* being complete, he can no longer act except in the infinite, and in consequence outside of both specific and general material boundaries. So, that is the Table of the progressive course of intellectual man: in childhood he does not think at all on account of his body; in youth he thinks through the body; in maturity he thinks with the body; in old age he thinks despite the body; after death, he thinks without the body.

It is this teaching which one cannot accuse of wishing to control the belief of men, for on the contrary it urges them not to take a single step without scrutiny. It is this doctrine which, showing in man the remains

---

[203] '*Les feux*' can be translated as 'fires' or 'conflagration', but in this instance this could be an abbreviation of '*feu du ciel*', or 'lightning' (lit. fire from heaven).

[204] '*Entier*' is the word used, or 'entire' to contrast with '*fractions*' in the preceding paragraph. 'Complete' seems the best word to use.

and ruins of a magnificent Temple, presents him with all the *actions* of wisdom and truth which ceaselessly strain to raise him up once again on his foundations; which teaches him that the ways indicated by enlightened men or the General Elect are needed by him in the middle age of his rehabilitation, but that the true light which acknowledges each in private comes by means of a still more natural channel and sheltered from all illusion, once man has practiced total self-denial for a long time, isn't at all filled with his own conceit, and does not believe himself wise and, like the daughter of Jephthah, has truly bewailed his virginity.[205]

It is this teaching which shows him that the crime of man subdivided all his *powers* in relation to him, whose vast ensemble he had previously contemplated in the blink of an eye, but as the nature of Beings is indelible, since man is the characteristic expression of the Supreme Principle, this Law must operate eternally.

It is this teaching which leads him to recognize that the multitude of facts, activities, *Agents* and *powers* spread across the Universe according to the Traditions of all Nations, are the fulfillment of that coeternal and indestructible Law which, having created man, accompanies him and will accompany him forever in every moment of his existence.

Finally, it is this teaching which makes him consider all the facts of Nature to be the expression of his true knowledge and of the sublimity of his original functions, as may be seen in the rainbow, a phenomenon which is only formed by the reflection of the solar rays – as the intellectual *powers* are the *reflections of the Action* of the Supreme God – and which appears when there are clouds, appears to set the boundary between their shadowy chaos and the abode of light; which bears a regular number in its colors; which appears in the form of a circumference so far subordinate to man, who himself forever occupies the center and makes it follow all his steps; which offers an immense Table to his eyes in which he can see what his first relationship with Unity was, with the submissive Agents which he commanded at will, and with the seat of disorder and confusion from which those faithful Ministers carefully kept him apart; which, in a word, presents so fertile an image that Wisdom could not choose a better symbol when, at the time of the Flood, He wanted to proclaim those

---

[205] Judges, 11:30-39.

Superior and Universal *Powers* which He made for all time the vehicles and the signs of His Covenant with man.[206]

With such a sublime doctrine, those who appear to guide us in the path of truth may merit our confidence, for if it happens that their course does not accord with their principles, those principles alone are sufficiently open to our minds that we will sense the error of their course, and the purity of our desires will render their efforts powerless.

In the same way, they would merit our confidence more if they taught us to discern knowledge with that wisdom which is the extension and goal of all knowledge.

One should not believe that this wisdom is at our sole disposition and that it depends completely on us, like the habit of bodily exercise by which we can shape ourselves by dint of repetition and be assured of success.

We have within us, it is true, many intellectual and spiritual abilities which can be perfected by our labors; these are the *secondary powers*, and also knowledge; but we don't come to wisdom through the force of strength: in the Court of the Kings we must walk with humility, submission, obligingness, and constant vigilance to captivate their benevolence, so that, at the moment they notice us they would always find us ready to please them and to sacrifice ourselves for them. It is as much through patience as through authority and violence that we should dispel the rivals who cross our path. Mildness and love are the paths which lead to happiness; moreover, despite all this care, the *Prince* may yet perhaps not judge it appropriate to honor us with a glance.

Let us now judge if wisdom is a precious thing and if there is nothing with which it may be compared.[207] Man must ask for it incessantly, but

---

[206] This comes from Proverbs 3:13 – 18: "Happy is the man that findeth wisdom, and the man that getteth understanding. For the merchandise of it is better than the merchandise of silver, and the gain thereof than fine gold. She is more precious than rubies: and all the things thou canst desire are not to be compared unto her. Length of days is in her right hand; and in her left hand riches and honour. Her ways are ways of pleasantness, and all her paths are peace. She is a Tree of Life to them that lay hold upon her: and happy is every one that retaineth her." As an aside, it may be of interest to the Reader to know that, in French, Wisdom (*la Sagesse*) is also feminine, as are several of the other words used by Saint-Martin to identify God. While this is merely a convention in French, where in most cases the use of the masculine or feminine is not connectioned with sex, it is intertesing to contemplate the fact that Saint-Martin uses feminine words to describe God almost as often as he uses masculine ones. It has been a challenge for the Translator to apply the masculine (i.e. 'He') throughout, especially when even the Bible and modern Gnostics attribute the feminine to Wisdom, or Sophia. Yet there is no doubt that Saint-Martin saw God, in all His mnifestations, as a masculine force.

[207] Saint-Martin is paraphrasing Proverbs 3:13-15 (see previous Footnote).

with words of Fire which express how much he desires it. His face must carry beforehand the joy with which this treasure would fill him; for it is a burning thirst, a voluptuous need: it is his whole inner Being which must speak.

We should listen to our Masters when they describe the imprudence to which man's mind is exposed during its journey because of too hasty judgments; when they tell us that however much knowledge, wisdom and *virtue* we might possess, there is always more to acquire than that which we already have; that the plants which pursue the course of their work in peaceful perseverance should serve us as models; that every moment that man uses to contemplate himself is taken from those destined for his *growth*; that not only should he not count the greatest pleasures which man can experience as having any value, he should also hold specific pleasures and enjoyments in even less esteem as being contrary to the Great Work; nor should he see any isolated part of knowledge as the sum total of marvels contained in man's Covenant with his Principle, for that false manner of seeing things would be the first obstacle to our progress; and if we suggest this to others, we may be assured that we will mislead them and that we will mislead ourselves.

We should listen attentively to those Masters if, having instructed us by means of those Principles, they urge us to consider whether there isn't an addition to the Great Work, and in that we will come to see the birth of a new order of things.

What would man's knowledge be, what would this Being be able to do to possess the whole of knowledge and truth if he had only been able to hope to know a subdivision of those Divine *Powers*? Since his very nature calls him to consider reuniting those very *Powers* and to be their living image, how could he ever recover his sublime privileges if he had only seen the scattered rays of that unity?

And who are those heroes, those demigods, those famous Agents whose relationship with the Earth are constantly depicted to us by our Historical and Fabulous Traditions? They have only been Agents of some of the *virtues* of unity. One of them manifested Fortitude by the *grandeur* of his enterprises and by his immense travails. Another manifested Justice through the punishing of *evil-doers* and by the enslaving of *rebels*. Still others manifested Kindness and Benevolence through the knowledge and assistance they brought to the *unfortunate*, and through the mildness they allowed to men of peace to taste. And one can even say of those Agents, without excepting those which are spoken of in the Hebrew Traditions, that they only showed man *individual powers*, temporal and fleeting, and that, in consequence, they did not give him that perfect concept of his Being, nor of the rights which are attached to his nature.[208]

He still lacks that addition to his knowledge to help him understand the sense of all those coarse symbols which truly represented the Law of men, but which only represented it in a material way, instead of that Law being shown through man's *power* and by the facts which emanate from man himself.

Therefore, a POWERFUL ACTION is needed to show the very real and potent existence of man, by facilitating the intellect of his Being and by raising him to a state of superiority towards which, ever since his fall, he never ceases to strain towards because of an irresistible Law of his essence; and so I tell you that a Third Age is required; a perfect pattern[209] is required who presents him with a Law which is simpler and more *one* than all those which had preceded it; a Law more similar to man's true nature, whose grandeur and sublimity we never cease to protect.[210]

Finally, it is necessary for Wisdom to *open* to human posterity another gate in addition to those which are contained in the *square* of man's power: that is to say that this Wisdom must *open* a fifth gate in order to abolish the *number of servitude* operated by the redoubled power of evil, so that man, having himself been delivered himself, might then be delivered from his confines. *And such was the spirit of that Hebrew Law which, at the end of fifty years, brought liberty to slaves and had*

---

[208] One might suggest that Saint-Martin is talking of archetypes. Thus, the ancient demigods tended to caricature and exaggerate one aspect of Divinity – Hercules/Heracles for strength, Venus/Aphodite for love – and we even see this in the Old Testament, such as Samson for strength. Thus, each demonstrates an aspect of the Divine Power (or Virtue); but none of those demigods exhibits the complete of rounded man, and so taken in isolation would lead to obsession or at best an incomplete image of original man, since in his glory man unifies all the powers or virtues. This is one reason why modern thought believes the Philosophers of early times understood well the concept of one god, but this was expressed in various aspects, which was taken by the less educated to imply polytheism.

[209] *Un type total* – lit. 'a complete type'. Saint-Martin is referring to 'Héli', the 'Repairer', or the 'Christ'.

[210] This Law is both the example of the Christ and also the Perfect Law which He gave to us, that one should love God and one's neighbor as oneself. The replacement for the Old Covenant for the New becomes very important in Willermoz' interpretation of the *Rite of Strict Observance* in the *Scottish Rectified Rite*. We have also seen references to the Virtues in this section, and the successive introduction of the Cardinal Virtues, and then the Theological Virtues forms a key progression in Willermoz' Rite.

dispossessed belongings returned into the hands of their original owners.[211]

By means of this new *power*, not only must man make the Laws of instinct and brute affection disappear from within him, but he must also replace them with the rights and habits of intelligence. Not only must he recognize all the *powers* of order and justice, but he must even learn to raise himself up above justice itself, by conducting himself by a Law different from that which had only been written for slaves and evildoers: in other words, he must learn to discern the true destiny of his Being, which was not created to be locked up in shackles, but to do good, like God, through his nature and through love; and not being compelled by the apparatus of reward and punishment.[212]

During the First Age of his expiation, man, like a child in the shadowy bonds of matter, no doubt experienced Wisdom's kindnesses. But like a child, he received those kindnesses without perceiving or recognizing the hand which showered them upon him; for he was still passive, and his true and intellectual Being had not yet tasted its true nourishment, comprised of activity and life.

---

[211] It is interesting to note that, while Saint-Martin saw the number 4 as being perfect, as well as the number of man, he also saw it as the product of 2 x 2; and since '2' was the number of confusion, or evil, 2 to the power of 2 was the number of evil redoubled as well. This reflects the idea that man contained two powers, both Good (since 4 comes from 10 and thus from 1 by Theosophical addition, and since 1+2+3+4 =10, which means from God or Unity), and Evil (being 2^2 as we have just seen), therefore containing both light and darkness. By opening the fifth gate the insertion of another '1' is implied. Now, the number '5' was the number of greatest evil to both Pasqually and Saint-Martin. However, in the approach of Theosophical addition, Saint-Martin saw it as the union of man with God (4+1), which reflects, too, the insertion of the Shin (ש) into Yahweh, the Tetragrammaton (יהוה), to create Yehesuah (יהשוה) or the Repairer. He thereby suggests the need for God to send the Repairer to bring in the Third Age, which also becomes a symbol of man discovering the spark of Divinity within himself, as we shall we shortly. He also supports his assertion by drawing our attention to the number '5' in the 'Jubilee Year' (again by Theosophical addition 5+0 = 5). Now, the 'Jubilee Year' of the Old Testament provided for a *double portion* of rest every 50th year. Each 49th year would be a Sabbath Year, followed by a Jubilee Year in the 50th, so that for two consecutive years the people would be bound to restore the land, restore personal and economic freedom and to depend on God for their livelihood and their nourishment. So, the allegory is that of a restoration to one's primitive rights and freedoms.

[212] This is another powerful case for man to move beyond the Mosaic Law, which he calls 'the Law written…for slaves and evil-doers', to seek the higher ground and embrace the single Law of Love, and to perform acts of love for Love itself, and not because he seeks reward or hopes to avoid punishment. It is fascinating indeed to read these words, written some two hundred and thirty years ago, and realize that many Christian denominations have still not achieved this understanding of the Holy Books in the intervening years.

In the Second Age, with his abilities more developed, he set about profiting from the gifts which he had squandered. It was then that the virtuous and enlightening Agents set themselves before him, and subjected him to sacrifices, to teach him about the state of violence and subjection in which all Nature found itself in comparison to him, because everything gave its life for him.

Through this, those Agents instructed him on the destiny of the various parts of the Universe. They taught him that there was not a single Being in Universal Creation which was not the image of one of the Divine *Powers*; that Wisdom had multiplied those images around man, so that when they were presented to him, Wisdom had them bring forth a new unction, so transmitting to man all the assistance he required; and so that, with the model thus uniting with the copy, man could come into possession of both.

This was to paint the Table of his destiny in vivid colors, representing the Universe as a Great Temple, in which the Stars are its Torches, the Earth its Altar, all corporeal Beings are the Sacrifices and man is the Sacrificer. Through this he would be able to recover profound ideas of the greatness of his original estate, in which he had been called to be nothing less than the PRIEST OF THE ETERNAL in the Universe.

But, despite this brilliant light which the Elect Ones of the Second Age had come to communicate to man, by explaining that he was the Priest of the Eternal, he still did not have a further explanation of this sublime title.[213]

The Table of relationships which the Elect Ones presented to him, magnificent as it was, only offered him images inferior to his true nature. In these he only saw powers as sparse and divided as the corruptible sacrifices. In these he saw neither sign of an imperishable offering, nor of the unity of the Agents which should join together so that, through them, he could enjoy the plenitude of his rights.

And so it was left to a Third Age for him to acquire a more perfect knowledge of truth; and for him to learn that, if simple and temporal

---

[213] Although it would be more grammatical to render *Éternel* as 'the Eternal One', the Translator has refrained from doing so, since this passage strongly reflects the work of the Order of the Élus Cohen. The members of this Order are referred to as Priests or Sacrificers, and many of the prayers they offer up during their ceremonies being with the words: *O Éternel*, which is norally translated in English versions as "O Eternal". Given the fact that this is one of the only times that Saint-Martin refers to God or the First Principle as *Éternel*, this would suggest that he is making that connection here. *Éternel* is normally rendered as 'Lord' in English.

images could have led him to discover some of the Superior *Powers*, then he must not place any limit on his hopes in presenting *Truth* with an image emanated from itself, and which, through the help it gives to man, animates him by means of the same unity, and assures him of the same immortality.

And it is through this that man, discovering the knowledge of his own greatness, learned that by establishing himself upon a Universal foundation, his intellectual Being becomes a true Temple; that the torches which must brighten his path are the light of thought which surround him and follow him everywhere; that the Sacrificer is his reliance on the necessary existence of the Principle of order and life; that it is before this burning and fertile persuasion that death and darkness disappear; that the perfumes and offerings are his prayer, his desire and zeal for the reign of unity alone; that the Altar is that eternal Covenant established by His very emanation[214], and to which God and man come together in concert to renew the Alliance of their love, there to find glory and happiness respectively. In a word, the Fire destined to devour the sacrifices, that Sacred Fire which must never be extinguished, is the divine spark which animates man and which, if he is faithful to his original Law, will forever make him burn as a bright and potent lamp placed upon the pathway to the Throne of the Eternal, there to illuminate the footsteps of those who have been separated from Him. Thus, at last, man may no longer doubt that he received his existence in order to be the living testimony of the light and the emblem of Divinity.

---

[214] For as we read above, man is the Sacrificer and in a way, being the Temple as both Priest and Victim, as was the description of the Christ. Here, Saint-Martin seems to describe man as the Altar as well, created by God's very emanation, and God meeting man at that Altar to renew the Covenant suggests, as all followers of Saint-Martin's writings know, that God is within us and that, by following the 'Way of the Heart', we can meet Him there.

Tzaddi (צ) – 1, 4 and 10, The Book of Man

To better convince ourselves how necessary it was for a *unity of powers* to be achieved before men gain sight of the Table of their Being – which had only been cursorily traced through specific manifestations – I am going to say something about *Numbers*. But first, I must warn you that this area of study is so vast that no man, nor any Being which God Himself created could understand it completely. Moreover, it is so worthy of respect that I can only speak about it to a certain extent, both because it is impossible to be very clear and open in a vulgar language, and because it conceals things which one must not state without preparation.

However, I will do so in order that the Man of Desire [215] may understand me, since it is necessary, and I will neglect nothing to procure his education with prudence.

But if it happens that he does not understand me, I beg him in his own interest not to discuss what I am going to confide in him with those Sages in title and influence in the opinion of humanity, for they have desiccated *knowledge* and have no substance; they are but fleshless skeletons and the most nourishing *juices* have evaporated before their eyes without them having the wisdom to grasp them. [216]

Knowledge is free. They have claimed they have determined its Laws, and have forbidden Mankind from hoping to discover anything outside their pronouncements: but it has fled before them and they walk in a gloomy void. Knowledge is as unrestrainable as water. They try to

---

[215] Subtle marketing, perhaps, as 'Man of Desire' was the title of his next book. However, as we have seen earlier, this description is also part of a series of stages of man's spiritual development, from Man of the Stream (asleep to reality, or the profane), to Man of Desire (awakened and seeking, or Apprentice), to New Man (on the Path, or Master), and finally, Spirit-Man (Enlightened, Adept, or Réau-Croix). It is worth noting, too, that this section reprises a significant part of his Saint-Martin's book *Of Errors & Truth* – though with the benefit of seven more years of meditation – which also links the point within the circle, '1', or Divinity, to the number '4', or man, who began in the center but now roamed the circumference of the circle, represented by the number '0'.

[216] This could be referred to as a 'hook'. Saint-Martin is suggesting that he is confiding secrets to the Readers, even going so far as to tell them not to share them with the profane!

restrain it, but it shatters the shackles they give it, and they are left in the desert.

Therefore, let the Reader not go to them to air his doubts, for they will only increase them or substitute lies. If something in what the Reader is about to read puzzles him, let him fall back on his own abilities and try, through *inner activity*, to make himself *simple* and *natural*, so that he won't be annoyed if success makes him wait. The *delays* he will experience are often the same paths which are being secretly prepared for him and which will lead him there.

Numbers are the invisible envelopes of Being, just as bodies are physical envelopes.

One cannot doubt that all Beings have an invisible envelope, for they all have a *Principle* and a *form*, and since that Principle and that form are at the two extremes, they are too far apart from each other to unite and relate without an intermediary. It is the invisible envelope or the number which fulfills this role. So it is that, in the body, Earth is the envelope of Fire, Water is that of Earth, and Air that of Water, though this order is completely different in non-corporeal Elements.

One isn't unaware of the fact that the Laws and properties of Beings are written upon their physical envelopes, since all the means by which they communicate with our senses are none other than the very expression and action of those Laws and properties.

One might say the same thing about their invisible envelopes. These must contain and wear the invisible Laws and properties of Beings, just as their visible envelopes indicate their physical properties. If they are written there, man's intellect must therefore be able to read them, just as his senses can read or experience the effects of physical properties drawn on the body and acting through the physical envelope of Beings. That is how the knowledge of numbers can allow him who does not take them as being simple arithmetic expressions, to know how to contemplate them according to their natural order and see in them those *Principles* which are *coeternal* with *Truth*.

One should know moreover that since Beings are infinite, and since the properties of these Beings are manifold, there is also an infinity of numbers.

And so, there are numbers for the fundamental constitution of Beings. There are numbers for their actions, their career, just as there are for their beginning and their end, when they are subject to one or the other; there are even numbers for the different stages of progression established for them.

And they are there just as many for the limits where the *divine rays* stop and reflect back towards their *Source*, not only to present Him their own images, not only to offer Him the glorious witness of His singular superiority and infiniteness, but also to draw *life*, *measure* and *weight* from Him, the sanction of their relationship with Him. Everything we have seen cannot exist except in the Original Source of Beings.

There are also composite numbers to express the different unions and compositions of Beings, actions and *powers*. There are central numbers, median numbers, circular numbers and numbers of circumference. Finally, there are impure numbers which are false and corrupt. And, we repeat, all those numbers tell us the various aspects under which we can consider Beings and the different properties, Laws and actions – whether visible or invisible – which we can be sure they have. And perhaps the real reason why numbers appear so chimerical to most men, is the custom by which Accountants make all numbers derive from zero, that is to say, to commence their geometric divisions from zero, before stating the first unity. They don't see that this visible and customary unity which becomes the first basis of their measurements, is simply the representation of invisible unity, placed before the first step in all those measurements since it gives birth to all, and that if they are forced to represent it with a zero, they should realize that this only depicts its inaccessible value, and not see it as a 'nothingness', since it is the source of all the bases on which man can operate.[217]

One sees here that just as numbers are infinite, so the idea one must have of them is of being simple and natural.

It will become much simpler when we note that this immense multitude of numbers, which subdivide and extend to infinity, directly sum to ten simple numbers, which return to four other numbers, and those into unity from which all comes.[218]

---

[217] This alludes to the Kabbalistic idea of God in his pre-Creative state, or אור (Aur): in that, if the number '1' is the manifested Deity, then the invisible '1' is Him before manifestation of Creation, and since we have no figure for that, if we use the number '0' we must understand that it doesn't represent nothingness, but rather potentiality.

[218] For in Theosophical terms, '10' is composed of 4+3+2+1, or '4' numbers. And as we see in his posthumously published work *Des Nombres* ('On Numbers'), 1 is the essential root of 4 because 1+2+3+4 = 10 = 1+0 = 1.

That is why, living amidst so many things in Nature, nevertheless we have only ten fingers, four limbs and a single body to touch those things, to approach them and to make use of them; *for our toes have no other purpose than to give us suppleness, elasticity and speed in our gait, as well as solidity and strength when we are standing still. And if you have seen men successfully make use of their toes through strength of practice, the forced exercise they have undertaken to get there and the useless attempts of so many others surely prove that those digits were not given to us by Nature to do such things; for, even if they have the number ten, like the digits on our hands, that is only because everything repeats itself, but with inferior qualities and properties according to the inferiority of the Order.*

The allegory of the *Book with Ten Pages* in the Work previous cited [219] clearly presents the different properties attached to the ten intellectual numbers. It suffices to add that from their various unions and combinations result the expression of all the Laws and actions of all the Beings, just as the active combination of different Elements results in the infinite variety of all corporeal products and Elemental phenomena.

From among the examples I have just given, I will limit myself to just one; but man is its subject, as he is the subject of this work, and from this example one may learn to consider the examples which I discuss and also to think about other properties of numbers.

The Ancient Philosophers have transmitted to us the addition of the number four which gives ten as a product, which offers a natural means of reading how to discover the immense *power* of the quaternary, Modern Philosophers are content to ridicule all these numerical concepts without understanding them or being able to refute them.

In that *Book* we saw man's original purpose, which was to be the *sign* and the *Minister* of the Divinity in the Universe. We also saw that he was marked with the *quaternary seal*.

It is a singular thing that this sublime destiny of man can be found written in the expressions of the Ancient Philosophers. For, in taking the quaternary number back to the result of all the powers which constitute him, he yields two numbers or two branches which, being reunited, form the number ten, in this manner:

---

[219] '*Of Errors & Truth*', referring to the Book of Man in Chapter 4.

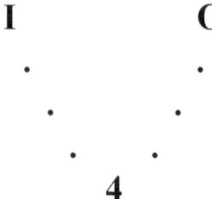

Now, the number four being placed between unity and the number ten, does it not seem to have the function of communicating unity to the Universal Circumference, or zero? Or, to put it another way, does it not appear to be the intermediary placed between Supreme Wisdom, represented by unity, and the Universe, represented by the zero? Out of this comes the natural figure:

$$I \ldots 4 \ldots O$$

Here I have drawn this figure using original numerical characters attributed to the Arabs, seeing that they had been transmitted to us by them, but the Sages of that country recognize that they belong to a more Ancient People.

These characters which, to the experienced eye, carry the exact imprint of the highest secrets of the Natural and Physical Sciences, can only have been drawn for common man by Sages; and for them by an even purer Hand, in order to help them walk with firm steps in the way of truth.

Thus, through the Law of Numbers and the figure I have just drawn, we can be sure of the original dignity of man who, being in correspondence with the Source of Light and with the Beings who were the most distant from it, was destined to communicate His *Powers* to them.

One also finds in these number the manner in which man went astray.

If, instead of being in the center of his eminent post, man, or the quaternary, became distanced from unity and approached the circumference indicated by the zero, until he was lost and became enclosed within it, he became material and tenebrous like it, and this is the new figure which his crime produced:

I ....

Could we not also discover indications of that union of the quaternary with zero in the number of days necessary for the human fetus to have life? The Physiologists assure us that it takes around 40[220], and so it would be hard to doubt that this had been the source and result of man's crime, since this number is recounted before our eyes in the reproduction of the human species.

Still, we should note, to calm the mind of the Reader to whom these truths might appear very strange, that we should not apply this number of 40 days to the crime of man, as we see it attributed today to corporeal reproduction. The true number of that Law is only a consequence and expiation of a false number *which acted at an earlier time.*

Finally, we also find in this simple figure:

I ....

clear evidence of all the principles previously outlined on the need to communicate the Superior Powers down to the unhappy abode of man.

From *one* to *ten*, there are many different numbers which are all attached to the first link of the chain through some specific tie, though we have the right to separate them in order to consider each in a particular light. If the quaternary, or man, has descended to the lower extremity of this chain, or down to zero, and yet the Supreme Source had chosen him to be His representative sign, would it not be necessary, for him to be able to recover knowledge of what he had lost, for all those numbers – or all

---

[220] This assertion is more likely taken from Aristotle, who proclaimed – without evidence – that life came to a male fetus at 40 days, and to a female fetus at 90 days. This came from his theory of Vegetable, Animal and Rational stages of development: the embryo being 'vegetative' until a certain point, when it became 'animal'; the 'rational' stage coming after birth. Similarly, in Jewish lore – Biblical, Talmudic and Rabbinical – the embryo is considered little more than fluid until the 40th day and, does not possess a soul נפש (Nephesh) until it is born. The website (as of June 2018): https://www.myjewishlearning.com/article/the-fetus-in-jewish-law, provides more detailed points concerning the contemporary controversy, and the use of the Bible in this argument.

those Superior and Intermediary *Powers* between *one* and *ten* – to come down to him, right down to his circumference, since he doesn't have the power to breach the limits prescribed for him, in order to ascend towards them once more? And here we see all the powers of subdivision whose relationship to man I have already explained, applied to all the Traditions and Allegories of mankind.

But that is still not enough for the complete regeneration of man. If *Unity* hadn't penetrated the circumference which he inhabits, he wouldn't been able to recover the complete concept, and he would have remained under its Law. It was also necessary that *Unity* be preceded by all the *intermediary numbers*, since the order was reversed by man, and he could not recognize the *Original Unity* which he had abandoned until he had known all the *powers* separating him from It.

This sheds much light on the nature of this *Universal Manifestation*, whose need we have recognized for the fulfillment of the Supernal decrees.

For, whatever Agent is charged with an operation, it is certain that it cannot be inferior to the specific Agents which have only manifested the Superior Abilities in their subdivisions; and if the specific Agents, though reduced to some partial *powers*, have nevertheless represented the Powers of Wisdom without which they would have been impotent in their efforts, so that is all the more reason that the *Universal Agent* must be the depository of the same rights and powers.

And so, this universal manifestation of Divine Powers, following the rigorous Laws of Justice which result in the subdivision of these Powers, must have crowned all the blessings that man could hope for by giving him a glimpse of those positive truths from which he took his origin.

We must at the same time acknowledge that nothing less than an Agent clothed in such immense power would be necessary to raise man from his fall and help him to reestablish his likeness and correspondences with the *Original Unity*.

If it was through the highest form of man that all the evil of his unhappy posterity has been brought about, it would be impossible for man to be redeemed[221] by any man of this posterity, for that would be to

---

[221] This is a most interesting word, since *reparer* means both 'to repair' and 'to redeem'. This means that the word used for Centuries to describe Saint-Martin's view of Jesus or Héli as 'The Repairer', might just as well be called 'The Redeemer', a term rather more familiar to us. However,

suppose that even degraded Beings, stripped of all rights and all *powers*, would still be greater than him who was illuminated by the *Light* Himself; and that would suggest that weakness was superior to strength. Now, if all men are in a condition of weakness, and if they are all bound by the same shackles, where from among them would you find a Being capable of breaking their chains and delivering them? And if one found such a man, surely one would have to wait until someone first came to break his?

So, it is true that since all men are in the same powerless condition, despite all being called through their nature to a state of greatness and liberty, they cannot be reestablished in that state by a Being who is their equal; which proves that the Agent charged with bringing them back to Divine Unity must himself be more than man.

Thus, we must admit that if *Divine Power* itself had not been handed down, man would never have been able to recover his knowledge. Then it would never have been possible for him to reascend to the place of light and greatness to which the rights of his nature had called him; and the seal of the Great Principle would have been imprinted on his soul in vain. Then that Great Principle Himself would have failed in the most wonderful of his Powers, love and goodness, through which He ceaselessly procures for man the means to be happy. And finally, that Great Principle would have been deceived in His decrees and in the ineffaceable Covenant which binds all Beings to Him.

When I say that there is nothing between man and God, I say this in the Order of our true nature, where indeed no Power other than that of the Great Principal can rule over us. In our present state, however, there is something between God and us; and that is this false manner of being, this transposition of powers which by imprinting universal disorder in us, creates our torment and the horror of our transitory situation in the temporal.

This is another reason why the *Divine Power* draws near us, in order to reestablish general order by restoring all the powers to their proper rank; by reestablishing *Original Unity*; by separating the *corruption* which had come together in the *center*; by distributing the *powers* of the center to all the points on the circumference – that is to say, by destroying the *differences*.

---

in line with all previous translations and authors, the Translator will continue to use the traditional term 'The Repairer'.

For this is a truth which is at the same time profound and humiliating for us, that here below differences are the only source of knowledge for us, since it is from them that the relationships and distinctions between Beings are derived; yet these are the same differences which steal away our knowledge of *Unity* and prevent us from approaching it.

Now, we know that if the *Divine Power* does not take the first step, man could never hope to return to that Unity. For with two separated *powers*, how could the weaker one – the one which is completely powerless – ascend alone and by itself in order to accomplish reunion?

Finally, without that Universal Agent, man may have known from all the preceding manifestations that he possessed powers and *spiritual virtues*: but he would never have known that there was a God, since there would never have been a *Unity* in all his *powers* which would have allowed him to know this.

And so, let us recognize with confidence that the Agent which is the depository of the Unity of all the powers, whatever name we give him, must possess the totality of all the Supreme *Powers* which, before him, had never been manifested except in their subdivisions: that this Agent would have to carry within him a divine character and essence, and that in penetrating the soul of men, he was able to make them feel what was their God.

Here I recall the preceding figure,

which represents the state of privation in which we all languish because of the separation we have from our Principle. We can see that in bringing these characters together and allowing Unity to penetrate into the quaternary of man, like this:

Universal order is reestablished, since these three characters:

$$I \ldots 4 \ldots O$$

are found once more in their progression and their natural harmony. This order certainly existed even at the time of the subdivision of these types, since it is eternally indestructible; but then it only existed horizontally, or on a latitude; whereas in the figure which unites them here under the same point and under the same center, this order exists according to its true number and true Law, which is *perpendicular*.

Finally, to speak without a veil, it is only in this age that the *Great Name* given to the Hebrews could have all its *action*. Under the Law of Justice, it had only acted externally. It had to penetrate right into the center in order to work in man that general explosion to which his intellectual Being is susceptible, and to deliver him from the state of concentration to which his fall had reduced him.

Given the profound concepts which we are presenting here, we should not be surprised at all by the various opinions men have held concerning the *Universal Agent*.[222] Whatever idea that they have formed about him, there is nothing of the *virtues, gifts* and *power* which they have not been able to find in him. Some have said that he is a Prophet; others a man with a profound understanding of Nature and of the Spiritual Agents; others a Superior Being; still others a Divinity. All are right, all have spoken in conformity with the truth, and all those variations only come out of the different places where men stand in order to contemplate the same object. The error committed by the early Philosophers was the desire to make their specific viewpoint both exclusive and universal. That committed by the later Philosophers was in not adapting their ideas to the weakness of their disciples, and in wishing to make them absorb the most fertile truths that the spirit of man may embrace without taking their level of intelligence into account.

Different levels of *knowledge* and will are therefore the only reason for the diversity of opinions reigning among men regarding this important

---

[222] If God is the First, or Universal Principle, then Christ or The Repairer is the Universal Agent. Since Saint-Martin refers to him as an Agent rather than a Principle, the Translator will use the lower case 'he', even though in traditional theology Christ is God. Since we see a couple of paragraph later that he had to take on human form to come to Earth, this would seem appropriate.

subject, for it is to them that the *Universal Agent* has come; to others for whom he comes; and others for whom not only has he not come, but for whom he will not come again.

The same principles which have been explained will help us to discover which should have been the most appropriate age for the manifestation of that Agent. For if he was charged by the Supreme Wisdom to heal the ills attached to the dark and foreign sphere which we inhabit, he would have to follow all of its Laws.

According to the Physical Order, an illness can only be cured after the remedy had penetrated to the very seat of life, to the center of the Being; which can be observed in most corporeal disturbances and which can only be properly remedied through the purification of blood.

But the blood is the center of the animal body. It is the most inner corporeal Principle, since being surrounded by other Principles it may consider itself to be in the center of the animal circumference, and it is from there that it sends forth emanations of its own life to the corporeal subdivisions of its extremities.

It must therefore follow that the *Universal Agent* charged with the Great Work of the reintegration of all *powers*, had to penetrate the most intimate substances of all impure Beings, to which he had to communicate his powers to the very *center* of all temporal things; and in order to accomplish this, he had to appear in the middle of time and in the middle of all the activity of emanated Beings, in order to act most efficaciously, and at a single point in time, both on the center and on the life of all the circumferences.

If one wished to identify a clear and identifiable age for this manifestation, it would be quite possible to discover it by bringing together various scattered ideas in the Hebrew Traditions. We must remember that their Scriptures teach us about the temporal Senary Law which directed the Creation of all things, and about the Sacred Septenary Law which was its complement.[223] One needs to understand the sense of the passage which says that: "*a thousand years are but as one day before God*"[224], since neither those who use it in their arguments nor those who

---

[223] Senary = pertaining to six; septenary = pertaining to seven. This refers to the six days of Creation and the seventh day on which God rested, as we saw earlier.

[224] 2 Peter 3:8: "But, beloved, be not ignorant of this one thing, that one day is with the Lord as a thousand years, and a thousand years as one day." It is odd that Saint-Martin quotes the New Testament when referring to the Old Testament.

debate it seem to have understood it any better than the rest. Finally, we need to know the relationship between all these expressions, both with the ternary and visible number of the corporeal Elements, as well as with the true number of the unity of their Principle. Then we will see that the Superior Laws and actions are also clearly designated in numbers, or in the intellectual envelopes of Beings, and that the Material Laws may be found upon the body.

But, just as we must give the Reader very detailed explanations of these matters, it would be useless to show him results which would be worthless for his education until he could be assured about all this through his own efforts. For now, I am content to lead him on the path, speaking to him further on the *quaternary number*, whose properties we have shown above.

Man, whom the quaternary number particularly suits, was emanated to occupy the *intermediary center* between the Divinity and the Universe. Through his fall, he was precipitated into a *circumference* very inferior to the place he had previously occupied, but since his nature had not changed despite his degradation, he had to occupy the center of this new region, as he had occupied the center of his previous one. And that was because, despite whatever degree of inferiority the Beings had descended to, their character was preserved and manifested itself.

If man, in his fall, still occupied a center, he therefore carried within himself his original quaternary number, though this number would have experienced some alteration on account of the new realm which was so contrary to it.

If man, in preserving his *quaternary* number, still occupied a center in the very abode of confusion which he inhabits, the Universal Agent, charged with providing him with a model, had to conform with all its Laws; that is to say, that in appearing in the middle of these times, he must have been imprinted with the quaternary number up at the time of his temporal manifestation. What I am saying is that the quaternary of time and the center of time are one and the same thing.

So, the quaternary which necessarily governs the Great Work, *must direct its results as it directed the various preparations; for that number which signifies both expiation and regeneration, expands or contracts by reason of the purpose the Beings must fulfill. The first man advanced by* forty *to obtain remission of his fault and the reconciliation of his temporal posterity; Jacob advanced by* forty *to obtain reconciliation for his spiritual posterity; the Liberator of the Hebrews advanced by* forty *to obtain deliverance of his people*[225]; *the Great Regenerator prepared the universal reconciliation by means of a* quadruple denary cube, *since in being its pivot, center and the first of all these types, it was to Him alone to perform the work of the middle of times, through which He embraces the two extremes, being both depository and complement of all the numbers.*[226]

Since his advent, this active quaternary number has reduced itself and will reduce itself more and more in future by reason of *extreme oppositions* for which it will be necessary for man to regenerate himself in less time than in the past; and this progression will continue to diminish until the quaternary *acts* so rapidly, so instantaneously that it will become confused with the Unity from whence it came. It is then that all temporal things will end, when love and peace shall reign in the heart of Men of Desire.

If one reflects on the sabbatical or septenary number which completed the origin of all things, one will recognize that this same number must complete its duration, and that four being the center of time, is also the middle of *seven*.[227] But we must guard against numbering the temporal course of the seventh action in the same way as the preceding six actions. This seventh action, not being marked upon our body[228], evades our calculations, and it would be impossible for man to calculate its length, since it is governed by *superior numbers* which man does not know how to command.

This is something to exercise the intellect, but there is also compensation for the work which remains to the done to calculate the age and antiquity of the World; and all I can say is that, to calculate this correctly, one must use a scale of terrestrial years.

Why use a scale of terrestrial years, you ask, and not days, weeks, months or even the revolutions of a planet other than ours?

Because, since time is the expression of the *six* and *one* first and the constitutive actions of Nature, there must be a direct correspondence to

---

[225] Moses.
[226] This seems to refer to the fact that the number '4' contains '3', '2', and '1', which can be used to create all numbers by Theosophic addition.
[227] In the progression 1, 2, 3, 4, 5, 6, 7: 4 is in the center.
[228] *Ne tombant point exclusivement sur le corps*: this implies that, since our envelope isn't marked with this number, being the number of Divinity, we can neither control it nor guess at its operation.

this in its periods and epochs. Therefore, it must present us with reduced – yet complete and proportionate – Tables to compare to the Great Table of the Origin of the Universe, its total duration and its destruction.

Now, we know that the terrestrial year is the period which most accurately represents these major traits of the Principle of Things, since it shows us in a short period the image of all which has been, which is and which is to come. This is because a year contains the universal production and destruction of vegetation, which is a true reflection of all things past, present and future. Finally, since it contains all these things, all ages, whether material or immaterial, it has been given to the intelligence of man to help him to be *reborn* and to assist him to leave the abyss.[229]

I would say we know this period is the same as all the terrestrial revolutions, that it is the true unit of computation of the Earth, and that during this particular time period the Earth depicts in living action all the traits of all time. This should be enough to prove that the terrestrial year is the symbolic number of universal time, and that as such, it becomes the basis of all our calculations.

We also find in this the proof which could avenge the Earth for the contempt shown it by ignorant men who wanted to find so little correspondence between it and the Universe as a reason to despise it. If the Earth didn't hold itself as closely as any other corporeal Being to the Laws and first Principles which have directed and produced all things, it would not carry with such clarity the number of all those characteristics.

---

[229] This appears to say that the annual cycle of vegetable life is a microcosm of the life of the Universe; and that these periods are given as a signs or lessons to help man learn how to reintegrate (the study of Nature to draw certain fundamental rules of existence is reminiscent of the 'Book of Nature' from *Of Errors & Truth*).

Qoph (ק) – The Work of the Repairer

Regarding the *revivification* connected with the *universal act*, both central and quaternary, we find signs of this in the Hebrew Traditions concerning the origin of the Universe. They teach us that the Sun was formed on the fourth day, and that before it came into being nothing animal had life. It was its reactive Fire which worked to draw forth all the corporeal Beings which inhabit the material Universe from the bosom of the Earth and the Waters. Was this not written to explain to us by means of that image that, if man became a criminal and subject to time, he would be only be able to recover his true light at the Fourth Age of the existence of temporal things? Was this not written to establish the number of that light and describe the Law by which it is governed and will be governed eternally?

It is for that reason that the Law given to the Hebrew People only carried the punishment of crimes unto the fourth generation. Now, the Universal Repairer, by appearing during the Fourth Age of the Universe, clearly satisfies the Law: in that Age he was able to accomplish a universal expiation for the prevarications of man's entire posterity, and therefore erase the impurity and illegitimacy of their own ancestors and any curse wherever his Ministry could expose them, on man's behalf.

However, should I suggest the formation of the Sun on the fourth day was a prophetic sign of a foretold event, for according to many the crime which took place could not have been predicted, for the Author of Things was not involved, and did not participate in the error of his creature? Should I not rather simply present the Sun's formation on the fourth day as confirmation of the universal action of the quaternary number which needed to be completed, before culpable and gloomy man could recover the life of his intellectual Being, just as the animals existed in an inert state – as it were in nothingness – until that moment when the elemental Sun gave impetus to the activity which was proper to them?

It is an established fact that, if so many mistakes have been made concerning Divine prescience, it is because those who discuss these facts confuse two very different Orders of things: the visible Order of corruptible things where we live, and the Order of incorruptible things, which was that of our true nature.

Instead of making this important distinction, they attribute to Supreme Wisdom an overall involvement in our works, which perhaps He has for some of us in our present estate where we are bound to the varied actions of Beings who are not free; but they are unable to see His Hand in our original estate without abusing Him and denaturing all His Laws.[230]

We will not spend much time on this question; it counts among the number of those which are useless and dangerous to approach by way of reasoning divorced from *action*. We should act to obtain the foundations for our meditations, rather than meditate before we have obtained those foundations. Without that everyone errs in the void, and in the shadowy space each man grasps a small piece which, in ignorance and recklessness, he uses to make generalizations. Everything is obscured since everything is divided; everything comes to nothing since man, left to himself, uses up his strength and receives nothing to renew it. And that is the origin of schisms and sects, that is to say, emptiness. Finally, I might add that one of the great signs of knowledge is knowing not to pay serious attention to these idle speculations.

Let us confine ourselves to recognizing that the Universal Agent, appearing in the middle of time in a Quaternary Age, and giving man the true catalyst he needed, put him within reach of returning to his former domain and travelling through all its parts; for if man's body exhibits two diameters, and if by that we mean that the body is a perishable symbol of the universal dimension, then his intellectual Being, holding to the Infinite Principal, is all the more clothed with a quaternary sign participating in the infinite, and with which he can forever measure all Beings.

But the two corporeal diameters of man are, as it were, confused, unconscious, distorted and inert in the woman's womb, until that moment when, on coming into the elemental light, he is allowed to make use of

---

[230] In this section Saint-Martin raises two important Theological points: that of free will and that of God's cooperation in physical works. He points out that, when people claim that the Sun was created on the fourth day as a prophecy that the Repairer would come in the Fourth Age to restore mankind, that would suggest that man had no free will, since why would God place a sign in the heavens to announce the termination of his punishment if man had been free to obey or prevaricate, and God did not know what he would do? So, Saint-Martin suggests the Sun was placed in the heavens as a sign to teach us about the Quaternary, and if it gained a further meaning concerning the Age in which the Repairer would appear, that was not the initial intention. Similarly, he points out that God is only connected with the spiritual or intellectual part of man, and not his physical part. In a way, perhaps Saint-Martin is suggesting that only prayer which speaks to the spiritual is efficacious; and that prayers offered merely to gain wealth (so popular in modern 'televangelist' ministries) and similar terrestrial and material gains, is pointless.

them. This, then, shows us that the quaternary measure of intellectual man was confined and as nothing after he committed the disorder, and that it could only extend and grow during the Age of great light, during that period when the *powers* of *Unity* were themselves *sensitized*, in order to flow in the four channels which form the hieroglyphic character of man.[231]

And so, this Age provided man with the positive means to exercise in his turn the same reaction on everything which was still obscure and hidden for him, and there was no longer anything in the Laws and nature of Beings which should have been able to hold out against his Empire, since all Beings are themselves subdivisions of the universal measure, and all belong at least in part to the *Great Quaternary*.

But for this universal development to produce such results, it had to be performed in the middle of universal time, and in the middle of the exact time which was its abridged reflection, and which divided the course of the Moon into *four*. The Agent charged with that work had to complete it not only between the new and the full Moon, but also in the middle of a septenary period of days being a sub-multiple of the lunar period. So in fact, it was in the middle of a week, in the middle of the *periodic* month of the Moon, and in the middle of the universal course of Nature that this Agent had to divulge to men the secret Law which had been veiled to them since their exile in this period of expiation, so that by acting simultaneously in these three centers, he opened as it were the passage to the *powers* of those three Supreme Abilities which alone could revivify man's three intellectual organs and bring *hearing*, *sight* and *speech* to all his posterity.[232]

---

[231] Saint-Martin plays with a number of symbols or images here, including the idea of the Fourth Age being that of the return of the Sun (or Son); and when the Powers of Unity – or God – were made *sensible* or material, meaning that He emanated His Agent, the Repairer, to show man the true path. The fact that he represents the Quaternary as being the intersection of two dimensions, or a cross, is far from coincidental too, since it was in that place, the very center of the intersection which original man, Adam, had occupied in the time of glory; and it is now the place which the Repairer must occupy in order to redeem mankind.

[232] This period of the cycle of the first moon of the year, in March, Aries, signifying the return of the Sun and the beginning of the season of growth, the end of winter and so forth, has been significant to nearly every civilization. In the story of the Christ, of course, once again identified with Moses, it is the very time of the last plague of Egypt, the death of the First Born that is linked to the Last Supper, which was a celebration of the Passover, and the subsequent death of God's firstborn, which is the reference of this passage. To the question of whether Adam was God's firstborn, the answer comes from the beginning of the Gospel of St. John: "In the beginning was the Word", which tells us that Jesus – or the Repairer – predates Creation. Another reason for the

It is during that Triple Age that he had to enter the *Holy of Holies*, dress himself in the *ephod*, the *robe of linen*, the *pectoral* and the *tiara* which had been used by the Grand Priests of the Hebrews in their sacerdotal functions, and which to them were only the symbols of the *true clothes* with which the Regenerator would one day cover the nudity of human posterity.

There he had to expound the *knowledge* to those whom he had chosen; he had to reestablish the *words* which had been erased from that *Ancient Book* formerly entrusted to man, and which man had disfigured; he had even to give them a *New Book* more extensive than the first, so that through that Book those who received it would know how to dispel the evils and the shadows which surrounded man's posterity; and so they would also learn to keep them at bay and to render themselves invulnerable.

There, he had to prepare the *ancient incense* described in Exodus, composed of *four aromatics of equal weight*, and which the Hebrew Priests could only use in the Temple under the strictest guidelines; he had to fill the *sacred censer* and, having *censed* all the *areas* of the Temple, he had to convince his Elect that they could do nothing without that *incense*.[233]

Finally, his work would have been useless to them if he had not initiated them into his knowledge by teaching them to *harvest* those *four precious aromatics* for themselves, to *create* in their turn this same incorruptible *incense*, and in burning it to *create* from it those *pure clouds of perfume* which, by their living wholesomeness have been intended since the time of the great disturbance to *confine corruption* and to purify the whole Universe.

For the Universe is like a great Fire set alight from the beginning of things for the purification of all corrupt Beings. Following the law of terrestrial Fire, it had begun by being covered with smoke; then the flame grew and endured to gradually consume all material and impure

---

references to the lunar cycles, as well as their connection with Passover, was the fact that this time was very important to the Élus Cohen, who had to operate some of their most powerful rituals during that time.

[233] No surprise, then, that the Élus Cohen were expected to create such an incense and burn it frequently during their Operations. That incense had three purposes: to create a sacred environment free from evil forces; to offer up a holy worship to God; and to provide a thick blanket of cloud in which *La Chose* might manifest itself following their Operations.

substances, finally to regain its *original whiteness* and to give those Beings their original colors.

It is for that reason that in the Elemental Order, when a flame has pierced and risen above the combustible materials, it continues its dissolution until it is completely destroyed. That is why, as it attracts to itself all its Principles of life, as it releases them and unites them with its own essence, it rises up with them into the air, and gives them that free and active existence which they had not enjoyed when in thr body.

The Universal Chief of all the Spiritual Creators of the pure and sacred Religion must, like them, relate on Earth everything which occurs in the Superior Order; and that accords with the great truth that everything physical is but the representation of that which is not, and that every action which occurs is the outward expression of properties of the hidden Principal to which they belong. The Universal Elect must even have fulfilled this Law Himself in a higher manner than all His Agents, which He had sent complete the Great Work, since on Earth they had only manifested the Religion of Justice and Severity, whilst he himself came to manifest the Religion of Glory, Light and Mercy.

Thus, in all those actions and in the Religion which he practiced, he had to show everything which took place in the Invisible Order. From the immense height of His Throne, Divine Wisdom never ceases to create the opportunity for our rehabilitation: here below, the Universal Regenerator never ceased to cooperate for the corporeal and spiritual relief of men by transmitting to them the various gifts relating to their own preservation and that of their fellow men, and by teaching them to distance themselves from the snares which surround them and to fill themselves with truth.

From the immense height of His Throne, Divine Wisdom never ceases to moderate the evil we commit and to absorb our iniquities in the immensity of His love; here below, the Universal Regenerator had to pardon the guilty, and when people stood accused before Him, He had to show that it was a greater Work to send them away absolved than to condemn them.

Finally, from the immense height of His Throne, Divine Wisdom provides His own *Powers* and *Virtues* to annul the *criminal pact* which submitted the entire posterity of man to slavery: here below, the Universal Regenerator had to give His sweat and even His very life to have us *physically understand* the sublime truths, and *remove us from death*.

Qoph (ק) – The Work of the Repairer

And so, the Visible and Invisible Orders, being linked by an intimate connection, show man the indivisible unity of the sacred motive power which causes all action. For to *Intelligence* nothing is greater or lesser among the Supreme Powers: and now in all the parts of the Great Work there is only a single ensemble, and in consequence a single Hand.

For this is an eternal truth: that all these facts would never have been understood by man if He who came to operate them had not lived in conjunction, through all the acts of his Ministry, with the *Unity* with which he was eternally linked by his very essence; just as all the possible manifestations of Divine Powers which Wisdom sends to assist man would have been meaningless to him if there was the slightest separation or division between these Powers, since as man is the final link in the chain, he would never have been able to see the *powers* of the Superior Part of the chain come if one of the intermediary links had been broken.

And to affirm our trust both in the necessary union of those powers with their Principal, and in the general possibility of the whole manifestation of which I have spoken, I will recall here that matter, however real it appears relative to the body and to material objects, is only apparent to the intellect; that it is because of the fact that it is apparent that the superior actions can come down to us and that we can raise ourselves up to them; that it would be impossible if the space which separated us were fixed, real and impervious; just as there would be no mutual influence between the Earth and the stars if the air between them were not fluid, elastic and compressible.

The only reward I desire from the Reader to whom I unveil these truths, is that he meditates upon the Law of Refraction, that he observes what is greater by reason of the density of the environment; and that he will then recognize that the object of man on Earth is to use all the rights and powers of his Being to rarify, insofar as he can, the *environment* between him and the *true Sun*, so that with all opposition being removed, the passage may be free and the rays of light will come to him without being *refracted*.

We should see that in man himself, however separated from that Wisdom from which he drew life, ignorance is a state only in relation to man and not to the Supreme Intelligence Who, embracing the universality of Beings and alone giving them existence, shows the impossibility for a Being to exist yet to be unknown to Him.

But since, despite our stains and our degradation, we can never escape from the intimate, total and absolute gaze of the Great Principal, perhaps He would be less far than we think if, in order to perceive His Presence, we were to follow truer and more illuminated paths. Perhaps every obstacle would become null and void if we were to use every effort we currently use to destroy our connections with Him, to reestablish them instead.

If from such connections comes the privilege of *pure powers*, which it pleases Wisdom to have communicated to us, it is because those *powers*, remaining unaltered unlike us because of our irregular gait, remain united to Him through their will as by their essence, and thus preserve the unity of all their abilities and all their correspondences with Him.

We must therefore admit that all superior manifestations, whose necessity we sense in order for us to retrace the rights of our original Nature, only present an appearance of separation relative to we who are confined in narrow limits and who, because of the weakness of our eyes, can only see a part of the overall Table; whereas He who holds the Table in His hand can bring it to life, contemplate it and see it forever in its entirety.

And so, for God, everything is connected, everything contains everything else, everything exists together. All *Powers*, whether inherent in Him or emanated from Him, all the Beings He has chosen, all the men whom He has caused to be born, and finally all the means He has employed from the beginning of things and which He will use until their end and in His own eternity, are ever present for Him. Otherwise His works would be perishable; He would produce only mortal Beings, and His universality would not be complete.

We should also reiterate that the false will of the free Being is the only cause which can exclude it from the universal harmony of *Unity*, since by its Nature it seeks this *Unity*; and from this we know that if man seeks to imitate the *pure powers* which manifest the *Divine Virtues* to him, his will would be united to the will of the Great Principal, and like them he would enjoy a complete relationship with that Principal.

It would appear to him through the indestructibility of his Being, founded on the Law of his emanation; he would be absorbed in the harmony of all his divine abilities; and among all the *powers* which Wisdom manifests in him, there would be none he did not recognize or in which he wouldn't enjoy, for otherwise he would not know their unity.

For since a love for the happiness of all Beings is the true essence of Wisdom, when He sends forth to us both the subdivided Powers and His own Powers, His purpose is simply to lead us back into that harmonious unity in which alone all Beings can rejoice in the fullness of their action.

And so He sowed all those *powers* around us, so to speak, so that we would harvest them, amass them and to make them our daily food; in other words, to make them ourselves a unity by removing all the obstacles and all the veils which cover our eyes and prevent us from seeing them.

Thus all these Divine *Powers*, ordained by the Great Principal to cooperate in the rehabilitation of men, permanently exist all around us, close to us, never leaving the confines in which we are enclosed; just as the creations of elemental Nature continually surround our bodies and are ever ready to communicate their salutary properties to us, to cure us of our ailments and even to preserve us from them, if only our false and contrary views did not so often keep us far from the knowledge of Nature's treasures, and the fruits which it could offer us.

Thus, without the obstacles which we ourselves put before the beneficent actions of the Great Principle, there would not be one of those *powers* which we wouldn't be able to harvest and gather, if we can put it that way, as we could appropriate all the *powers* of the wholesome substances of elemental Nature.

Thus, without the perverseness or weakness of our will, we would only be separated in appearance from all those Beings, all those salutary Agents whose benefits are recognized in all the various Traditions, and we would be close to them in reality.

All the works of that Great Principal would be shown to us, and from the beginning of time till now no Being, no *Name*, no power, no fact, no Agent would remain unknown to us; just as those Elect who have worked on the Earth that series of facts which have been transmitted to us through the Traditions of the Nations, so that all their knowledge, their understanding, their *names*, their wisdom and their actions would provide us with a single Table, a single point of view, a single ensemble, in which all the details were there for our instruction and provided for our use. This shows us how useless books would be if only we were *wise*, for those books are only so many collections of thoughts, and we live surrounded by *thoughts*.

Indeed, if all is fundamentally linked, inseparable, indivisible, and coming from the Divine Essence. If all the *powers* which emanate from the Great Principal are forever united and in perfect and intimate correspondence, it is clear that man, being unable to destroy or change his own nature which necessarily links him to universal unity, is forever encompassed about by all the Divine *Powers* sent in time; that he is surrounded; that he cannot take a single step or make a single movement without communicating with them; that he cannot act, think, talk even in the profoundest solitude without having them for witnesses, without being seen, understood, touched by them; and that if it was not for the fruit of his base and corrupt will between him and them he would know them as intimately as they know him; and he would have the same rights over them as they have over him; and it would not be going too far to say that then he could extend his privilege to actually knowing Fo-xi, Moses, and the Universal Regenerator Himself, since this privilege includes all the Beings who, from the beginning of time, have been called to the Earth.

Why would we then not believe that, without our corrupt will, we would have similar rights over those great facts and over the great acts to come? If our nature calls us to partake in the properties of *Unity*, would we not then, like Him, be able to embrace all of space and time, since we are, like Him, above all that is fleeting and temporal?

Yes! It is true that, in our essence, we are inseparably linked to *Unity*, and we must have all the things which belong to Him: those which existed before time, those which existed after the beginning of time, those which will exist until the end of time, even those which will exist after the dissolution and disappearance of visible and created things. For we would not strive towards *Unity* if our rights were only partial, and if we were unable to contemplate all the details of that immense spectacle in their entirety.

By this we see how simple an idea we have of the Prophets. Their glory and their illuminations become those of all mankind. All men are Prophets by their very nature, but it is their weakness and their depravity which prevents them from manifesting their privileges.

The etymology of that word is the proof. The Hebrews expressed it by the word *Roëh*, a participle of the verb *Raah, he has seen*. They also called their Prophets *Seers*. Perhaps one can derive from this the rights and *powers* of Kings, to whom, according to the true meaning, should principally belong the quality of *Seer*. And the first King of Israel received his titles and authority from the *Seer* Samuel, for at that time the temporal

Leaders of the Hebrews were *Seers*, as was man in his first estate, and as all his posterity should have been.

Finally, these *two worlds* are filled with treasures both born or to be born, which are manifested by man's will when he is wise, for there is a universal *Seed* in both. That *Seed* is without limit, without number, without end. It only awaits animation or a clear reason in order to produce and show itself, and this reason is the purity of man's desires. How can he then complain of his ignorance, and how can he have ills and pains when at every moment he has the power to educate himself or to pray to his God *efficiently*?

Besides, those who do not wish to believe they have a soul, because they have not been shown that in it is all that they are told they should be, show that they have little intelligence. Indeed, showing them the state of darkness in which they are buried would not be to show them anything at all. But before assuring them that all the wonders which we attribute to Him are not to be found in that darkness, they must make some effort to find them, and perhaps those efforts will help them to grow; so that they may recognize that it would not be so hard after all to think about it in order to be happy; for if they wish to be happy, they only have to *speak*.

Resh (ר) – The Acts of the Repairer

This leads us to an important question: that is, what are the physical means the Universal Agent has had to use to visibly demonstrate the unity of his *powers* to the Universe, in the middle of time and at the center of all the temporal, universal and individual immensites.

But I will say little on this topic, because we haven't forgotten that no Superior *Power* and no thought comes to man without being condensed, as if were, and united with the physical colors of the realm we inhabit, observing, however, that they follow the terrestrial Laws without being governed by them, and that they direct and perfect them rather than being bound and limited by their passive actions.

We haven't forgotten, either, the dignity of man's form. So, it is enough to know that this Universal Agent has had to follow the Law common to all the Agents which have manifested here. Let us add however that, just as through his Divine Nature he contained within himself the intellectual *powers* of all the Agents who preceded him, so his physical form had to contain all the subdivided *powers* contained in all the bodies in the Universe.

Let us also add that that if it is true, according to the Book already quoted, that the first terrestrial man had no mother, since before that first terrestrial man no *material* human body had existed, it must be true that he who alone could give light to his descendants had no father either. And that shouldn't surprise us if we focus on understanding the Principle Who first formed those bodies.

Finally, as the first man had placed evil alongside good, the Regenerating Being had to place good alongside evil in order to counterbalance that weight and the criminal act, and to bring the terms of the proportion into balance.

However, isn't the matter with which man is criminally united the source of the error and suffering he experiences? Doesn't it hold him as if chained to those things which, in the Physical Order, show him all the signs of reality, while they offer nothing to his thinking Being? The Universal Regenerator, uniting voluntarily and *in purity* with a physical form, must therefore have created the opposite kind, that is to say that he had to show material eyes all the signs of imperfection, of the fragility of which he was susceptible, without which none of the sources of that corruption would have been able to reach *him*. In other words, if matter had *charmed* man and subjugated the eyes of his Spirit, it was necessary for the Universal Regenerator to *charm* matter and thereby demonstrate its meaninglessness, by showing the *true*, the *pure*, and the *immutable* reign to it.

So, he appeared on Earth in accordance with its Laws in order to reflect to man his own situation, and to lay out the complete history of his Being: that is, if the Regenerator had to show man the portrait of his compound and degraded state, he also had to manifest in himself his simple and glorious state, and to that end, it was necessary for death to operate on him – with mankind as witness – a visible separation of the two substances which compose us, so that, through that visible process, we cannot doubt that what today forms this impure amalgam is the union of a superior and sublime Principle with a terrestrial and corruptible Principle.

In a word, the hieroglyph had to be effaced for the language *to appear, for we have seen that the hieroglyph came before languages, and it is this which could let it be said that all the previous Elect were but the hieroglyphs for which the Universal Elect was the* language.[234] *It is for that reason that he had two alphabets, since he had to knew two languages: that of the previous Elect and his own. The numbers of those two alphabets are easy to know, since they are double the number of man, and the number of man is found in his election, in his end, and in his progress in* one hundred forty-five thousand eight hundred and sixty-seven.[235]

At the same time this visible separation had to happen through violent means, to remind man that it was a violent event which had formerly joined his intellectual Being to blood.

It was also necessary for this separation to be voluntary, since the first union had been.

---

[234] Here Saint-Martin agrees with most Christian Exegists in saying that the Prophets and Priests (the Elect or *Élus* of the Old Testament) were the harbingers of the Universal Elect, the Repairer, the Christ.

[235] The Translator was unable to find a satisfactory answer to how this number was derived. Of the 145, 867, clearly 144,000 refers to the number of the 'Elect' referred to in Revelation 7:4 and 14:1. However, this still leaves 1,867 to divide between 'man's end' and 'man's progress/advancement/development'. By Theosophic Addition 1+8+6+7 = 22 (2+2) = 4, which is the Quaternary number of man. However, there must be a more satisfying explanation.

However, it wasn't necessary for the victim to voluntarily immolate himself, since then the act would no longer have been irreproachable, and the sacrifice would have had *no effect*.[236]

It was also necessary for those who sacrificed this victim to be utterly unaware of who he was, for else they would not have slain him.

Let us take a moment here to contemplate the universality of the Divine *Powers* opposed to the universality of disturbances which have soiled all Orders of Beings. Let us consider the Unity of Good erasing the Unity of Evil, by both taking on and at the same time negating all its efforts; let us bury ourselves in this abyss of wisdom and love where the generous *Victim sacrifices himself* without crime, and where the blind sacrificers, by destroying his visible [237] envelope, reveal the unique Exemplar of order and purity, and extract, without realizing it, a *Universal Electrum*.[238]

For the blessings which this Agent both provides and is the repository should not be limited to the places where he appeared nor to the men he had chosen, nor even to all those who lived on Earth at that time. In communicating his gifts to his Elect, he only gave them the germ of the Work: they then had to devleop it and operate it on a large scale in all the regions that the results of man's crime had reached; that is, in all Orders of Beings, since there were none which hadn't been affected by it.

And so those bodies and Elements which had been exposed through man's weakness and his crime to negative actions which ceaselessly try to interfere with their Laws, had to receive appropriate protections from him who came to regenerate all, to maintain them in that harmony which constitutes them and to safeguard them from destructive acts. Finally, this should have prepared them to see man's rights returned once more, now stronger and even more evident. And just as iron, when held in the same

---

[236] Saint-Martin says that the act of self-sacrifice must be violent, since the original act of prevarication had been a violent act; and the victim must be willing. However, it was not enough for the victim to kill himself, for that would be suicide, and therefore not a holy act.

[237] As in English, the word *apparent* in French can mean both visible and apparent, which leaves us to wonder whether Saint-Martin was using this vague term to hint as a more gnostic interpretation of the divinity of the Christ-Repairer on Earth. Was he hinting at a more Aryan interpretation of the Crucifixion?

[238] The Translator is uncertain as to the exact reference. The French used is *un électre universel*, and the word is masculine and not capitalized, so it is neither a proper name nor female. It could be 'electrum' in the sense of finding the alchemical gold having separated the pure from the impure through sacrifice, or in the sense of a universal catalyst, which makes it possible for all Bodies to follow that example?

direction as a magnet, can acquire some of its magnetic qualities, should we be surprised that men who have constantly followed the way of the *powers* of the Universal Agent would be filled with those same *powers*, and burning with zeal and confidence would be able to calm winds and waves, stop the effect of vipers' venom, give movement to the paralyzed, heal the sick, and even snatch victims from death itself?

This universal influence over the Earth and the Elements had to be demonstrated to us through physical signs by him who came to regenerate it: just as, at the time of the departure from Egypt, visible signs of aid and of a Superior *Power* appeared through that blood applied to the three different parts of the doors of the Hebrews.

Now, the signs of the work which the Regenerator worked invisibly on the Universe should be found in the Laws of the decomposition of his own body, since his body contained the purest and most active Principles of Nature.

He had to manifest three successive acts of purification, operated by the three pure substances of his material form in dissolution upon the three terrestrial Elements which serve as the Principles in all bodies; Elements which the original crime had infected, and through that all of Nature: Elements which had been soiled again through the prevarications[239] of man's first descendants, and whose purification the previous Elect, virtuous as they were, hadn't been able to complete.

Indeed, the ternary unity which had produced everything couldn't restore everything except through the same number, but with this difference: now acting on composite things, it could proceed only through separate actions, whereas in the beginning, working on the same Principles, it had produced everything in a single action.

Having regenerated the three fundamental bases of Nature, he had to regenerate the *powers* which he used as causes and reactions. He had to give all those invisible causes the actions they had lost through the criminal negligence of man who, charged with presiding over their harmony had allowed their purity and precision to alter. Or rather, he had to destroy all the obstacles which man's crime had allowed to come about in those causes, and in all the parts of the Universe. These, then, are the terrible barriers which all his posterity must broach before returning to the

---

[239] This is a clear indication that, at this time, being 1782, Saint-Martin was still closely adhering to the theosophy of Pasqually, since in his *Treatise*, Pasqually expressly refers to the subsequent prevarications of Adam's sons.

realm of light; these, then, are the various barriers presented to the mind as inevitable for man, once he will have separated from his physical form.

Now, it was over those invisible barriers that the Repairer had to extend his *powers*. By means of the rights to which he was heir, he was able to facilitate access to them, so that all those who had been stopped by them since the origin of the disorder, and all those who had not yet approached them, being fortified by these same *powers*, could now overcome those barriers without danger, once more bearing upon them the same *character* and the same *Name* which had formerly made all enclosures open to them, and procured respect and safety for them in the midst of the most terrible evil-doers.

The powers of those superior causes are retraced and physically put in action by the seven Planetary Stars. These have been discussed in the Book already quoted, in the Allegory of the seven trees and the geographical scale of man.[240] *They are the organs of the quaternary number, whose strength and existence are shown in the four types of stars which comprise the celestial region, namely: the Planets, the Satellites, the Comets and the Fixed Stars.*

As such, they are the greatest prize for man. They are, in effect, those powerful columns which were meant to serve as a bulwark, and which for him have become a the most formidable obstacle, until a beneficent hand might come to help him overcome them. These are the seven gates of knowledge, which can only be opened by him who posesses the quaternary double key. These are the seven gifts which, since his crime, have been taken away from men yet which still circulate continuously around us without us being able to enjoy them; and have led people to say that even the Just sin seven times a day because, according to the true definition *of the word* sin, *it is through that number that the walls of Jericho were brought down; it is by that number that Naaman's leprosy was cured. Finally, it is by the seven* types *of those seven* actions *which Hebraic Tradition portrays as having directed and completed the origin of things,*

---

[240] This is a reference to the comments in his first book, *Of Errors & Truth*, but remember that in that book he reminds us that, while people may see a reference to the seven planets in the allegory of the seven trees, found early in Chapter 1 concerning man's status before his fall, later in Chapter 7, he tells us that: "the throne of man was at the very center of the Country of his dominion, and from there he governed the seven instruments of his glory, which I previously designated under the name of seven trees, and which a great number will be tempted to take as the seven planets, but which however are neither trees, nor planets." So, the Reader should remember that the allegory refers to the higher *powers*, rather than to the planets themselves.

Resh (ר) – The Acts of the Repairer

and as before, for the time of their duration, serve as the Columns of the Temple which man should occupy in the Universe.

For since his crime, those seven types have remained inactive, waiting for the one who was to revive them. As soon as he appeared they came back to life; and reproducing themselves in their own powers, like God Himself, since then they have manifested their physical action. The first power of that manifestation being designated by the number forty-nine, it was seven weeks or forty-nine days after the consummation of the Work that those visible gifts should be spread abroad, because it was then that the fiftieth door should be opened, and for which all slaves wait to be delivered, and which will be opened again at the End of Time to those who, according to Daniel, will have the good fortune to expect and achieve after thirteen hundred and thirty-five days. [241]

Wasn't it also necessary for the one who was to pour out these gifts on the Earth to travel across the space which separates it from the First Author of Beings; that having purified the seven channels by which all the *powers* should flow into time, he went to take the *Shewbread* from the *Altar of Gold*, which is ceaselessly placed before the Eternal, and transporting it to all the regions of the Universe, he distributed it, not only to the men who from the beginning of time had travelled through the terrestrial habitation which we occupy[242], but to those also that have existed corporeally in this theater of expiation, seeing that they were all still lacking their true nourishment?

Moreover, we cannot avoid agreeing that this Great Act should take place by uttering a Word, since if we have no other instrument to express our ideas, it follows that the Principle Being, Whose sign and representation we are, could similarly only teach us the sacred designs He had had on us from the moment of our existence by means of Words, and which man had then defied. As a result, if He was to show us in the middle of time the unity of a Word, He would thereby show us once more the depth of all His thoughts and set us on the path to recover the true secret of His wisdom and all His *powers*.

---

[241] A reference to the prophecy of end times in Daniel 12:12.
[242] This comment is unclear. It suggests that the Repairer brought the Shewbread both to the worthy and the sinner (who 'existed corporeally in this theater of expiation'). However, bringing it to the worthy, described as 'travelling through this terrestrial habitation' makes little sense, unless he is referring to those who have travelled to the Earth across space, which would suggest the 'worthy' are the Elect and the Prophets, sent to Earth to teach mankind.

Now, here is the progression of the manifestation of His Powers: the material Universe is the expression of His *physical Word*; the Laws and treasures of the First Covenant of the *Principle Being* with man's posterity are the expression of His *spiritual Word*; the Great Work operated by the Second Covenant is the expression of His *divine Word*.

At the same time, it would appear necessary for the Great Work to be crowned on Earth by the multiplication of tongues.[243]

The first descendants of man, abandoning themselves to criminal excesses against truth had, as punishment, suffered that terrible *confusion of tongues* which rendered all individuals and all Nations foreigners to one another.

The remedies of the Supreme Wisdom being ever in proportion to our evils, therefore took the path most beneficial for us, which was now to increase the *gifts of tongues* in those it charged to proclaim those *powers* and to manifest them on Earth.[244]

For by means of that multiplication of tongues, they would find themselves within reach of bringing remedies wherever evil might have been victorious, and to call back to union, intelligence and life all those whom crime had delivered to dispersion, darkness and death; that is, that they could, through that multiplication of tongues, gather together and reunite all those which the *confusion of tongues* had *separated*. A profound Truth, instructive for those who aren't strangers to the rays of illumination, and fortunate enough sometimes to *contemplate* with confidence the *ways* and the *fruits* of wisdom!

Finally, if we here below can only know things through their signs and not by their Principles; if, in such an important circumstance, the designs of this Wisdom towards man had to be expressed in a manner

---

[243] In French the word *langue* means both tongue and language (rather like English); However, having the one word in French means that it conjures up both concepts simultaneously. So, for example, the same word can be used to refer to Pentecost, referred to earlier (in the reference to seven weeks or forty-nine days), when the Holy Spirit came down on the Disciples as tongues of fire; but also suggests the descent of different languages, or even the descent of the Word. Similarly, the word *mot* literally means 'word' in written form, whereas *parole* means the 'spoken word', and has been extensively translated in this Book as 'word' or 'Word', since it suggests the act of speaking, or the Word as a Verb.

[244] This refers to Pentecost, to which Saint-Martin draws a parallel with the story of the Tower of Babel. Whereas in Babel all men had their tongues or languages confused so that none could communicate with another; at Pentecost the gift of tonges or languages descended upon the Disciples, so that each could speak the languages of all the other Nations, and thereby spread the Good News.

which was protected from any ambiguity, any such physical signs would have to take on *tongues of fire*.[245]

That is how the Divine *Powers*, being still invisibly linked to one another, will be able to prepare the Universe anew for man, and at the same time restore man in his rights over the Universe.

It is then that the universal temporal work will be accomplished. For the Repairer couldn't bring calm in the Universe, or regenerate life in man's soul, without bringing peace and felicity to Beings of another Order, to those Beings outside of time by reason of their original functions, but who, through zeal for the reign of truth, have been in a state of disorder since their origin, whereas they were created in order to contemplate forever the living spectacle of perfection and *order*.

For if man's degradation has made them, so to speak, exercise functions foreign to their true purpose, the action which must be operated for his rehabilitation gives them hope of bring restored to their first happiness, which was to see regularity, justice and unity reign everywhere.

It is time to proclaim: the principle truth which this temporal and universal age should reveal to man is to teach him the true use of that beneficence which all Peoples have practiced since they have been outside their original estate, but which, since they were still separated from the estate of the Law of the intellect, had been limited to acts of humanity, the relief of the needs of the body and the duties of hospitality.

When the practice of that *virtue* began to develop, it continued to teach man those same duties, but it also taught him to render *other services* to his fellow man. It made him understand that he is accountable to them for all the *virtues* which are in him, since they were only given to him by the Supreme Wisdom as a *means to react*, to draw out in their turn all the *virtues* which are in others; and, to accomplish so a sublime an action man's task presents him with most rigorous duties, since he cannot remain inferior to what he should be without prejudice to his fellow man, since ultimately one of his *weaknesses* must cost the others a *virtue*.

But by uniting himself to his intellect, which should have been discovered after the great epoch, that beneficence becomes even more

---

[245] This is a play on the fact that *tongues of fire* are what are supposed to have descended on the Apostles at Pentecost; and also, the *language of fire* is a reference to the Hebrew language, which is sometimes also known as the Angelic language.

distinguished, in that it is connected to the immediate action of the First Principle with Whom our nature calls us to cooperate.

The ardor of his love for us leads him to detach from himself, as it were, his innumerable *virtues* and also his purest *powers*, both as active as himself. By detaching them he exposes them, if we can use such expressions, to *nudity*, to *cold*, to *hunger* and to all the *sufferings* of the temporal realm; and as he only detached them in order to send them into us, we can never honor them more, never exercise hospitality more to their benefit nor more advantageously for us, than by giving *shelter* to those he sends us, but who are *outside* and who ask only to *enter in*; by *clothing* those who have been *stripped* for us; by giving to *eat* and *drink* those who are suffering from *hunger*, *thirst* and utter *poverty*, so that they may come to be fed, refreshed, warmed, and clothed by man; and, if one can speak in this manner, moreover to revivify man himself by *transfusing* its own *blood* into his veins.[246]

Would it be unacceptable for the Universal Repairer to have chosen a material substance to serve as the foundation for his Divine and Spiritual *powers*, and, having had it enter into the Religion he had established, it received a virtue from him which it wouldn't naturally have? This idea is all the more likely since, given the understanding we have of man, he can transmit his feeble *powers* to any substance he judges appropriate, which physically – as well as morally – has unfortunately been the source of a great number of illusions on Earth.

The most favorable of all the substances of corporeal nature that the Repairer was able to employ in the Religion he had just established, is wheat. In addition to the specific qualities that make it special to man's nourishment, in the Hebrew language it bears the name of bar, *which also expresses 'purity', 'purification', and its root,* barar *or* barah, *means a 'choice', an 'election', from which are derived* berith, *'covenant', and* barouch, *'blessing'. Moreover, it isn't in vain that, according to Jewish Tradition bread, wheat, and the highest quality flour are so often used in*

---

[246] This paragraph refers to Matthew 25: 35 – 36, where Jesus gives the parable with the message that whoever performs any of those acts of kindness for the least of people is doing it for him. The last part of the paragraph is referring to the Eucharist and the act of ingesting the Body and Blood of Christ. At that time the dogma of transubstantiation was generally accepted, and Saint-Martin emphasizes this by stating that the physical ingestion of the wine is a transfusion (*transvaser*) of Christ's blood into man's veins. The following paragraphs continue this discussion concerning the logic of the Repairer selecting material or physical substances – wine and bread – to be the foundations for transferring spiritual and divine powers into man by means of a physical channel.

sacrifices, in men's covenants with Superior Beings, or in the preparations the Hebrews undertook to get ready for their festivals; and a thousand proofs taken from the Temporal Order can justify everything we have just said in favor of this substance.

Wine was also numbered among those things the Religious Law of the Hebrews prescribed to be used in their holy ceremonies. It doesn't offer, though, properties as vast, nor as beneficial as wheat; and the vine also demonstrates, by material signs, that its number *is opposed to purity. But the Universal Regenerator necessarily had to use wine in his Religion, because it is the symbol of the blood in which we are enclosed; which, like* iniquity, *must be consumed and disappear to show us the conditions that Justice requires for the traces of our deprivation to be eradicated.*

If men, seduced by the specius glimmers of their own judgment, are shocked to see that material substances truly have a place in the Religion established by the Universal Repairer; if they therefore see this Religion and sacrifice which should be performed as being simply figurative and just for appearance, they'd clearly be in error, because then this sacrifice would be void, and useless to the true Beings to which it should be offered.

From another aspect, if man's soul, wishing to contemplate the rights of this efficacious and true act, only seeks them among *passive numbers*, wouldn't we fear that he would then only find the appearance of reality, rather than reality itself? Wouldn't it lose sight of the essential fruit of this Religion which should restore *all numbers* to their natural order, so that we would see all at once, at the same moment, the sublimity of the *real numbers* appear, making the nullity of *passive numbers* disappear, and rectifying the irregularity of *false numbers*: that is, in that action, the fullness of numbers should be displayed before man to erase the deformity which follows from their separation.

Finally, would there be any danger in believing that in this action, both corporeal, spiritual and divine, in this action which only leads to man's deliverance from everything which is blood and matter, everything should be SPIRIT AND LIFE, like him who established it and vivifies it, and like man who should participate in it? But if it is certain that this Religion should exist on Earth, it is those who are its Agents who should declare it.

Let us limit ourselves to recognizing that all other parts of a Religion which is only SPIRIT AND LIFE should aim to illuminate us in our darkness.

They should be like a physical interpretation of the greatest truths that man may know, and which are truly similar to him. This Religion, considered in its *time*, in its *number*, in its various ceremonies, should be like a circle of *living actions* where intelligent and open-minded men may find the characteristic representation of the Laws of all Beings, of all ages, of all facts; that is to say that man should be able to recognize not only his own history from his primitive origin up to his future reunion with his *Principle*; not only that of all Nature and all the physical and intellectual Agents which compose it and which direct him, but also that of the Fertile Hand which ceaselessly assembles the most pertinent and particular traits for an explanation of the true nature of our Being.

That is what should be the physical signs of the gifts which the Universal Repairer has brought to Earth; and here is the abridged portrait of everything that he has had to operate, so that men might be linked to him by the unity of action, as he himself is linked by the unity of essence to the Divinity.

That will suffice to outline the powers of the Universal Agent, and the rights he should have to man's confidence. It is enough for us to recognize, through natural instinct alone, how necessary it is for us to have such an example before us. It would be imprudent and offensive to this Agent to claim to describe him more clearly, since to do that truly effectively, he would have to appear himself.

Moreover, to focus man's thoughts on so profound a study for a long time would seem to exclude simple and uneducated people from the privileges granted to all human posterity.

Man, whose burning heart ceaselessly consumes wild and unhealthy plants by which he is surrounded; man, who regards the *Agent* from whom he received thought to be a jealous Being who afflicts him when he loves something which isn't Him; man who, in sacrificing himself constantly is always humble and trembles before God, *because the secret of God reveals itself to those who fear Him*; the simple man who faithfully and trustingly follows the precepts which the Universal Agent must have taught, and which come from a source too beneficent to lead to illusion and nothingness: such is the man who can claim to enter into the council of peace, seeing that the highest knowledge one can acquire is but a frail and unsteady edifice when it doesn't rest on all those foundations which will always be its soundest support.

Because finally, if man directed his view towards the *Universal Electrum*[247], and warmed himself in the heat of a single ray, he would be so much purer, more luminous, greater that he could ever become through the discourse and reasoning of all the Sages on Earth.

Moreover, if it is truths which should be communicated, the more one should remain silent: and experience joins with reason to tell us to be reserved, by pointing out the inevitable harm which, throughout the Ages, has come from publicizing them.

Among the most famous Scholarly and Religious Institutions which have existed, there are none which haven't covered *knowledge* with the veil of mystery. As an example, let us consider Judaism and Christianity. Jewish tradition teaches us that king Hezekiah was punished for having shown his *treasures* to the Babylonian Envoys; and we see in the ancient Christians rites in the letter from Innocent 1st to Bishop Decentius, and in the writings of Basil of Cesarea, that Christianity possesses *things of great power and great weight which have never and could never be written*.

As long as these things *which could never be written* were only known to those who were its depositories, Christianity enjoyed peace; but when the Roman Emperors, tired of persecuting the Christians, desired to be initiated into their mysteries; when the rulers of the Nations set their foot in the Sanctuary and wished to cast unprepared eyes on the most sacred items of the Religion; when they made of Christianity a State Religion, and only saw it as a political resource; when their subjects were compelled to become Christians, and when this led to admitting everyone who presented themselves without examination; then were uncertainties, opposing doctrines, and heresies born. The obscuration became almost universal on every aspect of doctrine and worship, because the most sublime truths of Christianity could only be properly known to a small number of the Faithful, and because those who only glimpsed them were exposed to false and contradictory interpretations.

This is what happened under Constantine, called the Great. And barely had he adopted Christianity before the General Councils began, and that period may be seen as the First Age of decadence of the *Virtues* and illumination among Christians.

Following Constantine's example, his successors wished to expand Christianity, and used privilege and favor to procure followers. But those

---

[247] See Footnote 238.

they attracted by such means saw less the Religion to which they were called, than the favors of the Prince and the attractions of ambition.

From their side, the spiritual leaders themselves, in order to attract new support, indulged the wishes and passions of the Princes; and allying themselves every day to the temporal, they distanced themselves more and more from their original purity, so that some *Christianized* the civil and political world, while other brought the *civil world* into Christianity, forming a monster out of this mixture; and since its members had no connection, this could only give rise to discordant results.

The Sophists of the various pagan schools who were admitted to Christianity further increased this disorder, by mixing in a host of vain and abstract questions into this simple Religion which, instead of uniting and enlightening it, only produced division and darkness. The Temples of the God of Peace were converted into Scientific Schools, where the various parties disputed with more violence than the Philosophers beneath the porticoes of Athens and Rome ever did. Their arguments were all the more dangerous in that they confused things through words, because the great majority didn't know that *true knowledge* has a language which is all its own, which can only be expressed clearly by means of its own *characters* and by *ineffable symbols*.

In this confusion, the key to knowledge never ceased to be available to the Ministers at the Altars, as a *center of unity* they should never abandon, yet most of those Ministers never used it to enter the Sanctuary. They even prevented the Man of Desire[248] from approaching it, for fear that he would perceive their ignorance, and they prevented him from seeking to know the mysteries of the Kingdom of God, though according to the very traditions of Christianity itself, the *Kingdom of God is in the heart of man*, and thoughout all time, wisdom has pressed him to study his heart.[249]

Those spiritual leaders who kept themselves from corruption, wept over the straying of the multitude, and endeavored, through teaching and example, to keep men in the way of zeal, *virtue* and love of truth. But in

---

[248] While the term 'Man of Desire' is only used two or three times in this Book by Saint-Martin, its importance cannot be overestimated, and as mentioned before, his next book bore this title.

[249] This is a very Gnostic concept for the time, when the only means of salvation was seen to be through the Catholic Church. Given that the Gospel of Thomas, which explictly makes this point that a Church isn't necessary to have a personal relationship with God (Saying 77: "Split a piece of wood: I am there. Lift a stone, and you (plur.) will find me there"), wasn't discovered until December 1945 in the Nag Hammadi scrolls, this comment is extraordinary.

vain did they raise themselves above the abuse: the monster, who had already come into existence, was too advantageous to the ambitious desires of its supporters, so they took care to strengthen it. Still young under the first Greek Emperors, although it had already exhibited its pride, for a few Centuries it could only launch feeble and impotent blows; such as the trivial entrprises of Pope Symmachus against the Emperor Anastasius.[250] But, having reached the age where it could deploy its ferocity, the first French Emperors furnished it with the means. Charlemagne's father had seen the Pope at his feet, begging him to defend him against the Lombards, and beforehand the Prince had received his coronation at the Pope's hand as a reward of the services that he was going to provide. This bizarre commerce was not slow in having the oddest consequences. Those who had initially simply participated in a pious ceremony concerning the political rights of a sovereign soon claimed to have given him those same rights, then made themselves its depositaries, and finally claimed to be able to remove powers from those to whom they had given them.

Then Charlemagne's son, whose father had seen the Pope at his feet, not only ended up at the feet of the Pope but was even deposed by Bishop Ebbon during an assembly of his own subjects. This marked the Second Age, in which the abuses came from the spiritual leaders.

Now the torrent had broken its dykes, and there was no disorder which didn't occur: ambition and despotism, now covered with veil of Religion, led to the pouring out of more blood in ten Centuries than the hordes of Barbarians had shed since the birth of Christianity; and to shudder with horror, one only has to read the story of Comnenos in Constantinople, Philippe in France, Frederic in Germany, Suinthila in Spain, and Henry and Edward in England. However, the time was coming when eyes were beginning to be opened.

When the Leaders of Christianity confused themselves with the Temple and the Tabernacle when they should only be its columns; when they wished to sanctify their ignorance; when they indulged the extravagance of issuing decrees preventing anathemized Sovereigns from winning victories, even preventing Angels – in the same decrees – from

---

[250] While Symmachus was being elected Pope in one Roman church in 498 C.E., Laurentius was being elected Pope in another church, with the support of Emperor Anastasius, because of his overt Byzantine sympathies. Following years of intrigue, involving the intervention of the Gothic King Theodoric and several synods, Symmachus prevailed.

receiving the souls of those they had proscribed; and when finally several pretenders to the papal tiara were put forward, and seen to issue reciprocal anathemas and engage in bloody battles before the Christian Temples, the astonished people demanded to know if such heads could still be holy, being covered as they were with anathemas, and they allowed themselves to set aside their enthusiasm, and to substitute contemplation.

But in those unfortunate times, when the sacred and the profane were mixed together, when dispute was the sole science of public Christianity, where the clerics were only judged worthy of the functions of the Altar after passing frivolous tests in a barbarous academy, could the peoples' contemplations be capable of fairness and maturity?

Those coarse men, seeing the behavior of those who professed the sacred dogmas, weren't content simply to doubt their Masters: they took their imprudence so far as to suspect the dogmas themselves, and by dint of considering them in this spirit of defiance, they believed they saw insoluble difficulties there. This was the Third Age, in which the aberrations came from the members.

From this arose the various sects that came into existence three or four Centuries ago in the bosom of Christianity; which in their turn, serving as a pretext for ambition, have mutually been both its instruments and its victims.

But problems of another kind were mixed in with those errors, showing us both a *belief in true things* and *criminal credulity* confused and proscribed by barbaric sentences, which emboldened those *working for evil* and silenced more and more the *legitimate workers*.[251]

By then, those among the spiritual leaders who had preserved the deposit in its purity wouldn't have been understood if they had tried to direct man's thoughts towards the height of that *Ineffable Priesthood* which brought them before Divinity, and if they had tried to engage him in the search for *Divine Knowledge* by bending his action in on himself, stripping him of everything that was foreign to his Being in order to present himself completely with a pure desire for the rays of Intelligence.

And the passionate and bloody controversies of the most recent Centuries have only produced absurd systems and opinions still bolder yet than those which had already led men astray from the birth of Christianity.

---

[251] Saint-Martin is, of course, referring to the Inquisition, a cynical vehicle of the Catholic Church employed to terrify the general population back into line.

Resh (ר) – The Acts of the Repairer

For the Observers, revolted by the diversity and arguments over the most essential dogmas, attacked the very foundation of the Christian Institution, and didn't waste any time in rejecting it, having confused it with the monstrous edifice which pride and ignorance had planted in their minds.[252]

What should we expect of them, after they had struck this blow to the only Religion which has shown man the striking character of spreading far and wide without ever having bended before conquering Nations; of having conquered, not rough and barbaric Nations as we have seen in the Religion of Mohammad, but rather learned and well-ordered Nations; of having conquered them, not by arms, but through the sole charms of its gentle philosophy.[253]

The Observers who so misunderstood the basis of Christianity could not make any more favorable judgments of other Religions, so that, seeing no link between man and his invisible Principle there either, believed him to be so distant that no Religious Institution could have a relationship with Him. This is the Fourth Age of degradation, in which man, becoming Deist, is one step away from ruin.

The progress of error didn't end there, either. There are now new Observers who, in order to extricate themselves from the confusion which Deism has spread over the religious sciences, have taught even more destructive theories.

Not only have they said that the teachers of Christianity and all Religions were ignorant, misleading, even enemies of the moralilty they professed; that their dogmas were meaningless and contradictory since they had been disproved; and finally, that the basis on which those dogmas relied was imaginary, and as a consequence, man had no connection with higher *powers*; but they also went so far as to doubt his immaterial nature. Through this they have brought about that threat made against the

---

[252] Once again Saint-Martin is ahead of his time, in suggesting that, while the Catholic Church was corrupt and deserving of the contempt of the 'Observers' who ridiculed its bloody and intolerant history, they should be careful not to throw out the baby with the bathwater, to use a contemporary expression: that there is and has always been a kernel of Divine Truth concealed within the marrow of a Church led so far astray by the very human and political ambitions of its leaders. One is reminded of the 'Hidden Church of the Holy Grail' of A. E. Waite in this observation, or the Gnostic claims of an Esoteric or Inner Church following the teachings of St. Thomas.

[253] Again, Saint-Martin was writing before the major incursions by the European countries into foreign lands, the forcible Christianization of those Nations (one can guess the accounts about such colonists as Pizarro and Columbus were somewhat censored at the time), and the current trend of carrying Evangelizing messages of hatred and intolerance into Second and Third World countries.

Hebrews: that if they neglected their Law, they would eventually fall into such a degree of misery and abandonment *that they would no longer believe in their own life.*

Finally, they were led by that to deny the existence of the Principle of all Existence, since denying the immaterial nature of a creation such as man is to deny the immaterial nature of his generative Principle. This is the last and Fifth Age of degradation, when man is no longer anything but darkness, even below the insects.

Such is the dreadful theory which originated all the Philosophical irrationalities which have held sway in these recent times. The original descendants had sinned through *action*, wishing to equal God through their own powers; the latest descendants now sin through nullity, believing that in man there is neither *action* nor *virtue*.

It is from this that comes the delirium of the modern Atheist who, writing against Divinity, believes he has proved nothingness, since, according to him, if Divinity did exist, He would have punished his audacity.

Could we not to reply that Divinity can exist and not punish impotent attacks? That we must rather believe that He hasn't truly been attacked? That vain writings would hardly bring about the wrath of His anger? Finally, that he isn't *advanced enough* to *raise his voice* to Him, nor *educated enough* to *utter* real blasphemies against Him?

Since the beginning of Christianity, we have seen the progress of the confusion into which scientific disputes have led men, and which have produced an all too easy public dissemination of things which might not be properly understood by the profane or ceased to be secret though they were exposed to misunderstanding or incorrect interpretation. Then what is the path that man's soul should take in order to quit this disordered state, which is dedicated to uncertainty? It is the one which he would discover with almost no effort if he turned his eyes inwards.

A careful consideration of our Being would teach us about the sublimeness of our origin and our degradation; we would recognize around us and within us the existence of the Supreme *Powers* of our Principle; they would convince us that these Superior *Powers* must show themselves visibly to man on Earth, to remind him of the sublime functions he had to fulfil at his origin; it would prove the need for Religion, so that the presence of these *virtues* would be effective for us.

We can follow the signs of these truths in all Religious Institutions; and far from the variety of these Institutions leading us to doubt the foundations on which they are based, through knowledge of those foundation we could rectify everything defective in them; that is to say that we would gather those sparse but imperishable truths in our minds, which pierce through all the Doctrines and all the Religions of the Universe.

And here we are raising truths within truths, with the aid of simple, just and natural reflection; we are raising ourselves up to the height of a single and universal form, from whence we would rule with him over all the specific intellectual and physical Agents which were subordinate to him, for being the living torch of all the thoughts and all the actions of normal Beings, he could simultaneously spread the same light in all the abilities of all men.

And this is that brilliant light that man can bring to shine within himself, because it is the Word of all enigmas, the Key to all Religions, and the Explanation all the Mysteries. But man, when you will come to that happy understanding, if you are wise, you will keep your knowledge in your heart!

Shin (ש) – The End of Time

Given the Physical Law and the universal subdivision to which men have been subjected, and having subjected them to a material form, the Earth is too small for them all to live together; and it was necessary for them to live there successively in order to draw the strength and aid necessary to them to cross the space by which they are separated from the Source of all Light.

If man still doubted his degradation, this evidence alone should convince him, since it is impossible to conceive anything more shameful and depressing for thinking Beings than to be in a place where they can only exist with a small number of their *fellow citizens*, whereas by their nature, as numerous as they are, they were made to live and act as one.

That is why people who hadn't been born during the general manifestation in the middle of time, were therefore unable to receive the efficacious and direct benefits available to those who had already lived on this surface or who inhabited it during that time. One could even say that the *Universal Agent*, being subject to the Law of time, when he brought intelligence visibly to Earth, he was unable to manifest it through his actions in every place of our terrestrial habitation at the same time; that even if he brought his powers to all parts of this Earth, he could only put them in action in the places he lived, or perhaps in *a few other countries*, but in a manner foreign to matter and to benefit a few Elect intended to contribute to his work.[254] For the virtue and powers of those *visible signs* which always accompanied his thoughts here below, should dwell with complete superiority in him who produces all such thoughts.

Even today, since all men still haven't yet been born, human posterity cannot see all the facts concerning unity; it cannot see the universal work of Wisdom in action over all its species; that Great Work, whose purpose

---

[254] Remember that, if God is the Universal or First Principal, the Repairer, or Christ, is the Univeral Agent sent by the First Principle. Saint-Martin is making the point that, by being sent to Earth, the Repairer was subject to both time and matter, and could therefore only operate in his immediate sphere of influence, which was around two thousand years ago in Palestine. However, he also allows for the Repairer to act supernaturally to some extent, in that he could reach out to the Elect further afield through dreams or other means. One example would be the story of the Centurion, whose servant is healed *at a distance* (Matt. 8:5 – 13). Note, too, that his thoughts or his intellect allowed him to manifest unusual action on matter those *visible signs* which we would call miracles.

is for all Beings to have the true signs of the infinite before them at the same time, and that, when the limits of time have disappeared they will all, as they did before their crime, have intuitive evidence that it is God Himself who governs all.

Let us add that as the entire Universe is man's prison, and until the material Universe is destroyed the whole of humanity will not all be able to witness the great spectacle of the immensity from which it came, together at the same instant.

The course of man's life supports this truth. To the extent that his intellectual Being raises itself up toward the light, his body sinks and falls back on itself, and from this one should draw the lesson that, when he brings together within himself all the *powers* which comprise his terrestrial realm, his corruptible form can no longer exist with him; like certain fruit which naturally separates from its shell when it has reached maturity, so that the life of one is the death of the other.

By the same Law, when the total number of men required to exist physically on Earth has been fulfilled, the universal form, folding in upon itself, will disappear for them, and the fullness of that temporal number will make the Universe's existence unnecessary for man.

Finally, if an individual man's abilities cannot express the completeness of their own actions so long as he is bound to the least vestiges of his matter; if he cannot be truly free so long as he is subject to the influences of Beings contrary to his nature; if he cannot contemplate the totality of the sublime realm where he was born so long as the least corruptible particle remains within him and in those sublime images, it is the same for the species of man as a whole.[255]

Now, the Earth and all the great columns of the Universe still contain rays of those *pure substances* which had been brought along with him at his fall. Therefore, if man is destined to reunite with them, all the *debris* must disappear, so that on the one side the higher substances, and on the

---

[255] It is the work of Martinism, founded on Saint-Martin and Pasqually's teachings, that, having become a Man of Desire, one works upon oneself and, having reached a level of development, one then reaches out to one's fellow man to seek to bring them into an understanding as well. In this, we see both the idea of the Elect, those who become Men and Women of Desire and who are then destined to help others; and also, the idea that the individual is a cell in the body of humanity, and that the Great Work of the individual reflects that which is necessary for the entire human race.

other the *powers* of all mankind, by forming as it were two beams of light, can each animate the other and manifest all their brilliance.[256]

We know that the universal witness of the Nations agrees on this point. All of them regard the violent state of Nature and man as a result of disorder and as a preparation for a more peaceful and happier state. All await an end to the general suffering of the species, just as each day, death puts an end to the corporeal suffering of individuals who knew how to preserve their Being from all foreign mixture. Finally, there is no Nation, and one could say no man, left to themselves, for which the temporal Universe isn't a great *Allegory* or *Fable*, which must result in an important *moral*.

The general dissolution will follow the same Laws as the dissolution of the individual body. When the Universe is in the seventh power of its septenary root, all the Principles of life spread abroad at the Creation will gather at its center, just as the warmth of dying animals imperceptibly abandons the rest of the body to reunite in the heart. For we cannot ignore the existence of a fiery center in Nature, active and living, since the least individual body has a Principle or a center of *life* of some sort which makes it live.

Since this active and universal center is connected to the Earth, it is natural to think that all the other centers will reunite with this center; and when Christian Traditions give us the strange prediction that, at the end of time, *the stars will fall to Earth*, they are really speaking about the reuniting of those several centers with the universal center; which shouldn't be difficult to understand since the stars can only fall to the

---

[256] While this cannot be stated authoritatively, we should remember that Saint-Martin was still a close friend of Willermoz, still a Freemason, and a Réau-Croix in the Élus Cohen. It was also in the year this book appeared that the Convent of Wilhelmsbad began, which rectified the Rite of Strict Observance, giving rise to the Scottish Rectified Rite, or C.B.C.S., and Willermoz was in charge of authoring the new rituals. It is very likely therefore that this topic came up in their conversations, and that Saint-Martin was aware both of the preparations for the Convent and its agendas (both overt and hidden), and the fact that Willermoz was attempting to introduce Élus Cohen interpretations of the Trestleboards and Rituals of the Strict Observance into the proposed new Order. Given this, the Fourth Grade, or Master of St. Andrew was the pivot Grade which led the narrative from the Old to the New Testament and was dominated by the image of the fallen First Temple at Jerusalem. Since the Rectified Regime focused on rebuilding the Temple, clearing away the debris, and establishing the New Jerusalem as symbols for an internal process of Spiritual Alchemy, there is some merit in thinking that some of these thoughts were summarized in this paragraph. Remember that it would be another five years before Saint-Martin was introduced to Jakob Böhme, so at this time his thoughts were still strongly influenced by Pasqually, Willermoz and Freemasonry.

Earth by letting their form disappear, just as the different parts of our bodies dissolve and disappear to the extent that their secondary principles are reunited with their Generating Principle.

A single difference should be noted between the death of an individual body and the death of the Universe: corporeal individuals, as secondary matter, submit to secondary Laws after their death, which are putrefaction, dissolution and reintegration; whereas the Universe, being primary matter in the Physical Order, needs only a single Law to complete the course of its existence. Its birth and formation had been the result of the same operation; as it will also be of its death and total disappearance. Finally, if to bring the Universe into existence, it was sufficient that the Eternal *spoke*, it will suffice for the Eternal to *speak* for the Universe to be no more.

We have only to remember that, as the image of the Great Being, man uses the same means and the same abilities to give existence to his material works, and to destroy them.

Before that final demise, there will be disorders in universal Nature, such as a decrease in the warmth in individual bodies at that time, before they completely cease their activity. The *ternary powers* of the Elements which serve as columns to the Universe will be suspended, as strength and activity abandon us when we are naturally approaching our end. And this is the meaning of the Christian Tradition when it shows us all the ternary plagues manifesting at the *voice* of the *seven superior Agents*, that is, when those seven Agents return to the Great Being the rights and *virtues* with which he had filled them to accomplish His designs in the Universe.

This, I tell you, is the meaning of that Tradition, when it presents us with the various terms of that septenary Epoch: the deterioration, the conflagration, the destruction of the third part of the Earth, trees, green grass; the third part of the sea, fish, vessels, rivers and fountains; the third part of the Sun, Moon and Stars; the third part of men; when they tell us about the birth of new animals, rising up from the bosom of the Earth onto its surface to plague the inhabitants, such as worms and disgusting insects which sometimes come out of the flesh of man and devour him before his time; when they speak to us of the change in color of the stars, the reversal of islands and mountains; and finally, and when they paint a Table of the combustion of all the Elements, to show us, at the End of Time, the *disorders* which they have begun.

But a man advanced in years not only experiences decay in his body; he also experiences it in his mind if he has not taken care to take advantage of the aid offered to him in the various ages of his life, and to cooperate in the development of his abilities which are intended for continual growth. His spirit then suffers a double deprivation, enjoying neither the treasures of that wisdom he was unable to acquire, nor the activity of his youth whose age has passed for him.

Such is the fate of universal man as well: the aid sent to men has been increasing from the beginning of things to the middle of time, though the use they have made of it hasn't been in the same proportion.

This aid has also increased since the middle of time, because it has then opened the ways of the Infinite; but as they become more and more simple and become more intellectual, they would be imperceptible and useless to the posterity of mankind if that posterity didn't follow the same progression, so that then they might begin to lose sight of them; even the low-hanging fruit which that aid had begun to offer him.

Let us therefore paint the future posterity of man crushed by the disorders of physical causes, and by those they have allowed to dominate their intellectual Being. Let us paint men in the time to come, losing hope of seeing themselves reborn, and condemned to sterility as soon as they reach the full complement of the temporal number of men.[257] Let us paint the even more terrifying image of that sterility which shows them the unwelcome image of annihilation, that they will be even more tormented by *corrosive actions* which they will see heaped upon them, because there will be fewer individuals with whom that torment can be shared.

Let us paint those men exposed to the dreadful convulsions of Nature, having acquired in their intellect neither sufficient enlightenment or strength to prevent it, nor the resignation to submit to what is inevitable.

We see them so far removed from their *supports* that they are no longer able to understand their words, yet nevertheless still seek those *supports* because of the irresistible need of their nature. This is that hunger and that thirst which, according to the Prophet, *must be sent to the Earth, not a hunger for bread nor a thirst for water; but a hunger and thirst for*

---

[257] That is, once the last of all the men destined to live on Earth throught the ages have been born there will be no more children, and hence the reference to sterility. Note also the interesting comment about losing hope of seeing themselves reborn (*perdant l'espérance de se voir renaître*), which strongly suggests a belief in reincarnation which Catholic dogma denied. See Hebrews 9:27: "And as it is appointed unto men once to die, but after this the judgment"; and see Footnote 42.

the Word.[258] A desire all the more painful that, according to the same Prophet, *men will wander everywhere, seeking that Word, and shall not find it.*[259]

Finally let us represent those men as perhaps even cursing the Supreme God, whereas He does not cease to offer His hand to help them to pass over the *pits of the abyss* without accident. Because that beneficent Hand, which has never withheld His gifts from the children of man, will withhold them all the less at a time where their needs are dire.

To heap up the afflictions further, men in those future times will perceive the Table of the Centuries revealed, just as an individual approaching his end normally sees the entire circle of his past life traced before him in rapid and vivid images. Those unfortunate men will be tortured with pain, when in that portrait of the Centuries they compare the immense and inexhaustible abundance of *gifts* with which the Earth has never ceased to be filled, and the horrible prostitution that man's posterity has made of them throughout time. There they will see gathered on the one side, the many treasures of *powers* which since the beginning of things have been sent to help man and which have always been available to him; and on the other, he will be confronted with the unclean *fruits* of *iniquity* which have also accumulated in the crucible of the world, and which have delayed the purification of so great a number of those who have inhabited it.

In the midst of those disorders, let us paint ignorant, *impure*, cheating man, seeking to extinguish in their fellow man those last rays of natural light which enlighten us all, and trying to substitute that true and sole support from which men can expect help. Finally, let us paint those future times infected with the poison of a doctrine of *death*, which will distance men from their goal instead of bringing them closer to it. For what will make those blind Masters so dangerous is, since *criminal man* will then be more *advanced* than he currently is, he will assail men with *facts*, whereas up till now he could usually only attack them with rhetoric.

If human posterity has drawn so little benefit from the aid which has surrounded him, if it has only managed to substitute the light with darkness, how will it be able to withstand such Adversaries? Then one will only see there a terrible abyss whose darkness and horror can only

---

[258] Amos 8:11.
[259] Amos 8:12.

increase, until there being no longer any visible or invisible link between the corrupted Universe and the Creator, the general dissolution of the World will arrive to end both the errors and iniquites of men.

The very Law given to the middle of time has not destroyed the seed of those disorders which men are always masters at producing and multiplying. The *Universal Elect*, during his temporal manifestation, was only charged with bringing this Law to mankind and explaining it to them; but not to execute it without the agreement of their free will.[260]

It was therefore sufficient for him to give them a fair idea of *Divine knowledge* and to teach them that this knowledge is nothing other than that of the Laws used by the Supreme Wisdom to provide free Beings with the means of returning to His Light and His Unity. Once that knowledge had been given to men, time was given to them, not to forget it and profane it, but rather to meditate on it and profit by it.

When time shall pass away; when, according to the expression of the Prophets, *the Centuries will be returned to their ancient silence*, and the *stars*, having brought together their *seven actions* into one alone, their light will become *seven times* brighter: then, thanks to their splendor, man's intellect will discover *creations* which it had left to germinate within, and then his intellect will be nourished by the *fruits* it had itelf sown.

Woe to his intellect if those fruits are wild, corrupted, or unwholesome; for, having no other food, it will be forced to feed on them continually and experience endless bitterness; because those false and impure substances created within it from its own disorder, being unable to enter into reintegration, all that will be left to it is the violent operation of an *active Fire* that has sufficient power to dissolve it.

Woe to that intellect if it spilled the blood of the Prophets: not only has it contributed to the physical destruction of those who have born that name on Earth, but moreover, if it rejected those *intimate ideas*, those *living actions* which Wisdom had communicated to it at every instant, whose only goal was to present the truth to man so that he might see it as

---

[260] The *Universal Elect* was Christ, the Repairer, and the Law he was tasked to bring to mankind from the Great Principle is the Law of Love. By now, Saint-Martin was modifying or reinterpreting Pasqually's message away from the need to perform long and complicated rituals, and more towards the practice of love and beneficence as the means to reintegration; a path shared by Willermoz as he designed his Rite around the concept of *charity of the heart* in his *Knights Beneficent of the Holy City*. Eventually this would lead Saint-Martin to fully embrace what he termed the *voie cardiaque*, or 'Way of the Heart'.

the Prophets themselves saw it, then they would become true Prophets to him, whose *blood* would be asked by him again with inflexible severity, if he Had been negligent enough to let it flow without purpose, and depraved enough to prevent its influence over his fellow man!

Woe to the intellect, if only being able to act in concert with its Principle, it nevertheless wished to act without it; for after the dissolution of its physical links, it will again be reduced to act without that Principle, as it had done during the course of its earthly life!

For this will be the extreme difference between our current state of corporeal life and the state which must follow, which is still only perceptible to our mind. Here below we only know the living and intellectual action which is ours through desire; for during our sojourn in matter, the most effective means of that action are denied us: but when we leave this matter, if we have preserved the purity of our emotions during our corporeal life, those effective means will surround us and will be prodigious without measure, and pleasures unknown to terrestrial man will amply compensate for the deprivation he has borne.

Now, on death man loses all the objects, all the means, all the organs which were used for nourishment and the channel for crime; and if, during his corporeal life, he had nourished within him false inclinations and erroneous habits, all that would remain to him when he was separated from his envelope, is the disorder of his corrupt tastes and desires, with the horror of never being able to satisfy them.

Thus, the future predicament of the ungodly will be all the more terrible, for when the material envelope which now hides us from the light is dissolved, he will see the *living flame* of truth without being able to approach it, and this had previously been predicted in the temporal Universe by the *satellites* of *Saturn*, which, circulating around the ring whose star occupies the center, are unable to enter into its precincts.

We find yet another physical image in various Elemental substances. When they have suffered various operations by Fire, they become vitrifed and acquire a transparency which lets us perceive the light from which they previously acted as a barrier to us. In like manner, following the various *actions* undertaken by the Beings destined to carry out the intentions of the Creator of the Universe, they are liberated by the *powers* of a superior *Fire* from all substances of their temporal Law, which were but impurities compared to the first estate in which they should never have ceased to be. Then, they will take on a bright clarity; they will form a luminous barrier around the godless man through which his intellectual view will be able to penetrate, but which he himself will never be able to break through, so long as his will remains impure and, and so long as he hasn't vomited up to the last drop that draught of iniquity whose bitterness and horror he has been forced to experience across the Centuries.

That is where will be seen the complement of *a time, times and an half*.[261] For after universal childbirth there will be an *afterbirth*, just like individual childbirth, and that is the *half-time* of Daniel.

However, following the idea we have given concerning the will, it is impossible to attach any other period to that deprivation or that *half-time* than that which the godless will have fixed himself, for how can one then enumerate the duration of his actions? For they must be compared to time, and the *measure* of time will have been broken.

But because the godless will be close to the light and yet cannot enjoy it, his suffering will be inconceivable. He will know the tears and the gnashing of teeth which has been alluded to in the Book already quoted, by the number *fifty-six*, seeing that this expression represents both time and the principle of *idolatry*, and the boundary which separates him from the abode of perfection.[262]

Therefore, being excluded from order and purity, horror and despair will be his life, fury and rage his only emotions, until being reduced to tearing out his own *entrails* to *feed* himself and *quenching his thirst* on his own blood, he devours the very corruption with which he infected himself, and whose source he transmited by the *intense heat of his own Fire*.

If, on the contrary, man had only received and grown within him health-giving *seeds*, similar to his true nature; if he was content enough to occasionally water that *fertile plant*, which we all contain within ourselves, with his own tears; if he understood that he had to carry, like

---

[261] From Daniel 7:25 and 12:7, as well as Revelation 12:14. These prophecies are usually connected with the end times, which Saint-Martin is discussing here. There are, however, many different interpretations of these periods, which may be seen by a casual perusal of the internet. However, the later reference to *half-time* being like childbirth makes little sense if one adheres to the prevailing interpretation of the period of *time* as being one year, since *half-time* would then be six months, not nine. The only possible link is the fact that Revelation 12 is concerned with the 'woman clothed with the sun...travailing in birth'.

[262] In *Of Errors & Truth*, Saint-Martin, while introducing the Book of Man, mentions that the number 5 is associated with evil and idolatry; while the number 6 refers to the hexagram, or the six days of Creation placed in a circle which is the boundary of time.

Shin (ש) – The End of Time

all Beings, the characteristic signs of his Principle, and that none other than the First Principle could have given him existence; if he desired to resemble that Principle by conforming with His *images* sent in time; if he tried to make Him known to his fellow man, by loving them as He loves them, by tolerating their errors as He tolerates them, by transporting himself in his mind to those times of calm and unity where disorders can no longer affect him; finally, if he endeavored to cross this dark domain without entering into alliances with the *illusions* which comprise it; and in this laborious passage, only taking that which could *extend* his own nature and not corrupt it; then he will harvest the fruits whose *taste, color* and *fragrance* will soothe the intellectual senses of his Being, as they continually enliven all his abilities. Nothing will separate him from those superior spheres whose visible spheres are only imperfect images, and whose movements governed by inalterable relationships, brings about the most sublime harmony, and transmits Divine harmony to the universality of Beings.

There, like the Angels in Heaven, he will not be marked with the number of reprobation expressed today by the difference of the sexes, because the animal Principle, *the one whose generative and constitutive action is specifically concerned with the production of the sexes, will be returned to its source and will no longer act materially. There will, nevertheless, be bodies, but as these bodies will be animated by an activity more alive than that of matter, they will only be characterized as the parts of our form which serve to house the spirit and which manifest it, or those which may be used in the* pure exercise *of its functions.*

All the knowledge, all the *powers* of the Agents which Divine Wisdom put in charge of man's support and instruction from the origin of disorder will become part of him: he will have their strength, their zeal for the reign of truth, their intelligence to understand, and their purity to enjoy.

Having left allegories and emblems far behind, he will intuitively recognize those same *powers* which charity had detached from their Principle to come to guide and support man in the place of his laborious expiation. In him they will enjoy the fruit of their work; and in them he will enjoy in that indescribable pleasure of being touched and blessed by beneficent hands. As they will both be delivered from those cares and painful actions to which the Law of time still subjects them, they will cast their joyful and tender *eyes* with confidence towards the Source from

Whom they have received all their delight, and reclothing themslves in the simplicity of their *first character*, they will have the right to *lay their* hand on the censer and to offer, each according to their *measure* and their *number*, the pure *incense* intended for the One Who has permitted them to taste the *sacred* peace and *virtuous* delights of truth.

We know that the universal testimony of Nations accords with this consoling doctrine. If all Nations have had their *Minos*[263], if all have had the idea of his terrible Tribunal and that of *Tartarus*, where guilty men will spend their days in horror and darkness, they have also had their *Elysian Fields* where virtuous and peaceful Beings will enjoy without disturbance or fear the fruit of the fortunate gifts they will have spread over the Earth.

Then the pure man will therefore be able to recover access to that *imperishable Temple* whose wonders he must proclaim, and from which his crime had banished him. He will approach the *Holy Ark* without fear of dying, because being even more powerful than that described in the Hebrew Traditions, it will only permit those whom it has purified to enter its precincts.

There, no Being will be exposed to the punishment of Uzzah[264], because this *Holy Ark* is the source of clemency and life, and as it is both the *center*, the *seed* and the *source* of all *Powers*, it will forever be impossible for man to find himself admitted to its worship without the Ark itself opening the Holy of Holies.

The Grand High Priest of the Law before time, the same who has invisibly presided over the Religions of all the Nations on Earth, since there is not one which does not contain traces of the truth, he who had shown men in the middle of time the portrait of their Being and the reuniting of all the *Divine Powers* which his crime had caused to be subdivided for us, is also he who will preside over that future worship when time is no more, for being the sole Universal Agent of Supreme Wisdom, he alone can distribute the universal graces intended for all His children.[265]

---

[263] Minos was the King of Crete who demanded Athens sent youths to be sacrificed to the minotaur in his labyrinth. On his death he became one of the three Judges in Hades or Tartarus, along with Aeacus and Rhadamanthus.
[264] Who touched the Ark and died instantly (1 Chron. 13:10).
[265] In this instance Saint-Martin is referring to the Repairer, or Christ, who was called the Grand High Priest (Hebrews 4:14). However, this does muddy the waters a little, since one might ask: if God is the Supreme Wisdom, and the Repairer is the Universal Agent who is also the Grand High

He will therefore live among the chosen Levites, who, like him, having conquered corruption, will be judged worthy to fulfill the holy functions in the Temple. There, he will see them tirelessly set out the offerings of their praise and love about him and, he himself casting his *vivifying unction* upon those offerings, he will cause them to give out fragrant and *numerous* perfumes, which will spread sanctity throughout that august chamber.

These perfumes, succeeding each other with inexhaustible abundance, will rise up to the First Source of all life and intelligence, and this unquenchable Source, ever penetrated by their activity, will ever open up to let the sweetness of His own existence enter into man's soul with the same abundance and continuity. Thus, man will be able to nourish himself forever from the *life* of his Pattern, and the Great Being will be able to contemplate His image eternally, for by regenerating him ceaselessly He will allow him, by sublime right, to be the indelible sign of his Principle.

Finally, each man will enjoy not only the gift which is his alone, but he will still be able to participate with those of all the Elect who comprise the *assembly* of *Sages*; just as here below various men, by coming together could reciprocally increase their powers, each being nourished by those who shine among their fellow man, spreading among all of them the *talent* of a single one, and having germinate in a single one the *talents* of all; and such will be the future state of that mutual communication by which all men, uniting their possessions with those of the Great Being and all His creations, will ensure that all individuals will live in that Being and that Being in all individuals.

This future worship will therefore bear no resemblance to the rigorous and bloody sacrifices which were recounted in the Books of the Hebrews to teach man clearly about the severity of justice, and to remind him of the painful *separation* that he is continually obliged to make here below from all *substances foreign* to his true nature, if he doesn't wish to remain in illusion and death.

Priest, where does man, who is now restored to his primitive rights, fit in, since the purpose of his reintegration in *Of Errors & Truth* was for him to resume his role, which the Repairer (or the '*another*' who took his place) had temporarily filled during his prevarication. Also, the role of the Ark of the Covenant is unclear: as the abrogator of the First Coveneant and introducer of the Second, the Ark represents the Christ/Repairer, too. But again, this muddies the role of the Grand High Priest who was to offer up incense to the Shekinah seated upon the Ark, and the Grand High Priest *as* the Ark itself. Now the Repairer is the Ark, the Sacrifice and the Sacrificer!

This worship will be even greater than temporal worship, than the Law of Grace established by the Universal Repairer when there still needed to be times, intervals, composite and fleeting things; for then there will be no more *different seasons*, no more *rising* and *setting* of the stars which shine on us, no more passing from light into darknesss, no more moments marked for man's *prayers*, nor moments when his bodily needs or his stains oblige him to suspend them.[266]

Those admitted to the sacrifices will no longer be prevented because of differences in their language, for the Universal Order will be associated with the uniformity of all languages, and because the Supreme Principle is so majestic that there can be nothing less than the coming together of the *voices* of all Beings to praise Him.

And so, all the Sages together, at the same moment, at the same Altar and without cease, will forever be able to read without trouble or mistrust in the Eternal Book ever open before their eyes, THE SACRED NAMES WHICH MAKE LIFE FLOW IN ALL BEINGS…!

---

[266] In other words, man's worship will be unceasing and everlasting, since there will no longer be any time, and therefore no need to set various times of the day aside for prayer, work and rest.

Tau (ת) – Search Your Being

Men of Peace, Men of Desire, such is the splendour of the Temple in which, one day, you will have a right to take your place. Such a privilege should astonish you less than the fact that here below you can install the *foundations* of this Temple, you can start to *erect* it, and you can even *adorn* it every moment of your existence.[267]

All of Nature provides you with an example: when plants are sown in the earth, when animals are in their mother's womb, all work and continually use their activity to change their gross and unformed state in such a way as to become active, free and closer to the perfection which should be theirs.

But, to have the right to this sublime expectation, search your Being regularly, to ensure that it breathes only for the reign of truth and not for yours: this is compass of the Sage, the pact which he must constantly make with himself. Always preserve a noble image of the Principle which animates you, and believe that after Him who gave you existence, there is nothing worthier of respect than you yourself. This is a bulwark which will defend you from the approaches, not only of everything which is opposed to your nature, but also everything which is not worthy, and which has no true connection with you.

Since men are the expression of the abilities of the Great Principle, each of them is marked more specifically by one of these abilities; but though he must more normally display the properties which are analogous to it; though here below everyone is subjected to experiencing delays, to travelling along different paths and differing degrees in the acquisition and development of their unique gift; nevertheless, holding by their essence onto the Universal Principle of Beings, they all have connections with the universality of His *Powers* and His Light, but in a manner proportional to the sphere in which they live and to the inferiority of their creation relative to his Generative Principle.

---

[267] Another indication that Saint-Martin still recalled his roots in Freemasonry: the word 'adorn' or 'decorate' (*orner*) goes well with the Wisdom upon which it is founded and the Strength of the edifice.

Therefore, if a man, on coming to a mature age, is still a stranger to certain knowledge, certain illumination, if he is not able to have some pure, honest, natural and real *enjoyment*, then this isn't a complete man, for *knowledge* and happiness are nothing more than the application of the *active and living use of the Supreme Powers* to different things, different clssses and different situations in which he may find himself. Thus, the *unhappy man* is like the dead, since he doesn't know life. The *ignorant man* is a sick and crippled man which only became that by not having exercised his powers. Finally, the *misanthropic man who is without charity* is a cowardly and godless man, since he *doesn't act* on what he is reluctant to do, and he doesn't have enough confidence in his Principle to believe that this Principle has any power when he calls it to his aid.

Oh, man! I will try to show you a few methods of self-preservation, to protect yourself from these mistakes and the misfortunes which result from them.

Remember that, according to the teaching of the Sages the things which are above are similar to the things which are below, and understand that you yourself can contribute to this similarity by ensuring that the things which are below are similar to the things which are above. There, we are pure and simple like the Principle which has everything in Him, there the reign of ardor and zeal for the *Laws of the Temple* is intact and forever honored by the veneration of Beings. There finally, wishes and burning desires are ceaselessly given out before the Throne of the LORD, either to implore His clemency toward the unfortunate prevaricators, or to celebrate His *Powers* and kindnesses. So, learn from these sublime acts the *Ministry*[268] to which you are called: the Agents who exercise them only tell you of your obligations, and you would not have the *ability to read* them if you didn't have the ability to imitate them.

Do not neglect the aid of the earth on which you walk: it is the true Horn of Plenty for your present state, and it is not without reason that it is regarded by some Observers as containing a huge magnet *at its center, because it is indeed the rallying point of all created* powers. *It is also, in some manner, the reservoir of the true Fountain of Youth, whose fable has*

---

[268] A theme throughout Saint-Martin's teachings is the idea of man as a Minister, in the sense of being ordained, and therefore worthy to offer incense at the Altar of Gold. This theme runs from his first encounter with Pasqually, when he joined the Elect Cohen or Elect Priests, to his book which was published during his lifetime, *Le Ministère de l'Homme-Esprit*, or 'The Ministry of Spirit-Man', published in 1802.

transmitted so many wonders to us, since it is there that the substance which serves as the basis and the first degree towards regeneration – or the rebirth of all Beings – is prepared. Lastly, it is the crucible of souls as much as that of the body: happy is the man who knows how to discover its properties! For to not know things in themselves is to know nothing, and it is not enough to believe that everything endures, that everything is active: one must seek it out to be sure that it is and to feel it.

Then you will learn what it is to help the Earth to celebrate the Sabbath[269], *and why the Hebrews deserve so much criticism for having neglected that duty while they inhabited the Promised Land. Because in the active* physical *it is the same as in the passive physical, where we see that if man does not care for the Earth through cultivation, it gives forth only coarse and wild vegetation.*

The properties of Water are no less useful to know, since being the source of all salts, and containing in itself all the seed of corporisation, it is in Principle and in power what the Earth is only in deed, being matter which is already determined. There you will see that the color green is particularly attributed to the Vegetable Kingdom, which is really just the expression of the Principles of Water, and which occupies the same intermediate position between the Three Kingdoms that Water has among the three Elements, and green among the seven colors of the rainbow.

Don't despise the observation that over the entire surface of the terrestrial globe, Water is always lower than the Earth which surrounds it, although by its fluid and volatile nature it should be higher. In this image you will see a natural and physical representation of the inferior rank that all the powers *occupy today to come to your aid, although they were created to dominate all the realms.*

You could also consider Water from a different point of view; that is, with regard to the troubles it has caused across the Earth's surface, for in the physical all things are double, and Water especially bears this number. So, in comparing the different locations which it has submerged with those which it has left exposed; in considering, I tell you, the external figure of our globe, on which Water and Earth are so diversely mixed, you can extend your understanding of the progressive, general and specific effects of the crime, and on the true state of ancient, present and future

---

[269] This was another word apparently invented by Saint-Martin: *Sabbatiser*, which the Translator has rendered as 'to celebrate the Sabbath'.

intellectual Geography. But on this topic, like all those of this kind, don't limit yourself to the first observation. The more discoveries are capable of being expanded upon, the more it is important only to adopt them with much caution and prudence.

Finally, the properties of Fire, if you have the good fortune to acquire knowledge of them, will appear to you to be preferable to all of the other Elemental forces, because then you will touch on the very root of the great temporal tree which contains all the physical phenomena, and through which flows the sap which animates and nourishes all the physical Agents. And to note with confidence the true superiority of this Element over the other two, observe that the Sun is always bright in itself and in every direction, whereas the Moon and the Earth only have borrowed light, and half of their surface is always dark.

Then if you wish to judge the painful and degraded state of man here below, both in relation to knowledge of the Elements and with regard to the superior knowledge which they represent, you will notice that in these three Agents specifically meant for your instruction, the Sun is always full when it shows itself to us, the Moon is only full once a month, and the Earth never is, since we can only see a very limited horizon.

But to rekindle our hope amidst the deprivation which you suffer, pay attention to the example of the universal action of life, and that all fluids – be they aquatic, igneous, magnetic or electric – always tend to restore their equilibrium and to move to the places where they are absent. Note that the coarsest air, most concentrated in material bodies, is always related to the air in the atmosphere, that this air passes continuously through our body and penetrates into our smallest vessels, but when it becomes physical, *so to speak, and changes in accordance with all our situations and all the states of our physical form, for all that it doesn't stop maintaining its relationship with the purest, freest and most liberated ethereal air.*

If all this knowledge of the Elements appears to be meaningless to you, it is because you have not yet grasped the wholeness and universality of the Empire of Man. But Sages in all times have studied them thoroughly and have regarded them as a gift which is part of their domain, and as a favorable path to rise up to higher degrees. These same Sages have been too cautious to want to walk along such a path without having constant Laws and Rules, because they felt that there is nothing arbitrary in the worship which man is tasked to perform on Earth.

It is here that physical numbers wonderfully exercise their rights, classifying all the properties of all regions, all realms, all species and all individuals of the Elemental Universe into a precise order. It is here that we can begin to acquire a clear understanding of the original, median and terminal *Laws of all corporeal things, because these things, being composite, are susceptible to decomposition and analysis, and the number of their constituent Principles is the same as the number of all their actions, be they primitive and original, concerning existence and duration, or concerning death and destruction.*

Finally, it is here that the first applications of the true sense of the word to initiate *are made, which, in its Latin etymology means* approach, unite with the Principle; *the word* initium *meaning* Principle *as much as* beginning. *And since then, nothing conforms more with all the truths set out previously than the use of initiations among all Nations, nothing is more analogous to the situation and to the hope of man than the source from which those initiations came down to us, and than the object for which they have been used throughout: which is to close the distance between the light and man, or to bring him closer to his* Principle *by reestablishing him in the same estate in which he was* in the beginning.

When all the physical Agents about which I have just spoken have consumed, through their activity, the impure substances which defile your material organs; when they have corporeally regenerated *you through their own life and will thus have contributed to letting you regain your intellectual abilities, and that equilibrium and agility proportional to your infirm and painful situation; bring your gaze to bear upon the scattered and subdivided* powers *of all the Beings of that other Order who were the precedecessors of the age of intelligence, being their Agents and Ministers. Constantly making beneficial use of the thoughts they send you, work to make yourself as similar as possible to them to facilitate the joining together of their essence and yours. Through that union, they will convince you, once again and physically, that you are meant to contemplate them in their entirety and in their unity, and they will confirm the certainty of all the Elemental knowledge which you had previously discovered and acquired; because the same Principle which produced the Beings and Agents of all Orders, directs and governs them all by one and the same Law.*

Also, in the same realm, in the same phenomenon where you would have perceived a natural Elemental truth, rest assured that if you made appropriate use of your abilities, you will find a natural intellectual truth; be sure that you will find in this new Order the same plan as in the previous Order, and you will recognize similar properties which tend towards the same end, since everything holds together, everything touches, everything is one in means as well as in the purpose that the Author of Things intended. This is why in man, the corporeal organs which manifest the most perfect animal functions, such as those that are active in the heart and the head, are also the seat of the most beautiful traits of His immaterial Being, those being love and intelligence.

Finally, not only there is no physical fact which isn't linked to an intellectual truth, but there is nothing in the great phenomena and in the great movements of the Universe[270] that does not foretell one of those truths and which doesn't proclaim it when it comes to its term; so that this material Universe, when regarded from such a position, is the vehicle of true prophecy to an intelligent man.

These Superior Agents, serving as intermediaries between physical things and Divine things, will tell you by their action man's true destiny and the true place he should occupy; that is, that they will expose to you the true relationships which exist between God, Man and the Universe. One the one hand, they will show you the multitude and the subdivision of all Elemental and inferior things which, by reason of their number and multiplicity, only offer confusion and decay. On the other, through their mutual and general union and by their perfect correspondence, they will convince you of the unity of the Supreme Principle. They will show you, by their universal harmony, that unity is the only number in which resides all the gifts which our needs ceaselessly call to us, gifts which all men on Earth, without exception, pursue by means of secret movements of which they are not the masters.

They will make known to you the truth that if, in their example, we were constantly in line with that Unity, that is, underneath our Superior and Divine line, it would extend down to us a *pure and fixed substance* of power and action, which, amassing around us, would form a *foundation* which is more or less large, more or less broad, depending on how much we were to open our own *immaterial channels* to be filled by it.

Man here below, being more often the example of evil rather than of good, justifies this truth in distressing examples, instead of justifying it in

---

[270] In French, *jeu de grands resorts de l'Univers*.

comforting examples. So, what we experience most often is that the *foundation* of which I have just spoken decreasing in proportion to the extent that we close the *intellectual channels*, which are like the senses of our mind; and when we close communication completely, our *intellectual center,* no longer receiving this substance which was to form its foundation, falls in on itself, overturns and sees itself exposed to the revolution of the inferior and horizontal circumferences which sweep it away, and make it wander according to their disorganized Laws. *That is what is meant by the custom of human Magistrates when they cause the ashes of criminals to be cast to the winds.*[271]

On the contrary, these pure and intermediary Agents only being able to offer types of good, must make us understand that if we were to close none of our *immaterial channels*, we would see our *foundation* extend to an immense distance, and perhaps acquire enough breadth to cover the entire Universe.

We cannot even doubt, reflecting on our primitive destiny and remembering that such was the majesty of man, that he needed nothing less than all the *Powers* of the Universe to contain him and serve as his seat; just as, in his present state, the corporeal form in which he is imprisoned could not contain and sustain his intellectual Being in the extent of all its abilities if it wasn't the most regular of all the forms and the most perfect summary of the great Universe.[272]

So, it is only from a *foundation* so extended and a support so solid; I tell you, it is only through the general union, and through that vast assembly of all those pure and intermediary Agents which, hovering above the physical world, offer to assist you, defend you and surround you, that you can raise youself like them with certainty, and with a true light, up to that Universal *Unity* Who dominates them and vivifies all.

Therefore, those same pure and intermediate Beings will teach you that the Agent who is custodian of that unity, bearing within him life and clarity, can produce in you, as he does in them, the strength and peace that

---

[271] Freemasons will recognize, too, a reference to the penalty of the Third Degree, which is hardly surprising given Saint-Martin's continued interest in the Craft at this time.

[272] This is a common Theosophical and Hermetic theme: man as *microcosm* to the Universal *macrocosm.* 'As above, so below' – and Saint-Martin has already alluded to the *Emerald Tablet* earlier (see Footnote 60). By bringing this to our attention here, Saint-Martin reminds us that this isn't simply a static state, but a dynamic one, in which man can affect the Universe through his actions.

are his, because the most beautiful of his powers is the desire to share it all with you.

And so this Agent, being the dispenser of all the gifts and all the aid which can come to you, will become the motive for all the movements of your Being, when all your abilities working according to your desires "by earth, by oil, by salt and by fire", will have recovered the level of purity which is required of them for you to be able open the first doors of the Temple, there to be adopted by the faithful *Guides* who must transmit to you here below the *powers* of the Sanctuary, until you have acquired the right and the power to go and draw them up youself at their source.

Therefore, recognize that, from the lowest to the highest degrees, you can hope for aid in every step you have to take to travel along the path and reestablish yourself in the rights of your origin.

Recognize, too, that none of these aids are foreign to that Universal Agent who had to establish the Age of Intelligence and bring men the addition of all powers and all enlightenment. As his essence is inherent in the very center from which arise all essences, all *pure facts*, all *supports*, nothing which works for good may happen without his attachment and without him being either the mediating or the directing Principle.

Thus, when you work to attract the various *powers* of those immaterial Beings charged with activating your thought, it will be the aid of the Supreme Agent that you will receive, since those Beings are simply His organs and administrators. Even though you only work with Elemental things, if you feel you are expanding your knowledge and your *powers*, be assured that it is still him who is working through them to achieve the success you are obtaining, as it is him who at all times is responsible for their existence and all their regular activity.

It is therefore only in pure works, of whatever kind they might be, that you can recognize His power and, so to speak, communicate with him. The sole difference that distinguishes these various operations, is that in some he acts by means of simple active emanations; and in others he acts by means of intelligent emanations; that in some he preserves, he animates, he instructs; and in others he renews, he elevates, he sanctifies. But in this diversity of actions, and under the names of *Preserver*, *Instructor*, *Renewer*, *Sanctifier*, you cannot avoid seeing the same Being, the same Agent – Supreme and Universal – through whom everything moves, through whom everything exists, and who only clothes himself in those different characters to better provide for all our needs, all our circumstances, and to fulfill to its full extent the vast designs He has on us.

Because we should not forgett that if men were attentive and careful to lend themselves to the views of wisdom, they would each see specifically working within them and in relation to them, that same order of things, that same succession of manifestations that we have previously recognized as being operated in general upon our entire species for the accomplishment of the *Great Work*.

If, by these intermediate and secondary paths, you can to some extent always receive the aid of the Supreme Agent who, in all Ages, has been the author and the support of that Great Work, and to taste without end his special consolations, it is easy to judge the extent of your enjoyment and your success if, through your confidence in this aid and this consolation, you were to elevate yourself enough to be supported directly through his own power.

So, when your hurts become too strong, when the *waters* of your dark domain are ready to inundate you, and when the shadows of ignorance appear to be harsh and unbearable as well, ask the Repairer to intercede with WISDOM for some rays of His Fire to dispel them. Could He, without forgetting Himself, go against the wishes of His own substance, and the *powers* of him on whom rests both His NUMBER and NAME? Ask, I tell you, through his intercession to Wisdom, for Him to lend His support to your impotence, and put His thought in the place of your thought, His intention in the place of your intention, His action in place of your action, His very words in the place of your words, and when He has thus renewed your whole Being, when He has made you as invincible and incorruptible as Him, He will not be able to refuse your offerings, since it will be His own gifts which you offer Him.

By that He no longer brings your hopes to an end; by that, He ensures strength for your Being if it is languishing, abundance if it is lacking, knowledge if it is ignorant; and moreover, He assures him of life and light, even when he seems dead and buried in the deepest abyss. For, if this Supreme Principle has, through His active abilities been able to give birth to the harmony of physical Beings, and through His thinking abilities been able to produce your intellectual Being, how could it be more difficult for Him to regenerate your *powers* that to have given them existence?

THE END

Appendix I – The Martinist Pantacle

(AS ENVISAGED BY PAPUS)

In the comprehensive diagram, we see the number of perfection, 4, represented by the square (in this case the vertical and horizontal lines forming the cross) in the center of which is the still point or the Seventh Day of Creation, as well as the point where Man was placed, following his creation by the First Priniciple.

The encompassing circle represents the First Principle, while its thickness reminds us that it is a temporal barrier; and the Hexagram represents the Six Days of Creation, further symbolizing the six Agents of Creation, or the Elohim. The Hexagram denoted by the white asacending and black descending triangles represents the evolutionary and involutionary forces, which act within Creation yet only reach as far at the six Agents, and not to the First Principle Himself, Who is outside of time.

This diagram purports to summarize all of Creation in one Table.

www.ingramcontent.com/pod-product-compliance
Lightning Source LLC
Chambersburg PA
CBHW070353050526
44400CB00013B/1045